Cultural & Social History

THE JOURNAL OF THE
SOCIAL HISTORY SOCIETY

Volume 4, Issue 1

⊛ **BERG**

Cultural and Social History

Cultural and Social History: The Journal of the Social History Society (ISSN 1478-0038 print; ISSN 1478-0046 online) is published four times per year by Berg Publishers, 1st Floor, Angel Court, 81 St Clements Street, Oxford, OX4 1AW UK. Four parts form a volume.

2007 Subscription rates
Print
Institutional (1 year): £155/US$290; (2 year) £248/$464
Single issues: £30/US$60

Online only
Institutional (1 year): £120/$230; (2 year): £192/$368
Free online subscription for institutional print subscribers.
Full colour images are available online.
Access your electronic subscription through www.ingenta.com

2007 Membership rates
Membership of the Social History Society is open to all interested individuals, not just professional scholars and students. To download the membership form go to www.socialhistory.org.uk

Individual: £40, Postgraduate: £15, Partner: £18
Members of the Social History Society receive the journal as part of their membership fee.
See http://www.socialhistory.org.uk or http://www.bergpublishers.com/uk/cshistory/cshistory_subscribe. htm for further details.

Orders and payment
Turpin Distribution handle the distribution of this journal. Institutional orders accompanied with payment (cheques made payable to Turpin Distribution) should be sent directly to Turpin Distribution, Stratton Business Park, Pegasus Drive, Biggleswade, Bedfordshire, SG18 8TQ, UK.
Tel: +44 (0)1767 604951. Fax: +44 (0)1767 601640. E-mail: custserv@turpin-distribution.com

Enquiries
Kathryn Earle, Managing Editor
email: kearle@bergpublishers.com
Production: Ian Critchley
email: icritchley@bergpublishers.com
Advertising and subscriptions: Veruschka Selbach
email: vselbach@bergpublishers.com

Articles appearing in this journal are abstracted and indexed in America: History and Life; the British Humanities Index; Historical Abstracts; International Bibliography of Book Reviews; International Bibliography of Periodical Literature; PAIS International; Linguistics and Language Behaviour Abstracts; Social Services Abstracts; and Sociological Abstracts

Berg Publishers is a member of CrossRef.

Submissions
Submissions should be sent in electronic format (either Word or Rich Text Format) to culturalsocialhistory@bergpublishers.com

Reprints
Copies of individual articles may be obtained from the publishers at the appropriate fees. Write to: Berg Publishers, 1st Floor, Angel Court, 81 St Clements Street, Oxford OX4 1AW, UK

Typeset by Avocet Typesetting, Chilton, Aylesbury, Bucks
Printed in the UK

The Social History Society

Objectives

The society was founded in 1976 to encourage the study of the history of society and cultures by teaching, research, publication and other appropriate means. Since then it has organized a conference annually and acted to represent the interests of social and cultural history and of social and cultural historians both within higher education and in the wider community. The society is based in the UK but is concerned with social history internationally and in all its broadest forms. It welcomes not only contributions and members from overseas, but also historians and interested individuals from both inside and outside the formal academic community. It actively seeks to maintain links with other historical societies and bodies, nationally and internationally.

Cultural & Social History

THE JOURNAL OF THE
SOCIAL HISTORY SOCIETY

Volume 4, Issue 1

CONTENTS

AUTHORS' BIOGRAPHIES

Karl Bell studied for his PhD thesis on the magical imagination and modern urbanization at the University of East Anglia and is currently employed within the School of History as an associate tutor. He has published an article on millenarianism in mid-nineteenth century Norfolk in *Social History* and is due to take up a lectureship at the University of Portsmouth later in 2007. His research interests include magical mentalities, folklore, popular nineteenth-century literature and expressions and functions of the fantastical imagination in popular culture.

Ulbe Bosma is senior research fellow at the International Institute of Social History. He has published various books on Creole history in Dutch and English and articles in various journals. He recently co-authored *Being Dutch in the Indies* (Singapore University Press, 2007) and co-edited *Sugarlandia Revisited* (Berghahn, 2007). His current research interests are on (post)colonial migrations and on commodity production in colonial economies.

Stephen Lovell is a reader in modern European history at King's College London. He is the author of *The Russian Reading Revolution: Print Culture in the Soviet and Post-Soviet Eras* (2000), *Summerfolk: A History of the Dacha, 1710–2000* (2003), and *Destination in Doubt: Russia since 1989* (2006).

Fernando Rosa Ribeiro is Professor at the Faculty of Philosophy and Human Sciences at the Universidade Estadual de Campinas, Campinas, Brazil. He has published on Dutch colonialism in Asia and South Africa, and on the Caribbean region.

James Sharpe is a professor at the University of York and has published eleven books and over forty articles and essays, most of them on early modern English social history. His publications on witchcraft include *Instruments of Darkness: Witchcraft in England c. 1550–c. 1750* (London, 1996), and *The Bewitching of Anne Gunter: A Horrible and True Story of Football, Witchcraft, Murder and the King of England* (London, 1999). His main current research interests are the court system of the early modern Isle of Man, and violence in early modern England.

Jonathan Wild is lecturer in Victorian literature at the University of Edinburgh. He is the author of *The Rise of the Office Worker in Literary Culture, 1880–1939* (Basingstoke, 2006) and has also published articles on topics including George Gissing, Jerome K. Jerome, and the popular literary magazine *John O'London's Weekly*. His current projects include a monograph on literary culture in the Edwardian period. Wild is the Deputy Director of the Centre for the History of the Book and he is also a member of the editorial team of the Duke-Edinburgh edition of *The Collected Letters of Thomas and Jane Welsh Carlyle*.

J. Carter Wood is a research fellow at the International Centre for Comparative Criminological Research/Department of History at the Open University. He is the author of *Violence and Crime in Nineteenth-Century England: The Shadow of Our Refinement* (London, 2004). He has written several articles, essays and reviews on the history of crime and violence and he is currently researching topics related to victimization in interwar Britain.

OBITUARY

EMERITUS PROFESSOR JOHN BURNETT

Professor John Burnett, who died on Sunday, 5 November 2006 aged 80, was renowned as a social historian whose interest in ordinary people's lives led him to embark on a programme of describing the life of the people of Britain in the nineteenth and twentieth centuries in every aspect: from what they ate and drank to how they were housed, from what schooling they received to what work they did, and how they spent their money. The one gap in this agenda was dress and at the time of his death he was half-way through 'Clothes Make the Man', which Yale University Press was to publish.

John Burnett was born in Nottingham in 1925, the son of Arthur and Evelyn Burnett. His father was a tailor and owner of a gentlemen's outfitters' shop. He attended High Pavement School, Nottingham, and won a scholarship to Emmanuel College, Cambridge, where he read Part I History and Part II Law. He followed this with the Ll.B. postgraduate degree at London University and began teaching law and history at Guildford Technical College and later at Borough Polytechnic. During this period he undertook research at the London School of Economics, being awarded the University of London PhD degree for a study of nineteenth-century adulteration of bread, tea and beer. He enjoyed teaching social history for London's Extra-Mural Department and was stimulated in this work by Professor O.R. Macgregor and H.L. Beales. John Burnett was later appointed Head of Department of General Studies in the School of Social Sciences at Brunel College, Acton. Brunel was one of the Colleges of Advanced Technology converted into universities in the 1960s, and which later moved to Uxbridge to become Brunel University. John Burnett was awarded a chair in social history in 1972 and later served a term as Pro-Vice-Chancellor. An inspiring and popular lecturer, he continued teaching into his 70s.

John Burnett's first major work was a social history of diet, *Plenty and Want*, initially published in 1966, with later editions in 1979 and 1989. It was followed by *A History of the Cost of Living* in 1969 and *A Social History of Housing 1815-1985*, in 1986. During the 1970s, with the rise in popularity of oral history as source material, John Burnett became convinced that ordinary people in the nineteenth and early twentieth centuries were more literate than previously thought and that oral history did not tap into the longer time span of modern social history. He felt that people often experienced the desire, as they grew older, to record the facts of their lives on paper and that many had left autobiographical memoirs – which he distinguished from diaries – that offered unique historical insights into the lives of common people. This led to a notable contribution to social history: the creation of autobiography as source material for the study of working-class lives. It resulted in part from a radio broadcast made on the BBC's 'Woman's Hour' programme. This elicited a remarkable response, including one from Winifred Foley on her upbringing in the Forest of Dean which she later developed for publication as *A Child in the Forest*. John Burnett published an edited selection of these narratives in 1974 as *Useful Toil: Autobiographies of Working People from the 1820s to the 1920s* and followed it with *Destiny Obscure: Autobiographies of Childhood, Education and Family from the 1820s to the 1920s* in 1982. In all, over 800 autobiographical writings were received and an archive of some 230 items, not held privately or in record offices, was formed and is held in the library of Brunel University. In collaboration with Professor David Vincent and David Mayall, John Burnett published, between 1984 and 1989, *The Autobiography of the Working Class*, a three-volume annotated bibliography which recorded all known examples of material written by authors who were working class, at least for part of their lives, wrote in English and lived for some time in England, Scotland or Wales between 1790 and 1945. As a postscript to this phase of his work, he produced *Idle Hands: Experience of Unemployment, 1790-1990*, in 1994.

Throughout this phase of his writing John Burnett retained his interest in diet, regularly attending meetings of the Historians and Nutritionists Seminar at Queen Elizabeth College (now once more part of King's College, London). At the invitation of Professor Hans-Jurgen Teuteberg, he attended the founding meeting of the International Commission for Research into European Food History (ICREFH) in Münster in May 1989, raising the funds and organizing the first research symposium of ICREFH, which took place at Brunel University in September 1991 to mark the harmonization of European Union food policies. In collaboration with Professor Derek Oddy, he initiated the workshop approach to facilitate discussion at these meetings. The proceedings of the Brunel symposium were published as John Burnett and Derek J. Oddy (eds) *The Origins and Development of Food Policies in Europe* in 1994. John Burnett attended further ICREFH symposia in Wageningen, The Netherlands, and Vevey, Switzerland. In all, he contributed chapters to six ICREFH books on food history. His interest in food consumption continued unabated and he published *Liquid Pleasures: A Social History of Drinks in Modern Britain*, in 1999, and *England Eats Out: A Social History of Eating Out in England from 1830 to the Present*, in 2004.

John Burnett was a longstanding member of the Social History Society of the United Kingdom and served as Chairman from 1985 to 1991, thereafter becoming one of its Honorary Vice-Presidents. John was recognized by many historians with his trademark pipe in his mouth, but relatively few suspected that behind this exterior was the leader and clarinettist of the Brunel All Stars jazz band.

Professor John Burnett, teacher, broadcaster and prolific writer on social history, is survived by his wife and son.

WITCHCRAFT IN THE EARLY MODERN ISLE OF MAN

James Sharpe

Department of History, University of York

ABSTRACT This article examines evidence relating to witchcraft beliefs and official attitudes to witchcraft in the Isle of Man during the seventeenth and eighteenth centuries. It is based mainly on court records, and above all those of the Manx ecclesiastical courts. It demonstrates that there was a rich popular culture relating to witchcraft on the island, with a number of individualistic features. It places Manx witchcraft beliefs in relation to two other phenomena that were central to the island's popular culture: fairy beliefs and the belief in the efficacy of the curse. It also demonstrates that the island's authorities maintained a relatively low-keyed approach to witchcraft (only two people are known to have been executed as witches in the island), treating it as a sign of popular ignorance and a regrettable source of neighbourly disputes rather than as a satanic heresy.

Keywords: Isle of Man, court records, attitudes, cursing

I

Thomas Wilson was Bishop of Sodor and Man between 1698 and his death in 1755. He was one of the more remarkable Anglican bishops of the early eighteenth century and, *inter alia*, his fame was to be perpetuated posthumously by a much-republished collection of his sermons. One of these sermons, preached on 29 September, the feast of St Michael and all the Angels, in one year of his lengthy incumbency (unfortunately we do not know which) took as its theme 'The nature, the power, and the malice of evil spirits, and the necessity of a steadfast faith in the protection of God.'[1] Wilson's text was a passage dealing with perhaps the most celebrated of the exorcisms attributed to Christ in the New Testament, His curing of a man possessed with a legion of devils. Christ commanded them to leave the sufferer, and, in Wilson's words, the evil spirits 'knew that they must obey, and besought Him that they might go into a herd of swine that were feeding hard by; the very nature of them being to do mischief whenever they are permitted'. Christ, 'that He might convince the world how dreadful their malice is, and how great their power when left to themselves, and not restrained by God', granted their wish.[2] And, as the text, Mark V.13, put it, 'the unclean spirits went out, and entered into the swine: and the herd ran violently down a steep place into the sea (they were about two thousand), and were choked in the sea', the legion of demons being drowned with them.

Address for correspondence: Professor James Sharpe, Department of History, University of York, Heslington, York Y010 5DD. E-mail: jas19@york.ac.uk

Cultural and Social History, Volume 4, Issue 1, pp. 11–28 © The Social History Society 2007

Wilson's sermon, although couched in the measured tones of the early Enlightenment, was based on a theological position which demonological writers had made familiar from the mid-fifteenth century. 'Now from this history', Wilson commented on the scriptural narrative:

> we learn three truths of great importance. *First*; that the devil is a spirit of great malice and great power; *Secondly*, that both his malice and power are altogether under the government of God. And *thirdly*, that God often permits him to do great mischief for the punishment of wicked men, and for the trial of the faith of good men.[3]

Wilson did not add that element into the demonic equation that was so familiar in early modern demonological treatises – the input of the human servant of Satan, the witch. But he did allude to the belief in witches by noting the tendency to despise evil spirits and their power 'as if we had nothing to fear from them' and the converse tendency 'to ascribe too much power to evil spirits, and to be too much afraid of those whom we suspect to have dealings with them'. The bishop assured his listeners that 'we are wrong in both these extremes'.[4]

Towards the end of his sermon Wilson commented on the popular superstitions of the less theologically well-equipped of his flock, particularly those superstitions relating to the Manx equivalent of what were known in England as cunning folk.[5] 'I know', he declared, 'that simple people have been persuaded to make use of these instruments of Satan, because they make use of some good words, as they say, or scripture expressions.'[6] He also, following a line frequently employed by writers sceptical about witchcraft, urged his listeners 'never to make a rash and wrong judgement of the misfortunes that befall other people', the inference being that the troubles attributed to witchcraft would be better ascribed to the Almighty's mysterious purposes. Again very conventionally, Wilson reminded his audience that 'such afflictions' could be removed 'never by charms, which are certainly of the devil, who by this means would draw men from trusting in and looking up to God, to trust in vanities.' And, finally, Wilson deplored 'that great wickedness of wishing the devil may take either man or beast', since 'you see what mad work he can make when he has his liberty . . . you discover, by your horrid wish, the most wicked disposition that the devil can inspire any man with.'[7]

Thus at a time when concern with witchcraft might be thought to be diminishing among the educated, Wilson, a dedicated clergyman who was devoted to the spiritual welfare of his Manx flock, felt that attacking witch beliefs in the very public forum of a sermon was a worthwhile exercise. His concern was with superstitions about witchcraft rather than the reality of malefic witches, but he was evidently convinced that such superstitions were embedded in the psyche of the Manx peasantry.

II

This article has a twofold objective. Firstly, it will carry out a preliminary examination of these 'superstitions' and attempt to delineate some of the main contours of witchcraft beliefs. Secondly, it will present an analysis the reaction of the island's authorities, and in particular its ecclesiastical authorities, to witchcraft. It will be argued that such an analysis makes a useful and distinctive contribution to our understanding of the variables affecting witch hunting in early modern Europe.

Our starting point must be that, however firmly embedded witch beliefs were in Manx culture, charges of malefic witchcraft were rarely brought before the island's equivalent of the English assizes, the Court of General Gaol Delivery.[8] One woman was convicted of witchcraft before that court in 1569, but was reprieved on grounds of pregnancy.[9] Another, accused of witchcraft in 1598, escaped trial because of a slip in legal procedures.[10] So far as is known, only two people were executed for witchcraft in the early modern Isle of Man: Margaret Ine Quayne and her son John Cubon, burnt for witchcraft at Castletown in 1617.[11] On this evidence, it might seem that witchcraft was hardly a major phenomenon in the island and that it is one of those locations that add little to our knowledge of early modern witchcraft. But deeper analysis of Manx court records reveals a rich and distinctive set of witchcraft beliefs in the early modern Isle of Man. Such an analysis also reveals that the island's authorities, and in particular its ecclesiastical authorities, adopted an idiosyncratic attitude to witchcraft accusations.

Despite its economic backwardness and its lack of any significant claim to importance in European cultural life, the early modern Isle of Man enjoyed a complex and sophisticated administrative system.[12] Between 1406 and 1736 secular rule on the island was invested in the Stanley family, from 1485 earls of Derby, who as Lords of the Isle enjoyed essentially regal powers. Normally, ruling the island was the responsibility of a governor appointed by the Stanleys, under whom served a hierarchy of officials. There was also a complex system of courts, both secular,[13] and, more importantly for the purposes of this article, ecclesiastical. The Manx Church, whose history for the pre-Wilson era awaits detailed research, was essentially a poor one, its clergymen relatively uneducated and not invariably of the highest standard.[14] Yet it possessed in its courts a formidable tool for social discipline, which could impose severe and sometimes ornate penances, and could also fine offenders, put them in the stocks or make them wear the scold's bridle, imprison them, or bind them over to be of good behaviour.[15] The records of the Manx Church courts do not survive from before the early seventeenth century, and it is not until fairly late in that century that a continuous set of presentment books survive.[16] Nevertheless, the records of these ecclesiastical courts, together with such witchcraft cases as are noted in secular court records, provide a substantial body of evidence on Manx witchcraft in the early modern period.

Let us turn initially to a relatively well-documented case of 1658–9 tried in the secular courts on a commission issued by governor James Chalenor to major Thomas Huddlestone, involving accusations against Jane Caesar, wife of John Caesar, the Island's Attorney General. The accusations originated when a servant in the Caesar household, Ellinor Crowe, began to spread stories of her mistress's dabblings in witchcraft. According to two witnesses, Thomas Bridson and Randle Shymyne, mature men aged about fifty and sixty respectively, Crowe recounted how one morning Jane Caesar got up and asked her 'where is the water and herbs that was in this vessel?' When Crowe responded that she had 'thrown them out of doors', Caesar allegedly exclaimed 'thou whore, thou hast cast away the *tarra* of my cattle', supposedly adding (one suspects this was a gloss made for the benefit of the court) 'the luck, good, substance, and essence of my cattle'.[17] Here we encounter a central element in Manx witchcraft beliefs, and one which was still present when folklorists investigated Manx witchcraft two centuries later.[18] Probably underpinned by some equivalent of what anthropologists have described as the concept of limited good,[19] the Manx held that the witch had the power to take away the *tarra*, or increase, from a household's cattle and crops, and either destroy it, or perhaps more frequently, transfer it elsewhere. This 'magical transfer of productiveness' was regarded as one of the defining activities of Manx witches.[20] Something like it was referred to in another of the rumours surrounding Jane Caesar, that she had asked Crowe to get her the parings of the hooves of a cow that John Caesar had sold. Elizabeth Kenvig, also a servant in the Caesar household, reportedly told how she and a third servant, Isabel Shymyne, were sent out on May Eve with twigs of rue to stick in the cattle and sheep in the fold, presumably as a protection against witchcraft on what the Manx held to be the most witch-ridden of nights. Another witness deposed that Jane Caesar's daughter Margaret shook tallow over the family's sheep on May Eve, while yet another related how Isabel Shymyne had told her that Jane Caesar had shaken oats over the sheep that evening. More equivocal evidence was offered by Daniel Comish, John Caesar's ploughman, who said that he saw 'a white thing like salt' on some of the oxen, but that 'he never did see or know his Mrs [i.e. mistress] Jane Caesar seek for or use witchcraft', and Finlo Quirke, who deposed that 'Mrs Jane Caesar did never seek for any witchcraft from him, neither could he do her any, but coming to the house he made a charm for a sick cow.'[21]

The witchcraft that lay at the centre of this case, firmly embedded in popular belief, was, as we shall see, characteristic of the witchcraft that came to the attention of the Manx authorities in the seventeenth and eighteenth centuries. The outcome of the case was likewise typical. The jury of six men convened to try the case declared that Ellinor Crowe, Elizabeth Kenvig and Isabel Shymyne had committed 'slander touching sorcery' since they had not proved their accusations against Jane Caesar. The jurors also stated that they were 'ignorant of the law in this case', and that it should be referred to either the ecclesiastical courts or the governor.[22] It was, indeed, governor Chalenor who ended the affair with a decision obviously geared to meet its peculiar circumstances. In an order dated 10 September 1659 he directed that, although Jane Caesar had been found innocent, she should acknowledge her renunciation of witchcraft in Malew church the following Sunday, and admonish others to reject such delusions, 'which are of great inducement to greater temptations and are too frequently practised in this island, as is daily observed.' Chalenor issued a further order, to be made public in writing in Malew church, that anybody further slandering Jane Caesar or her descendants for witchcraft should pay £10 to the Lord of the Isle and also pay reparation to the offended party as was usual in such cases.[23] Jane Caesar had an influential husband, which may have helped turn the case against those spreading rumours of her involvement in witchcraft: but Manx court records of the period suggest that this type of outcome was frequent with more lowly witchcraft suspects.

Jane Caesar's case is well documented, but most references to witchcraft in the Manx legal records are relatively brief. Many of them, indeed, arise from a few words, hastily spoken, which formed the basis of a slander case. Thus William Cowle received damages in the secular courts in 1615 after Edmund Cowle slandered his wife as a witch. In 1655 Katherine Kelly was fined 12d for slandering Ann Creere as a witch, and a year later fines of 2/- were imposed on Phillip Keneene who slandered Jony Kneale 'to be a witch and that she should be burned', and John Quaine who slandered the wife of Mark Quinney 'to be a witch.'[24] Long memories about witchcraft were demonstrated in 1693, when Alice Cowle of Castletown was reported to the ecclesiastical courts by Mistress Margaret Moore of Ballasalla and others 'for speaking scandalous and defamatory words against her mother Jane Caesar late deceased', who had, as we have seen, been the subject of a witchcraft accusation in 1659. It was ordered that Cowle, 'for her unjust and uncharitable expressions and reflections on the dead', should make '7 Sundays penance in several parish churches and ask the relations of the above Jane Caesar forgiveness before the congregation.' She was also sentenced to fourteen days imprisonment in the bishop's prison at St German and ordered to pay all the legal costs arising from the suit and enter into a bond guaranteeing that she would perform her penance.[25] Obviously, some of these slanders of witchcraft arose from words spoken in anger during a more general altercation. Thus in 1632 it was deposed that a Mr Anglish had called Anne Creghan 'a witch & apprentice to ye greatest witch yt ever was in this isle', and also called her 'a whore and a Manx term meaning strumpet and daughter of a beggar.' Further statements relating to this case suggest that there was rather a lot of name calling surrounding the incident.[26]

What is evident from some of the better documented cases is the magical power attributed by the Manx to earth and dust. Taking dust from the witch's foot, identified by later Manx folklorists as a means of countering the witch's power, was already a known antidote against witchcraft among the early modern Manx.[27] Thus in a case of 1695 it was reported how the wife of William Cairn attributed an illness she was suffering to witchcraft, and asked another woman 'to get Mrs Robinson to come and see her, yt she might get ye dust of her feet, for she thought there was more upon her than the hand of God since Mrs Robinson and she fell out.'[28] Earlier in the seventeenth century John Moore was presented for taking 'some earth from ye church stile', which he sprinkled over a sick calf 'for to prevent an evil eye'.[29] In a case from Patrick in 1733, Isabel Sale, afraid of the witchcraft of Thomas Bell, 'scraped the dust where he had passed on horseback' as he went to church one Sunday, '& sprinkled it on the cattle'.[30] The association between witchcraft and earth was, however, a wider one, probably reflecting concern over *tarra*. In 1605 John Rawscrafte was found guilty of witchcraft and sorcery in that on May Eve he picked up three handfuls of earth from his neighbours' land.[31] In 1750 William Callow or Calow of Lonan petitioned the vicar general of the island to the effect that his wife had been falsely accused by William Corlett of the same parish. Corlett, according to Callow, 'maliciously reported that his wife was taking up dust or earth out of his folds to perform charms therewith, which vile expressions have caused great uneasiness to your petitioner, wife, and all their relations.' A witness, John Skillicorn, deposed that Corlett had told him that Callow's wife Mary had come into his sheepfold, gathered dust and dung from there, and had taken it home in her apron. Another witness, Katherine Callow, deposed that Corlett had told much the same story to her, apparently adding that 'he was sorry he did not give her a witch's mark, & that she would not be doing anything there but mischief & harm.'[32] It was probably earth that Alice Kewne and Alice Quirke of Arbory were collecting when they were seen a little after daybreak on 19 February 1663 'with their hair loose about their ears and had no clothes on them but their petticoat about their heads barefooted.' The women were apparently walking around the landmarks indicating the boundaries of Arbory parish putting something in their aprons.[33]

Sometimes the charges involving witchcraft and dust were more elaborate. In 1677 a slander was reported against Henry Corrin and his wife 'that they do wear about them herbs which their servants have several times seen', the servants allegedly reporting further that 'the said Henry Corrin's wife did take dust from their several neighbours' mear hedges at sowing time, part whereof she laid up in the doorstead & part did sow or cause to be sowed with ye first oats they did sow that year.'[34] Fertility of the crops was also clearly an issue in a case of 1697, when it was alleged that Henry Kelly of Marrown had 'sent his son to carry earth out of the field of Thomas Chicase of Cottin (which field was newly sown) to his own field where he was sowing.'[35] A more extreme case came in 1733, when Daniel Cowl of Ballaugh was presented by John Bridson, the rector of the parish. Cowl had apparently taken umbrage when the clergyman had walked past him without bidding God speed to his plough team, which, according to Cowl, made one of his bullocks lay down 'before the said minister's face'. Cowl, who allegedly declared subsequently that 'some of the ministers are worse than the devil', told how he 'went and took some of the earth off the said minister's foot and threw it on the beast', at which 'the said beast got up and never laid down . . . before nor since.' It was probably Cowl's further comments that 'I say he [Bridson] is the devil, and the devil is in him, for the devil is more busy about ministers and clerks than he is about others, for they are the worst sort among us' that earned him the censure of the ecclesiastical courts. But his getting dust from Bridson's foot and sprinkling it on his seemingly afflicted cow, that standard Manx remedy against witchcraft, is noteworthy.[36]

It is also clear that another peculiarity of Manx witchcraft beliefs noted by later folklorists, the significance of May Eve and May Day, was already present in the seventeenth and eighteenth centuries.[37] Thus in a case of c. 1716 a Jurby woman complained to the ecclesiastical authorities about gossip that she and her husband had been out early on May morning, walking on the dew in their neighbours' fields with the intention of harming the increase of their crops.[38] In 1695 William Lacey of Kirk Andreas complained to the ecclesiastical authorities that he had seen Jony Cowle, widow, 'in his lands on May Day in the morning with her petticoats ab[ou]t her head and neck. And that he thought she was in no good ways (which is, as understood, that he suspected her of sorcery).'[39] Henry Quayle deposed in 1733 how Henry Sale of Patrick had come to him 'last May Day two years' and told him how the previous evening Thomas Bell's maidservant and children had walked on his land, and was clearly unconvinced by Quayle's assertion that 'they could do no harm there.'[40] And one is left wondering exactly what circumstances lay behind a case of 1794, in which John Corjeage of Michael reported laying hold of a woman on May Morning, who said if he did not let her go, she would bewitch him, and then confessed that to do so was not in her power, as he had 'a cross made of round [rowan?] tree' in his pocket.[41]

As might be expected, charmers figure prominently in these Manx witchcraft cases. Bahy Quayle was accused in 1706 of being a charmer, having apparently been presented for the offence several times before, while one of her clients, John Cubon, was presented for going to her for a charm.[42] When Ewan Corkhill of Ballaugh was presented as a sorcerer in 1664 it was noted that a number of his neighbours had resorted to him.[43] The neighbours of Elizabeth Kewin alias Cubon of Kirk Arbory reported in 1666 how she came home 'with burdens of corn, meal, fish, etc.', and suspected that she had 'gotten the same for sorcery and wicked practices, and by deluding poor ignorant people; also (by report) many resorting to her house to get of her sorcery, and bad signs seen by credible people.' By the time the jury met to investigate this case, the evidence against Kewin alias Cubon had extended to comprehend not only using evil charms against cattle, sheep and crops, but also the ability to increase or lessen the productivity of a farm or household, and to change herself into the shape of a hare.[44] Generally, however, the Manx tended to see charmers as benevolent. One well documented charmer, Alice Cowley, who fell foul of the ecclesiastical authorities in 1713, apparently advised married women about barrenness, advised farmers on how to make their crops and herds flourish and advised parents on the curing of a sick child, all of these problems seemingly being ascribed to malefic witchcraft.[45] We have occasional insights into the techniques of charmers, among the most frequent of these, in the Isle of Man as elsewhere, being the use of the sieve and shears for divination.[46]

On occasion, the punishments awarded to witches and charmers could be severe. Thus Alice Cowley, the charmer apprehended in 1713, was imprisoned for thirty days in the bishop's prison, and then had to stand in a white sheet, holding a white wand and carrying a paper saying 'for charming and sorcery' on her breast for two hours in each of the island's four market towns, this to be followed by public penance in Ballaugh church, where she was publicly to renounce her practices.[47] Generally, however, the penalties inflicted by the Manx courts in witchcraft cases were not onerous. Under Manx law, allegations of witchcraft were first screened by a jury of six men appointed by the ecclesiastical courts, whose role it was to decide if the allegations were serious enough to pass on to the secular authorities.[48] Almost invariably these juries decided to the contrary, and thus witchcraft allegations were usually dealt with by the Church courts, where they were routinely either redefined as cases of charming or sorcery, or reformulated as slander cases. The outcome of these cases was usually the imposition of a relatively light punishment upon the offender. Typical was Bahy Quayle, who, presented as she had been several times before for using charms, was directed in 1706 to find sureties ('bondsmen') against future offences of that nature, and to make public acknowledgement of her faults before the congregation of her parish church.[49]

The tendency for tensions concerning witchcraft to surface as slander cases left the way open for the courts to seek to engineer a settlement between the parties involved rather than the punishment of alleged witches. This might involve official attempts to forestall future problems. Thus, in 1652 deputy governor Captain Samuel Smith, following ecclesiastical court practices and, indeed, anticipating the action taken by governor Chalenor in the Jane Caesar case, ordered that whoever in the future slandered Christian Kermode of Douglas for witchcraft would be severely punished, and directed that this order should be published in the island's parish churches.[50] Sometimes, however, especially in Church court cases, a simple, albeit officially sanctioned, apology on the part of the witch's accuser was thought to constitute sufficient remedy. Thus in 1673 it was certified that Thomas Clarke 'hath this day very penitently confessed his offence in calling Mally Fayle the daughter of a witch, and upon his knees in full congregation craved forgiveness.'[51] In 1750 William Corlett 'justly incurr'd a severe censure' for what were thought to be scandalous accusations of witchcraft against Mary the wife of John Callow. 'Yet upon the intercession of several persons', it was noted, 'the said Mary Callow is prevailed upon to accept of William Corlett's asking her solemn forgiveness, which he has accordingly done in public court.' Even in this instance, however, the verdict was to be 'published' in the parties' parish church, as was an order that any person reviving the slander would forfeit £3, be subject to forty days' imprisonment, and suffer further punishment 'as the law directs'.[52] The same decision was reached in a case of 1754, when William Killey of Lezayre slandered Mary the wife of Ewan Kinread by saying she was a witch. In this instance Killey acknowledged 'that he must have uttered some expressions rashly tending that way, & for which he asked her the said Mary Kinread solemn forgiveness on his knees.'[53] Here as elsewhere the objective of officialdom was obviously to defuse the neighbourly tensions that so often underlay witchcraft accusations rather than root out alleged witches.

We should not come away with too benign an impression of Manx witchcraft beliefs: witches were to be feared and they certainly on occasion were seen to be potentially harmful. In gossip surrounding the witchcraft activities of Thomas Bell and his family in 1733, Isabel Quayle claimed that Bell's wife had told her that 'as long as you are in favour with the sorcerers you are safe enough', and also alleged that Bell's daughter had killed a heifer by witchcraft.[54] A case of 1707 in which John Cottier was found guilty of slandering Isabel Gawn for witchcraft turned mainly on allegations that Gawn had killed a horse worth £5 belonging to Cottier by witchcraft.[55] The potency with which witchcraft was regarded was indicated by an incident of 1617. In that year Phillip Costeane, accused of a bloodwipe (a Manx term equating with serious assault) had the charges dropped by the court after claiming that he did it 'in defence of his life or to avoid other harm that might befall to him' by the witchcraft of those he assaulted, namely Margaret Ine Quayne and her son John Cubon who were to be executed for witchcraft that year, and possibly other members of the Cubon family.[56] And, of course, that central attribute of Manx witchcraft, the ability to lessen or increase a household's prosperity, clearly implied malefic powers. When investigations against Elizabeth Kewin alias Cubon of Arbory were taking place in 1666, one of her neighbours deposed that the supposed witch had told her 'it was as easy to take away the substance of one man's corn to another, as it was to turn a cake of bread upon the girdle [i.e. griddle].' Another deponent reported that she could not make cheese nor raise a calf due to her troublesome neighbour's witchcraft, and that 'for a long time they were very low in estate every way while the said Elizabeth used and frequented the house'.[57] What is striking, however, is that such suspicions almost never surfaced as a formal accusation in the court of General Gaol Delivery.

III

Thus with early modern Manx witchcraft we have unusual evidence of a body of popular beliefs about witches, evidence which constitutes a useful addition to our growing knowledge of witchcraft in the Europe of the period. The Manx records are less rich than, for example, the Inquisition records, which have been used to such effect in the study of popular beliefs by Carlo Ginzburg,[58] yet they do reveal a remarkable local witchcraft culture. Obviously we have done little more than delineate some of the main issues in this article: a full discussion must be postponed until we have a deeper knowledge of the everyday life of the island in the early modern period, of work practices, of perceptions of gender, and of the symbolic significance attached to thresholds, hearths, clothing, uncovered female hair, and many other matters. Yet it would seem overcautious to neglect this issue completely, even at this early stage of investigation. Manx court records rarely note the occupational status of persons involved in legal cases, so it is difficult to establish the precise social status of witches and their accusers. Conversely, although the nature of the relevant records makes exact quantification on this point difficult, it is clear that the overwhelming majority of those suspected as witches or charmers were women. But what the sources do convey very forcefully is a clear sense of a deeply embedded peasant belief in witchcraft and charming, important aspects of the island's culture whose distinctiveness was probably in large measure connected to the broader linguistic and cultural separateness of the Manx.

Our investigation of Manx witchcraft raises issues about the relationship between witchcraft and other elements of the popular belief system of the period – elements that can be found in other parts of the British Isles. Perhaps the most important of these relationships is that between witchcraft and fairy beliefs. There was in Scotland, as the statements of some confessing witches suggests, a close connection, and on occasion confusion, between fairy and witch beliefs, while a similar relationship, although less powerful, was also present in England.[59] Fascinatingly, a very definite link between fairy and witch lore can be found in an early Manx case. Alice Ine Gilbay, saved by pregnancy from execution for witchcraft in 1569, had allegedly told Anne Watson not to be afraid of her, but that nevertheless she had 'a concubine of the fairies which I might send att any time to kill thee', a spirit that had obvious parallels with the English familiar.[60]

Some very pertinent comments on the relationship between witchcraft and fairy beliefs have been made by Ronald Hutton in relation to Ireland. There, he argues, there existed 'a rich traditional rural Irish cosmology, in which the fairy folk were constantly held responsible for untoward events and uncanny misfortunes.'[61] This, claims Hutton, helps explain why there were so few witch accusations among the early modern Irish: 'Gaelic Ireland affords a classic case of a society which did not fear the witch-figure because it ascribed misfortune to other sources.'[62] Much the same situation may have obtained among the Manx. At the very least, several eighteenth-century English observers, while having little to say about witchcraft, commented extensively on Manx fairy beliefs. One such was George Waldron, an English government official resident on the island in the early eighteenth century who wrote at length on Manx superstitions, and especially fairy lore.[63] Another visitor to the island, albeit much later in the century, was David Robertson. Unexpectedly spending a night in a cottage in the upland zone of the island, Robertson was regaled with an account of Manx fairy lore by his host, an elderly peasant. The old man assured Robertson that the island was still full of fairies, and that there existed both good ones, and (in Robertson's words) 'those who were sullen and vindictive'. These latter, 'who were neither beautiful in their persons, not gorgeous in their array . . . delighted in procuring human misery', Robertson's informant adding 'that to them, Manksmen imputed all their sufferings.'[64] The Manx believed in witches, but just as in (on Hutton's interpretation) Gaelic Ireland, the presence of a strong image of the malignant fairy may have inhibited among them the development of the concept of the malefic witch and, indeed, in so far as they would have come into contact with it, the notion of the demonic witch of the learned demonologists.

Secondly, these Manx materials emphasize the relationship between witchcraft and cursing. Early modern sources indicate that the Manx were fully aware of the power of the curse, with presentments for cursing figuring prominently in the correction business of the island's ecclesiastical courts until well into the eighteenth century.[65] Most of these presentments do not give much information on the words spoken, frequently reference being simply made to one person wishing 'the curse of God' or 'God's curse' upon another. Sometimes, conversely, more elaborate details of the curse were noted. Thus in 1695 William Moor of Arbory was presented for wishing God's curse on two other men, and also 'for cursing in common, and saying God's curse upon them that took the top off his ling stack, and that they may both lose their hands and their feet, and the devil put out their eyes that did the same.'[66] In 1659 another relatively elaborate curse was uttered by Catherine Cottier alias Kneall against John Casement, the woman declaring her wish that 'he might have neither son or daughter about his fire or hearth to the third of fourth generation and that his house might be ruinated', sentiments that led to her performing penance at five of the island's parish churches, being whipped, paying a fine of 6d, and spending an hour in the stocks at Ramsey.[67] Belief in the power of the curse might have been reinforced by a folk-memory of the pre-Reformation Church's pronouncement of the curse of God against miscreants. In 1695 William Lacey of Andreas reported that he had seen the widow Jony Cowle in his fields on May Day morning, and suspected that she had been performing witchcraft. He expressed the wish, in the words of the court documentation, that she might be given 'the curse of the church which had been our old obsolete custom practised in this island in cases of yt nature.'[68]

Folklorists noted that belief in the potency of cursing was still alive among the Manx in the late nineteenth century, most notably in the form of a ritual of seven bitter curses. The most powerful of these was that of the *skeab lome*, a Manx term which translates literally as 'the naked broom or besom', but which is perhaps better rendered in this context as 'the besom of destruction'. This was a curse of annihilation, accompanied, so the folklorists found, by an elaborate ritual on the part of the curses. In this ritual the curser with her (for the curser was normally a woman) face to the door of the house of the object of her hatred, and with hair uncovered, would make a gesture of sweeping with a besom, and utter a severe malediction.[69] Seventeenth- and eighteenth-century sources make it clear that this most potent of curses was already current. Sometimes the full formula of the curse is recorded, as in a Rushen case of 1744: 'may the besom of destruction come upon thyself, upon thy hearth, upon thy health, upon thy possessions and upon thy children.'[70] More usually, the it would simply be noted that the curse of the *skeab lome* had been invoked, for example at an unknown parish in 1673, at Rushen in 1675, at Rushen again in 1678, and at Patrick in 1735.[71] The Manx curse is clearly a topic that would repay further investigation, yet it is evident even from an initial analysis that in the curse, and especially in the curse of the *skeab lome*, the Manx had a well-defined notion of the power of one individual to harm another through occult forces. This raises the issue of the relationship of the curse to that parallel concept which was apparently less central in the Manx belief system, fear of the power of the malefic witch.

Such a relationship was suggested by Keith Thomas in his classic study of English popular beliefs,[72] and was certainly one that was familiar to English demonological writers. Thus William Perkins, one the most important Protestant theologians of the Elizabethan era, declared that witchcraft should be suspected, 'if after cursing there followeth death, or at least some mischief', adding that 'witches are wont to practice their mischievous facts by cursing and banning.'[73] Thomas argued that among the population at large 'it was widely assumed that certain types of curse still retained their efficacy', and that 'the more justified the curser's anger, the more likely that his [sic] imprecations would take effect.'[74] These ideas have been developed further in a recent analysis of Welsh witchcraft cases, where it has been argued that:

> the idea of cursing was linked with notions of justice, and it is clear that different assessments of justification led to accusations of witchcraft after formal cursing. Apparently successful maledictions could be explained alternatively as justifiable curses or unjustifiable bewitching. From the standpoint of the suspected witch, curses were a justified response to injustice; but from the standpoint of the accuser the reputed witch's malediction was an unjustified response to a relatively innocuous offence.[75]

One suspects that similar considerations were at play with instances of cursing among the Manx. Interestingly, however, the author of the analysis of Welsh cursing argues that the curse was considered to be at its most dangerous, and hence most likely to result in an accusation of witchcraft, when it crossed the boundaries of age, gender or status.[76] The nature of the relevant records makes it unlikely that we shall ever gain a sufficient grasp of the contexts of the Manx cursing cases to see how often these boundaries were crossed on the island, but it might well be that they were not crossed often enough to result in numerous witchcraft accusations. Moreover, the island's ecclesiastical authorities were clearly concerned to contain and defuse those tensions that underlay and were released by both cursing and witchcraft accusations.

IV

Parallels to the Manx witchcraft belief system doubtless existed throughout Europe. Elsewhere, especially under the impact of the more rigorous Christianity demanded by both the Reformation and the Counter Reformation, such belief systems were attacked, and either marginalized as superstition or redefined as demonic witchcraft. In the latter eventuality, the equivalents of our Manx witches and charmers might be burnt in large numbers.[77] If one of the earls of Derby, or, indeed, one of the island's governors, had been a rabid witch hunter, things might have been different. But over most of the early modern period the Lords of the Isle were happy to rule from a distance, their major concern the collection of rents and dues. Thus there was little by way of proactive campaigns for reform or more intensive rule from the island's secular authorities.

The Manx Church was much more important when considering the relationship between officialdom and the lack of witch hunting in the island, not least because, as we have noted, most accusations of witchcraft were initially screened by juries appointed by the ecclesiastical courts. The history of the Manx Church in the pre-Wilson period is, we must repeat, very much uncharted territory, but there can be little doubt that the island was one of the 'dark corners' of Europe. The Reformation did not really arrive on the island in any meaningful way until Bishop John Phillips's Manx Convocation of 1610, and throughout the seventeenth century the spreading of post-Reformation religious standards was hampered by the poverty of the Manx Church, the low quality of its clergy, the uneven commitment of the Bishops of Sodor and Man to the spiritual improvement of the island's population, and the linguistic problem (there was no Manx bible until well into the eighteenth century).[78] Had there been an aggressive Calvinist Church on the Scottish model, a full-scale witch hunt may have developed.[79] As it was, witchcraft on the island seems to have been regarded in a manner that Stuart Clark has identified as typical of many other parts of Protestant Europe. It was seen essentially as an issue that reflected not so much the devil's input (although that could never be ignored entirely) but rather the superstition and ignorance of the population, and the lamentable capacity of Christians to fall out with each other rather than dwell together in Christian charity.[80] Unfortunately, we have no policy statements on witchcraft from John Phillips, or from later active bishops such as Isaac Barrow (1663–70). But we do, to return to the clergyman with whose sermon we began this article, have a number of orders on the subject from Thomas Wilson.

One of these came in the aftermath of the censure of two charmers, Alice Cowley and Isabel Gawne, in 1713. In a circular to his clergy, Wilson noted that the two women had wandered 'about the country deceiving the people, and drawing them from their dependence upon God, and trust in vanity and lies.' The clergy were instructed to tell their flocks to have nothing to do with such persons:

> My earnest desire therefore is, that you will not fail to take the occasion of representing unto your people, after as plain a manner as may be, the sin, and the consequences, of seeking to those wicked deceivers, and make them sensible that all charms, let the words be good, bad, or unintelligible, or mere jargon, are of the devil, with whom there is a compact implied by the very practice: that is a forsaking of God when we have most

need to fly to and trust in Him, viz in time of trouble and distress . . . In short, these wicked devices being contrivances of the devil, to draw men from trusting in God for health and security and prosperity, we should endeavour the very knowledge of them, if possible, be rooted out from among us; that our people be taught to look up to God, to trust in His goodness and providence, to fear none but Him.

Wilson also, perhaps significantly, noted that such practices, 'may, if not timely discouraged, end in downright witchcraft.'[81] But overall, he is here following the standard theological line that witch beliefs, although essentially the devil's work, should be treated as an aspect of popular ignorance rather than as evidence of the existence of an heretical sect. In this, on the strength of what can be inferred from the records, he was following the established attitude of the Manx Church and, indeed, that which was by the early eighteenth century prevalent more widely in the Anglican Church of which the Manx Church was part.[82]

Peter Burke has commented that 'in any study of witchcraft over the long term, evidence from the European periphery is absolutely central.'[83] What I hope to have demonstrated here is the importance of witch beliefs in what was culturally and geographically very much a peripheral region of early modern Europe. In particular, I feel that there are two issues that need to be re-emphasized. Firstly, there is the presence of a distinct set of popular beliefs about witchcraft in the island – here as in so many other places apparently little affected by contact with 'learned' models of demonological witchcraft. As eighteenth-century presentments and the writings of nineteenth-century folklorists demonstrate, the Isle of Man was one of those places where these popular categorizations of the supernatural were very resistant to being replaced by official theological and legal ones. And, secondly, and very much related to this first point, Manx materials provide yet more evidence of the variations with which officialdom in this period might confront the problem of witchcraft. The desire for higher standards of Christian belief and Christian behaviour that were integral to the Reformation and the Counter Reformation did not lead automatically to witch hunting. It was just as likely to lead to clergymen shaking their heads in dismay at the ignorance of their flocks, and at their inability to live in peace with each other.

NOTES

1. John Keeble (ed.), *The Works of the Right Reverend Father in God, Thomas Wilson, D.D., Lord Bishop of Sodor and Man*, 6 vols (Oxford, 1847), vol. 2, pp. 236–45. The most probable date for the sermon is 1713, in which year Wilson was involved in the prosecution of two charmers, or 'good' witches. Wilson is a figure who is in urgent need of a modern scholarly reappraisal. For a recent discussion of at least one facet of his career, see John Owen Mann, 'Thomas Wilson and Anglicanism', unpublished M.Phil. thesis, Queen's University Belfast, 1998.

2. Keeble (ed.), *Works of Wilson*, vol. 2, p. 237.

3. Keeble (ed.), *Works of Wilson*, vol. 2, p. 237.

4. Keeble (ed.), *Works of Wilson*, vol. 2, p. 236.

5. The importance of cunning folk in early modern English witch beliefs was first emphasized by Alan Macfarlane, *Witchcraft in Tudor and Stuart England: a Regional and Comparative*

Study (London, 1970), ch. 8, 'Cunning Folk and Witchcraft Prosecutions'. For a more recent and fuller study, see Owen Davies, *Cunning Folk: Popular Magic in English History* (London, 2003).

6. Keeble (ed.), *Works of Wilson*, vol. 2, p. 244.

7. Keeble (ed.), *Works of Wilson*, vol. 2, p. 244.

8. On the Court of General Gaol delivery, see J.R. Dickinson, *The Lordship of Man under the Stanleys: Government and Economy in the Isle of Man, 1580–1714* (Chetham Society, 3rd series, vol. 41, 1996), pp. 65 - 6. Aspects of the business of the court are discussed by Dickinson, 'Criminal Violence and Judicial Punishment in the Isle of Man 1580–1700', *Isle of Man Natural History and Antiquarian Society Proceedings*, 11/1 (2000): 127 - 42. I am grateful to Dr Dickinson for commenting on an earlier draft of this article.

9. Manx National Heritage Library (hereafter MNHL), Libri Placitorum (Books of Common Pleas: hereafter Lib. Plit.), 1569, unfoliated, Court of General Gaol Delivery, Session 9 May 1569.

10. MNHL, Libri Scaccarii (Books of the Court of Exchequer: hereafter Lib. Scacc.), 1598, f. 6.

11. MNHL, Lib. Scacc. 1617, f. 1. This entry contains no details of the nature of the witchcraft allegedly committed in the case: it does refer to details contained in a Church court 'book of presentments', but this appears to have been lost.

12. For an excellent discussion of this system, see Dickinson, *Lordship of Man*, ch. 1, 'The Government of the Isle of Man'.

13. An analysis of the work of the secular courts formed the basis for a project funded by the Leverhulme Trust, E.224R, 'Crime, Litigation and the Courts in the Isle of Man, c. 1550–1704': for a preliminary report on the findings of this project, see J.A. Sharpe and J.R. Dickinson, 'Courts, Crime and Litigation in the Isle of Man 1580–1700', *Historical Research*, 72 (1999): 140–59. Further analysis of the archives of these courts was facilitated by an Arts and Humanities Research Board award, RLS-AN6397/APN10423.

14. Anne Ashley, 'The Spiritual Courts of the Isle of Man, Especially in the Seventeenth and Eighteenth Centuries', *English Historical Review*, 57 (1957): 31–59, remains the best general introduction to the history of the Manx Church in the early modern period. For a more general, if dated, overview see A.W. Moore, *Sodor and Man* (Brighton, 1893). Later developments are traced in John Gelling, *A History of the Manx Church 1698 - 1911* (Douglas, 1998).

15. The sanctions available to the island's Church courts are discussed in J.R. Dickinson and J.A. Sharpe, 'Public Punishments and the Manx Ecclesiastical Courts during the seventeenth and eighteenth Centuries', in Simon Devereaux and Paul Griffiths (eds), *Penal Practice and Culture 1500–1900: Punishing the English* (Basingstoke, 2003).

16. The main sources relating to the Manx ecclesiastical courts are: the Libri Testamentarum, listed currently as either Episcopal Wills or Archiadiaconical Wills, in which presentments are scattered among records of testamentary business, volumes relevant to this article being available on microfilm as MNHL EW1-31 and RB512-26; Presentment Books, which survive in a broken series from c. 1640 and in a complete series from the late 1690s until 1874; and the Libri Causarum, recording the business of the bishop's consistory court, these 'Libri' being bound collections of loose papers relating mainly to administrative matters, but also including presentments, depositions, notes of compurgation and orders of penance. These ecclesiastical court records are usually unfoliated, and hence citations from them in this article are made to the relevant parish (where possible) and the date of the presentment, etc. Jennifer Platten is currently preparing a Liverpool University PhD thesis

on the work of the Manx ecclesiastical courts in the late seventeenth and eighteenth centuries.

17. MNHL, Lib. Scacc. 1659, ff. 21–2, 22–6. Despite their surname, the Caesars were an established Manx family of some standing, while Jane Caesar was the daughter of one of the branches of another such. Here as elsewhere I have modernized the spelling of the original documentation.

18. The most important of these later works on Manx Folklore was A.W. Moore, *The Folk-Lore of the Isle of Man, being an Account of its Myths, Legends, Superstitions, Customs and Proverbs* (Douglas, 1891), which contains a lengthy discussion of Manx witchcraft beliefs in the Victorian era. For a more modern study, see Margaret Killip, *The Folklore of the Isle of Man* (London, 1975). The work of Moore and other students of Manx folklore is discussed by Stephen Harrison and Yvonne Cresswell, 'Folklore', in John Brewer (ed.), *A History of the Isle of Man. Volume V. The Modern Period 1830–1999* (Liverpool, 2000). See also the discussion of witchcraft and related beliefs in a work written by a pioneer student of Manx archival materials, David Craine, *Manannan's Isle* (Douglas, 1955), pp. 13–30.

19. The concept was introduced by G. Foster, 'Peasant Society and the Image of the Limited Good', *American Anthropologist*, 67 (1965): 293–315.

20. The phrase is used by Craine, *Manannan's Isle*, p. 18, in the course of a general discussion of *tarra*.

21. MNHL, Lib. Scacc. 1659, ff. 21–4.

22. MNHL, Lib. Scacc. 1659, f. 24.

23. MNHL, Lib. Scacc. 1659, f. 25.

24. MNHL, Lib. Plit. 1615, unfoliated, Court held at Douglas 8 May 1615; Lib. Scacc. 1655, f. 56; Lib. Scacc. 1656, f. 42.

25. MNHL, Liber Causarum 1659–1704, Depositions 25 May 1693; Order of John Pass and John Christian, Vicars General, 8 June 1693.

26. MNHL, RB513, Bishop's Court at Peel, 31 May 1632.

27. This was one of a number of peculiarities in Manx witchcraft beliefs to be noted by later folklorists, such as Moore, *Folk-Lore of the Isle of Man*, p. 78. Killip, writing in 1975, noted that the belief had been current within living memory: *Folklore*, p. 55.

28. MNHL, Liber Causarum 1659–1704, Examinations 21 Aug 1695.

29. MNHL, RB513, Presentments Aug 1630.

30. MNHL, Presentment Books, 1733, Depositions 24 July 1734.

31. MNHL, EW1, Presentment 4 May 1605.

32. MNHL, Presentment Books, 1750, Petition of William Callow of Lonan, and Depositions 21 July 1750.

33. MNHL, David Craine, '1663: Sorcery in Arbory', *Journal of the Manx Museum*, 3 (1934): 38–9.

34. MNHL, RB519, Petition of John Kewley, 2 Dec 1677.

35. MNHL, Liber Causarum 1659 - 1704, Note from 'a jury sworn concerning witchcraft' 29 June 1697.

36. MNHL, Presentment Books, 1733, Ballaugh Presentments, 22 May 1733.

37. Moore, *Folk-Lore of the Isle of Man*, p. 111; C.I. Paton, *Manx Calendar Customs* (London, 1939), pp. 42–54, discusses both witch beliefs relating to May Day and the elaborate May Day celebrations enjoyed on the island. This work notes little witchcraft significance for other dates, including Hallowe'en.

38. Keeble (ed.), *Works of Wilson*, vol. 1, p. 303. Nearly two centuries later Moore noted that

on May Morning 'the maidens went forth to gather the dew, and wash their faces in it, as it was supposed to ensure a good complexion, as well as to render the hostility of the witches innocuous.' *Folk - Lore of the Isle of Man*, p. 111.

39. MNHL, RB522, Order 10, June 1695.

40. MNHL, Presentment Books, 1733, Depositions 24 July 1733.

41. MNHL, Presentment Books, 1794, K.K. Michael Presentments. The wood of the rowan tree was regarded as an antidote against witchcraft throughout the early modern period: see Iona Opie and Moira Tatem (eds), *A Dictionary of Superstitions* (Oxford, 1989), pp. 333–4.

42. MNHL, Presentment Books, 1706, Michael Presentments 24 Nov 1706.

43. David Craine, '1664: Ballaugh Presentments for Charming', *Journal of the Manx Museum*, 3 (1934): 219.

44. MNHL, EW17, Order 14 July 1666; undated Depositions of Daniel Bell, George Houldinge, Catharine Norris *alias* Fargher, Ellin Norris, and others. The unusually full documentation for this case is dated between 1 July 1666 and 31 March 1667.

45. Keeble (ed.), *Works of Wilson*, vol. 1, p. 302.

46. For example, Craine, *Manannan's Isle*, p. 22, where details of a Braddan case of 1733 are given.

47. Keeble (ed.), *Works of Wilson*, vol. 1, p. 302.

48. Mark Anthony Mills (ed.), *The Ancient Ordinances and Statute Laws of the Isle of Man: Carefully Copied from, and Compared with the Authentic Records* (Douglas, 1821), p. 302.

49. MNHL, Presentment Books, 1706, Michael Presentments 24 Nov 1706.

50. MNHL Lib. Scacc. 1652, ff. 28–9. The order noted that 'no probable evidence' could be found to prove the allegations against Kermode, and that 'by the general opinion of all her neighbours she is a very civil woman and of good behaviour.'

51. MNHL, RB519, Certificate 25 May 1673.

52. MNHL, Presentment Books, 1750, Order 21 July 1750.

53. MNHL, Presentment Books, 1764, Lezayre Presentments 19 Jan 1754.

54. MNHL, Presentment Books, 1733, Depositions 24 July 1733.

55. David Craine, '1706: a Kirk Christ Rushen Farmer doing Penance for calling a Woman "*BenKalliagh ny Bishag*" and "*Ben Kalliagh ny Olssyn*"', *Journal of the Manx Museum*, 2 (1932): 58–9.

56. MNHL, Lib. Plit. 1617, unfoliated, Session of 3 May 1617.

57. MNHL, EW17, undated Depositions of John Stile and Catherine Norris *alias* Fargher.

58. Carlo Ginzburg, *The Night Battles: Witchcraft and Agrarian Cults in the Sixteenth and Seventeenth Centuries* (London, 1983).

59. For Scotland, see J.A. MacCulloch, 'The Mingling of Fairy and Witch Beliefs in Sixteenth and Seventeenth-century Scotland', *Folklore*, 32 (1921): 229–44, and Lizanne Henderson and Edward J. Cowan, *Scottish Fairy Belief: a History* (East Linton, 2001). For England, see Keith Thomas, *Religion and the Decline of Magic: Popular Beliefs in Sixteenth- and Seventeenth-Century England* (London, 1971), pp. 606–14. See also Dianne Purkiss, *Troublesome Things: a History of Fairies and Fairy Stories* (Harmondsworth, 2000).

60. MNHL, Lib. Plit. 1569, unfoliated, Court of General Gaol Delivery 9 May 1569. For possible connections between the English fairy figure and the witch's familiar see James Sharpe, 'The Witch's Familiar in Elizabethan England', in G.W. Bernard and S.J. Gunn (eds), *Authority and Consent in Tudor England: Essays Presented to C.S.L. Davies* (Aldershot, 2002), pp. 228–9.

61. Ronald Hutton, 'The Global Context of the Scottish Witch-Hunt', in Julian Goodare (ed.),

The Scottish Witch-hunt in Context (Manchester, 2002), p. 31.

62. Hutton, 'Global Context', p. 32. Witchcraft in Ireland has not been much studied, although it is interesting to note a comment from an observer in County Kildare in 1683, who remarked that despite the widespread tendency to attribute misfortune to witchcraft among the local population, 'of witches there are very rarely heard any detected or convicted amongst then': Raymond Gillespie, 'Women and Crime in seventeenth-century Ireland', in Margaret MacCurtain and Mary O'Dowd (eds), *Women in Early Modern Ireland* (Edinburgh, 1991), p. 45. St John D. Seymour, *Irish Witchcraft and Demonology* (Dublin and London, 1913) remains the classic work on Irish witchcraft. For the continued potency of Irish fairy beliefs into the modern era see A. Bourke, *The Burning of Bridget Cleary* (London, 1999).

63. George Waldron, *The History and Description of the Isle of Man: viz its Antiquity, History, Laws, Customs, Religion and Manners of its Inhabitants, its Animals, Minerals* (Dublin, 1742), pp. 36–48. Waldron's account of Manx superstitions is of special interest as it was heavily drawn upon, and extensively quoted, by Sir Walter Scott in his partly Manx-based novel, *Peveril of the Peak* (Edinburgh, 1822).

64. David Robertson, *A Tour through the Isle of Man: to Which is Subjoined, a Review of the Manks History* (London, 1794), pp. 76–8. For later Manx fairy beliefs, see Moore, *Folk-Lore of the Isle of Man*, ch. 3, 'Fairies and Familiar Spirits'.

65. On the Manx curse, see Craine, *Manannan's Isle*, pp. 22 - 5.

66. MNHL, RB522, Arbory Presentments 4 Feb 1694 [?5].

67. David Craine, '1659. Doing Penances in Five Parish Churches', *Journal of the Manx Museum*, 3 (1935): 58.

68. MNHL, RB522, Order 10 June 1695. For a discussion of what William Lacey probably meant by 'the curse of the church' see Lester K. Little, *Benedictine Maledictions: Liturgical Cursing in Romanesque France* (Ithaca, 1993).

69. On the *skeab lome* see Craine, *Manannan's Isle*, pp. 23–5; Killip, *Folklore*, p. 60.

70. Craine, *Manannan's Isle*, p. 24.

71. MNHL, RB519, Presentment 2 Feb 1673; Rushen Presentments 25 May 1675; Malew Presentments 24 Feb 1678; RB520, Rushen Presentments 16 June 1678; Craine, *Manannan's Isle*, p. 24.

72. Thomas, *Religion and the Decline of Magic*, pp. 502–12.

73. William Perkins, *A Discourse of the Damned Art of Witchcraft. So farre forth as it is revealed in the Scriptures, and Manifest by True Experience* (Cambridge, 1608), p. 202.

74. Thomas, *Religion and the Decline of Magic*, p. 505.

75. Richard Suggett, 'Witchcraft Dynamics in early modern Wales', in Michael Roberts and Sion Clarke (eds), *Women and Gender in Early Modern Wales* (Cardiff, 2000), pp. 93–4.

76. Suggett, 'Witchcraft Dynamics', p. 90.

77. For a classic statement of the impact of this more rigorous Christianity, see Jean Delumeau, *Le Catholicisme entre Luther et Voltaire* (Paris, 1971). For an important study emphasizing the connection between witch hunting and the rise of the confessional state, see Christina Larner, *Enemies of God: the Witch-hunt in Scotland* (London, 1981). These post-Reformation processes were, of course, in many ways a continuation and intensification of late medieval developments: see, for example, Michael D. Bailey, *Battling Demons; Witchcraft, Heresy and Reform in the Late Middle Ages* (University Park, Pennsylvania, 2003).

78. The Manx bible was published in instalments between 1763 and 1770 under the aegis of Thomas Wilson's successor, Bishop Mark Hildersley: R.H. Kinvig, *The Isle of Man: a Social,*

Cultural and Political History (Liverpool, 1975), p. 126.

79. One is reminded of the comment made in a recent study of Scottish fairy lore, that 'the activities of the kirk do indeed seem inextricably linked to witch - hunting and the changing attitudes to folk culture more generally': Henderson and Cowan, *Scottish Fairy Belief*, p. 121.

80. Stuart Clarke, *Thinking with Demons: the Idea of Witchcraft in early modern Europe* (Oxford, 1997), pp. 445–54, 461–8; see also Clarke's earlier discussion of this topic, 'Protestant Demonology: Sin, Superstition and Society (c. 1520–1630)', in Bengt Ankarloo and Gustav Henningsen (eds), *Early Modern Witchcraft: Centres and Peripheries* (Oxford, 1990).

81. Keeble (ed.), *Works of Wilson*, vol. 1, pp. 303–4.

82. For the decline of elite witchcraft beliefs in early eighteenth-century England, see Ian Bostridge, *Witchcraft and its Transformations c. 1650–1750* (Oxford, 1997). For a major early eighteenth-century sceptical work written by a future bishop see Francis Hutchinson, *An Historical Essay concerning Witchcraft. With Observations of Matters of Fact, tending to clear the Texts of the Sacred Scriptures, and Confute the Vulgar Errors about that Point* (London, 1718).

83. Peter Burke, 'The Comparative Approach to European Witchcraft', in Ankarloo and Henningsen (eds), *Centres and Peripheries*, p. 441.

LATE COLONIAL ESTRANGEMENT AND MISCEGENATION

IDENTITY AND AUTHENTICITY IN THE COLONIAL IMAGINATION IN THE DUTCH AND LUSOPHONE (POST) COLONIAL WORLDS

Ulbe Bosma
International Institute of Social History, Amsterdam, Netherlands

Fernando Rosa Ribeiro
Universidade Estadual de Campinas, Campinas, Brazil

ABSTRACT This paper attempts to reassess the work of two contemporary writers in the 1930s: Gilberto Freyre in Brazil and E. du Perron in the Netherlands Indies (Indonesia). Their famous narratives (respectively, *Casa-Grande e Senzala* and *Het Land van Herkomst*) present a (post) colonial world where inequality, violence and racism are almost as conspicuous as mixing and contact across the colour lines. In fact, although one work is a sociological and historical interpretation of colonial and imperial Brazil and the other a literary reworking of personal reminiscences related to Indies society in the early twentieth century, both construct worlds that present several important similarities.

Keywords: postcolonialism, literary imagination, Brazil, colonial Indonesia.

INTRODUCTION

Literary imagination has now become widely and fruitfully used as a critical source to analyse colonial cultures. Some critics have pointed out that this might privilege colonial discourse, as the overwhelming majority of these testimonies carry the stamp of the colonial master narrative of colonial and racial dichotomies. We would like to focus, however, on E. du Perron (1899–1940) in the Dutch East Indies and Brazil's Gilberto Freyre (1900–87), both of whom have featured prominently in colonial and postcolonial literature. Their work is complex and their view of their respective societies sophisticated. Freyre and Du Perron have been able to relate colonial history, their personal biography and their countries' future within a common imaginative framework. They both wrote about the world of their youth and the past of their societies in order to reflect upon a new postcolonial nation in the making.

Addresses for correspondence: Ulbe Bosma, International Institute of Social History, Cruquiusweg 31, 1019 AT Amsterdam, Netherlands. E-mail: ubo@iisg.nl
Fernando Rosa Ribeiro, Departamento de História – IFCH, Universidade Estadual de Campinas, Campus Zeferino Vaz – Barão Geraldo, 13081-970 Campinas – SP – C.P. 6610, Brazil. E-mail: frosaribeiro@yahoo.fr

Cultural and Social History, Volume 4, Issue 1, pp. 29–50 © The Social History Society 2007

One might argue that E. du Perron is a late colonial author whose work has become part of the Dutch literary canon, but was never translated into Indonesian. In contrast to that, Gilberto Freyre's work has been enjoying an unstinting prestige in Brazil, where, as a matter of fact, literature is not divided so neatly between a colonial and postcolonial canon but rather between a colonial and 'imperial' and 'republican' one. Though in some quarters – especially but not only among black scholars and activists – his work has been denounced as being part of the elite's ideology, Freyre has never been considered a white 'colonial' author, and his work is never considered to be part of colonial literature as has been the case with Du Perron's. However, neither author belongs to any international canon of postcolonial literature. Theirs are not usually conceived to be subaltern voices. On the contrary, their voices clearly originate in the 'masters' class', so to speak, and bear many marks of that origin. In this sense, Du Perron and Freyre may only have counterparts in Latin America and the Hispanic Caribbean, and to a lesser degree South Africa, where a class of indigenous whites developed a distinctive, non-metropolitan, Creole thinking. However, both Du Perron's and Freyre's voices bear criticisms and dislocated perspectives that do not necessarily subscribe to views current among their contemporaries. We believe that it is precisely this dissonant character that has helped to ensure that the works of both authors should become classics largely canonized in their respective language domains (Dutch and Portuguese). Freyre in particular has managed to capture and rework in a very cogent and convincing way (at least inside Brazil) themes that are deeply rooted in the Brazilian *imaginaire*. This may offer a clue to the continuing success of his work locally. Yet, a comparison with Du Perron's work could allow for some important interrogations about the contours of a thematic of domination, violence and sexuality that pervaded the societies where various groups of whites and non-whites interacted together both inside (post) colonial homes and outside of them. Both Du Perron and Freyre tried to make sense of that complex interaction, and by doing so reworked the colonial bourgeois way in which 'the discourse of sexuality articulated with the politics of race'.[1] Their most important work appeared precisely at the juncture of the defining moment of the nation: in Java: the increasing intensity of anti-colonial struggle and in Brazil the migration of blacks to urban centres and their increasing presence in the urban labour force, besides the appearance of a small but very vocal black middle-class. Also, Brazil's largest black political and social movement – Frente Negra Brasileira, or 'Brazilian Black Front' – came up exactly in the 1930s, before it was suppressed by the Vargas dictatorship as from 1937.

No doubt, the two colonies themselves are very different. To use the Eurocentric and therefore in some ways rather misleading dichotomy between settler and exploitation colonies, Brazil clearly belonged to the former category and the Dutch East Indies to the latter. Viewed through those lenses, there is not much to compare. Moreover, Brazil formally ceased to be a colony already in 1815, after which it was governed by an emperor, who was a member of the Royal House of Portugal, until the proclamation of the Republic in late 1889. Slavery was abolished only as late as 1888 and non-whites, though formally citizens, would in fact be excluded from the formal structures of power in the new republic for at least another century. Being comparatively poor and weak, the Portuguese crown had always relied on private entrepreneurs and the landed elite to colonize and govern its vast American *conquistas*. As Carvalho puts it, Brazil grew out of an 'archipelago of captaincies' privately governed by local elites, who were in fact an imperial elite trained at Coimbra (Portugal's oldest university).[2] Tradition, of course, also included Catholicism and attachment to the monarchy (in fact, both were closely intertwined, as the king was the representative of the Pope). This shared tradition and training created a 'basic consensus' among an otherwise very diverse elite of various origins.[3] This is similar in a way to the Dutch *patriciaat*, which was closely connected, to both the court and the Indies. No doubt, the autonomy of the economic elites of Brazil – the slaveholders – was greater than that of the East Indies planters whose ascendancy was closely linked to the metropolitan banks and industries that provided for the markets of tropical products.

What unites these elites of colonial Indonesia and nineteenth-century Brazil is their peculiar blending of local and imperial attachment, though the Brazilian elites were arguably even more insulated than those in the Dutch East Indies were. Little or nothing stitched the different Brazilian regions together. Like the Indies archipelago different parts of the country had to be connected by boat well into the twentieth century. The Emperor in Rio and the *tuan besar* (viceroy) in Bogor (near Batavia) were the centres where all the bureaucratic strings were pulled together. Emperor Dom Pedro II was particularly aware of that fact and he and his family adroitly used imperial symbols and regalia to stress local attachments, while they kept close nuptial alliances with the royal houses in Europe. The Governor-General of the Dutch East Indies was, like his counterpart in British India, endowed with regal qualities and often called Viceroy. But the Indies never were a 'European monarchy in the tropics', as the *tuan besar* in Bogor ruled over a country in which Europeans had to stay outside the indigenous society.[4] Official colonial ideology had proclaimed that the country had to be ruled on behalf of the natives by the Dutch crown. Though Brazil and the Indies had the same role in providing the world market with coffee and sugar, the Brazilian landed elites were eventually able to shape their country, whereas the Dutch-Creole elite, in spite of its crucial role both in the development of colonial capitalism and even in early Indonesian nationalism, eventually was not.[5] Both Freyre and Du Perron belonged to these landed colonial classes and were well aware of their exploitative nature and violent role in history, their mixed racial origins, and their aristocratic pretensions. But whereas Freyre portrays the self-confidence of a class who successfully forged a nation, Du Perron is full of self-doubt and hidden irony. And precisely this contrast makes a comparative reading of their work a critical appraisal of the roots and limitations of what we tentatively call Creole settler discourse – a discourse that was hybrid by nature and tried to inhabit the crevices between 'settler' and 'native'.

THE LOCATION

Du Perron and Freyre were born almost in the same year, respectively 1899 and 1900, therefore at the apogee of imperialism. Their local attachment was merged with a singular cosmopolitan outlook, even though Freyre was more of a city dweller than Du

Perron was. Both conceptualized their work during long years of absence. Du Perron left in 1921 with his parents who retired to a small castle in Belgium. He lived a luxurious life and travelled around in the Netherlands and Belgium until the Great Depression depleted his family capital. Then he lived a few years in Paris before returning to the Indies in 1936, disappointed at a failed attempt to translate his *Land van Herkomst* and to escape from poverty, as well as an increasingly fascist Europe, only to discover that his old Creole, or Indies, society had been afflicted by the same fascist virus.[6] Freyre wrote both abroad and in his native postcolonial Pernambuco in Nordeste (the North-eastern region of Brazil). In 1916 he went to study in the US, and spent time there and in Europe (France and Portugal) until 1933. Later he would also spend some time in exile in Portugal. In 1951, as an official guest of Salazar's government, Freyre would go on a tour of the Portuguese African colonies and to Goa in Portuguese India.[7]

The educational careers, and the intellectual environments, of the two men were rather different. Whereas E. du Perron was practically a school dropout, who at a later age seriously considered becoming an academic historian, Freyre was an academically trained scholar (who studied under Franz Boas at Columbia).[8] Contrary to current legend, however, Freyre spent most of his time at Balliol College in Texas, not in New York. Therefore, rather than being steeped in the latest anthropological discourse, he was in fact immersed in the discourse of the post-bellum South whose fiction and literature he read extensively while at Balliol. Du Perron lived in a far more cosmopolitan environment and was heavily involved in anti-fascist movements during the thirties. In contrast to his friend André Malraux, who kept his belief in communism, Du Perron eventually concluded that Hitler and Stalin belonged to the same category and that an intellectual could never honestly become enmeshed in politics. Freyre, however, acted for a while as an all-out propagandist of the Portuguese empire under dictator Salazar, and was sympathetic towards the Brazilian military dictatorship that came to power in 1964.[9] Du Perron was attached to literary naturalism and sobriety (*vorm of vent* – 'style or guy'), while Freyre was easily carried away by his own grandiloquent enthusiasm.

What unites the two writers, however, is the way in which they grapple with the question of how to integrate their past into an evolving sense of nationhood. In their best known works they both use a procedure that combines sociological descriptions, a long-term perspective on colonial history, and striking autobiographical elements.[10] According to Veloso and Madeira, Freyre introduced into historical research new sources of empirical data that are now widely used, namely, newspapers, photographs, diaries, etiquette books, recipe books, wills, etc.[11] Peter Burke has also pointed to Freyre's originality in that regard.[12] Interestingly, Du Perron is also considered to be a writer of great originality, mixing, as he does, stories, opinions, memoirs and letters, both real and fabricated. Therefore, the writing of either author cannot be easily fitted into a single genre. Du Perron's intimate and documentary portraits of his Creole family life reveal at close reading a very precise sociological catalogue of Creole and mestizo life in the first decade of twentieth century colonial Indonesia. Du Perron meticulously describes a colonial *temps perdu* in his 'country of origin', equivalent to the

Indies expression *tempo doeloe* that gained currency just about the time when he was writing. It made him appreciate the political aspirations of his Indonesian friends, without being able to participate in their endeavour for a new Indonesian nation. Gilberto Freyre also looked for the *temps perdu* of Brazil's colonial past in order to, as he puts it, 'find my own ancestors'.[13] In that process he not only appropriated Brazil's history but also that of Portugal in an attempt to demonstrate an innate drive towards miscegenation that could bring masters, slaves and indigenous peoples in a single national future. Grandiose historical depictions, based on archival and other sources, were forged into a compelling nation-building master narrative. He contrasts Brazil with the US, or in fact the Anglophone world at large, to give his own country the credits of producing a different, universalist and racially unmarked culture based on contact and – to employ a word that Gilberto Freyre uses time and again – *miscegenation*. Despite his grandiose detours, the basis of Freyre's work is the narrative about private life. It is in the *casa-grande* (big house or master's house) and the *senzala* (slave quarters) that he locates the uniqueness of Brazilian society.[14]

Strongly rooted in locality and the tropical 'grand house', both books, *Casa Grande* and *Land van Herkomst,* are also, paradoxically, dislocated and written from a marginal man's perspective. Du Perron calls himself the *smalle mens* (the thin, or perhaps even better, marginal man).[15] Because of his Creole background *and* his position as intellectual in the era of mass politics, he realizes that he is the marginal man in a double sense. Leo Spitzer mentioned the ambiguities and contradictions in lives in-between in his well-known work, which often coincided with a deterritorialized position.[16] In a way, both authors start from a position in between (former) colony and (former) metropolis, between white and non-white, between Europe and South America or Southeast Asia. There are not only colonial voices in both texts; there are also the voices of the Old World's Europeans – Du Perron's friends in Europe, to whom he retells his life in Java – and Freyre's various English and other travellers whose works he quotes throughout, besides his American teachers, whose opinions he mentions time and again. And, finally, there are their own voices: voices that are not easy to categorize as solely either 'colonialist' or 'racist', but are singular and original, and still fresh today. Their books stand out in the literature of their time and their appreciation has grown ever since, reaching the status of classics in their own language domains and even, as is the case with Freyre, far beyond.[17]

To be sure, whereas Freyre's work has become part of the grand idea of 'racial democracy' on which Brazilian nation-building narratives would be constructed, Du Perron's is apparently part of a *temps perdu* of a Creole colonial aristocracy. With great sophistication they tried to transmogrify the colonial (and, in Brazil's case, colonial and imperial) past, some times painfully aware that they were not able to present their societies as common fare to outside readers (an important part of their audience) as well as to some critical insiders, such as nationalists in Java or the emerging black middle class in Brazil. They do not justify (post) colonial oppression, but candidly acknowledge that their identity is bound up to that of the colonial oppressors. They were both born and raised in the (post) colony as scions of old local 'patriarchal' (in Freyre's favoured expression) families with deep roots outside Europe. They knew what it was to live in intimate contact with alterity – with nonwhites of various kinds. In fact, they were both, to some degree, non-white themselves. Freyre famously writes: 'Every Brazilian, even the light-skinned one with blonde hair carries about with him on his soul, when not on soul and body alike . . . the shadow, or at least the birthmark, of the Indian or the Black.'[18]

Du Perron's search into his own roots consists of two elements. First, the search of his father – in which he was personally involved as his biographer Kees Snoek found out – for French aristocratic roots and second the truth about his Asian maternal ancestor.[19] In his book, Du Perron mentions that Ducroo's father had paid a professional genealogist to trace his family roots in France, which indeed was a truly biographical element. It was hoped that the man would be able to identify living, if distant, relatives in Bourgogne. It was all in vain. Alas, Ducroo as he moves to Europe, eventually finds out, after his father's death, that, according to a colonial genealogical work, the Ducroos in Java descend from two adopted sons of a (possibly Swiss) French colonel of the Dutch colonial army, who was stationed in Ceylon.[20]

A further comparison between novel and biographical and historical data is revealing. From 1930 to 1936 the professional genealogist, Bloys van Treslong Prince, published the genealogies of all those old wealthy landed Indies families who had made their fortune in colonial business. For many of these families this proved to be an embarrassing exposé as they were intent on demonstrating their respectability by laying claim to European noble ancestry. They were to discover, almost without exception, that at least one of their maternal ancestors was just a slave at one of the East Indies Companies settlements. When Van Treslong Prince published about Du Perron's pedigree in the respectable *Bataviaasch Nieuwsblad* in 1930, Du Perron already knew that his great-grandfather Louis du Perron was the son of a Ceylon stationed officer and his concubine.[21] According to his biographer Kees Snoek, he was even quite shocked, as he had always denied being of mixed descent. Du Perron's family claimed that since Grandfather Louis' features were unmistakably *totok* (white and born in Europe), he could not possibly have been the son of a Ceylonese female slave.[22]

But E. du Perron's denial that he was a mixed blood should not be taken at face value. He very well knew that there was some Asian blood in his veins. Mixed blood, was however too crude an expression for a man, whose parents or grandparents were all Europeans under law and legitimate. On the other hand, Du Perron consciously takes a position outside the Dutch bourgeois world, the Dutch newcomers in the colony, not only by claiming French aristocratic lineage and placing himself in the class of 'colonial patriciat', but also by stressing his Creole credentials, which leave room for a mixed ancestry, as long as it is remote. Reading carefully *Het Land van Herkomst*, one could even arrive at the conclusion that he is strengthening his Indies-rootedness by providing his alter ego, Ducroo with a shortened pedigree, leaving out his grandfather, the metropolitan trained lawyer Hendricus Wilhelmus du Perron, who married a daughter of the Menu family, thus linking up to the West Java landed Creole *patriciaat*, which was, as anyone knew but no one admitted, racially mixed. His mother, Madeline, was a widow Polanen Petel, born Bédier de Prairie. Again she belonged to a wealthy and respected West Java family. Her family came from French Réunion (Ile de

Bourbon) in the Indian Ocean. But in his novel, he situates his mother's place of birth in Malacca, a former Portuguese and Dutch enclave turned British.[23] And here he admits, in this typical Indies way, that his mother's first husband was 'half-Spanish', which is nothing else than a euphemistic, and encoded, way to say that there is 'native' blood in the family. She was a devout Catholic who studied at the nuns' school, but she also believed in 'native superstition' (*inlandse bijgeloof*). The truth was that she was an enlightened lady, being part of that easy Sundanese network of local nobility and Creole planters. Du Perron's mother taught Dutch to a Sundanese *patih's* (high indigenous civil servant) daughter.[24] The differences between genealogical and biographical facts and Du Perron's fiction, provide us with an important entrance to how he constructs his identity as Indies, French, aristocratic and deeply colonial. The ambiguities and doubts that attend this process could also have followed Freye's one-liner about miscegenation: we all know it, and it's part of our identity, but we are not 'halfcastes'.

Here it is perhaps the place to note that, interestingly, Freyre's work has been comparatively both more eulogized and more criticized inside and outside Brazil than Du Perron's work either in the Netherlands or in Indonesia. Though we are unable to go into detail here as regards the long and complex history of the reception of Freyre's work, we can point out to its current status inside Brazil (and the larger Lusophone world). Beside a strong tendency to revere his works – and, importantly, his figure as a great *national* intellectual (in this regard he has become almost a sacred cow) – there are of course many different possible readings of his work and his main ideas. For instance, both Freyre and his work have been sharply criticized as they are considered to be largely responsible for (or else at least representative of) a supposedly rosy view of Brazilian 'race' relations that has dominated both in official and non-official circles. Regardless of its author's (at best ambiguous) personal reputation, and in spite of hardly being a rallying point for major intellectual debate nowadays, Freyre's work remains nonetheless at least an important beacon in a wide-ranging literature that imagines the nation in Brazil. It is in this sense that we take an interest in his work here.

CASA-GRANDE

Du Perron's *Het Land van Herkomst* and Freyre's *The Masters and the Slaves* make the (post) colonial big house (*casa-grande*) of their youth the central place in their universe. It is the setting where the colonial and (in Brazil's case) postcolonial dramas unfold. It includes the servant quarters (*senzala* or slave lodgings) besides the *herenhuis* or master's house. In Du Perron's text, it is Gedong Lami in *Kampoeng Melajoe* or the 'Malay Quarter' outside Batavia (today's Jakarta). Du Perron himself describes it as a *herenverblijf* (gentleman's mansion)[25] In this space the entire repertoire of sexual and hierarchical relations exists: slaves and servants (in Gilberto Freyre's case), servants and workers (in Du Perron's text). The characters are somewhat more limited in Gilberto Freyre's book: blacks, Amerindians, and the Portuguese, various mestizos plus the occasional Jew or English traveller. In Du Perron's Creoles, Javanese, Sundanese, Chinese and Arabs abound, besides all kinds of Europeans and shades in-between.

Both describe people's complexion: darker, whiter, more native or Chinese looking. In neither text is anybody simply an individual, but is instead confined to his place in the racial or colour taxonomy.

Again, Du Perron did not write his autobiography, but an autobiographical novel that described the world of his youth grouped around his own family. His father owned a rice-husking plant, and ruled as a patriarch over the inhabitants of his realm who were almost *corveable à merci*. The landlord rejected any interference from the colonial civil service. The struggle between landowners and colonial government was fierce in those years and often went public in the colonial newspapers, as Du Perron mentions. Ironically, the Du Perron family lived mostly from their Batavia real estate agency, which made huge profits in those years because of an acute shortage of decent housing in the colonial capital.[26] Du Perron therefore romanticizes the seigniorial features of his father, who actually was never able to make a career as a planter. This romanticization finds a parallel in Freyre.

Freyre uses his black-and-white illustrations to give himself a place in history, whereas Du Perron brings the colonial political economy into his family life. Besides, the photographs in the text insert, so to speak, Freyre into the Brazilian history he is about to tell. They portray him as the master or patriarch. The first photograph comes right after the table of contents and takes up a whole page. It shows Freyre standing at the foot of the steps leading to his own grand Solar dos Apicucos, namely, his own stately big house in Pernambuco. Even before opening the book, the reader is regaled with stunning views, in drawings or photographs, of different *casas-grandes*. These are not the only casas-grandes depicted in the book.[27] At the foot of the first photograph there is Freyre himself, standing watch over his own *casa-grande* and looking ahead of him, away from the viewer, left arm slightly raised, right arm hanging by his side. It is almost as if he were part of the statuary adorning the spacious veranda above him: the master in the master's homestead. We will come back to this stunning photograph later. There are four pictures of Freyre in the book: a face close-up just opposite the title page, with a caption with a quote from the Aspen Award Jury's speech at the University of Oxford when it awarded him a prize in 1967: 'As a philosopher, scientist and literary writer, Gilberto Freyre has transformed the image that Brazil made of itself. He now inspires the whole of mankind to reach a clearer understanding of its purpose and destiny'; then comes the photograph described above; next there is an autographed photograph of a mature but still somewhat young and smug-looking Freyre, (the caption is a quote from the chancellor of the Sorbonne praising Freyre to the skies); finally, there is a photograph of Freyre receiving the Great Cross of the Rio Branco Order from the Brazilian Minister of Foreign Affairs. Therefore, before the main text even begins the reader has already been fed no fewer than three pictures of the author, plus assorted drawings, illustrations, and various kinds of texts – prefaces, bibliographies, opinion pieces from famous people – among them Roland Barthes in Paris and Ortega y Gasset in Madrid – praise poems by well-known poets, etc. The reader is left in no doubt that she is about to tackle a renowned masterpiece by an internationally famous writer. Of course most of these were added to later editions of the book and were absent in the original.

Freyre's emphasis is on the uniqueness and singularity of the Portuguese character and therefore of Portuguese colonialism, which poured out over three continents and across two oceans. Here we have the Portuguese *miscibilidade* or the ability to mix, which has become a trope in postcolonial historiography often contrasted – first and foremost in Freyre's own work – to an assumed protestant Anglo-Saxon colonial seclusion. Most of it is based upon hastily made comparisons, and of course open to debate. All the suffering of the colonial encounter here eventually created a society that was, according to Freyre, in comparison with other societies, 'harmonious',[28] especially because intimacy between masters and slaves could exist inside an ethos of violence and inequality. We will come back to the trope of 'harmony' later. Freyre will spend the rest of the book (not to mention the rest of his long writing career) trying to describe the colonial encounter and the formation of Brazil's singular society in detail.

While the cruelty-harmony oxymoron eventually takes global dimensions in Freyre's overall work,[29] Du Perron frames it in the immediate setting of his personal memories. Somehow, the contacts between whites and different shades of non-whites often come across in more vivid detail than in Freyre's case, where the grander picture almost excludes any agency of his personae. Yet, it is precisely the encounter that is central in their work. Take, for instance, Du Perron's description of his literary persona, Ducroo's wet nurses and child minders. First and foremost, there is Ma Lima or Alima, his 'Native' *baboe* or wet nurse. She slept in his bedroom for most of his childhood. She would bathe him and feed him. She would carry him in her *slendang* (cloth used to carry children against the chest), where he would fall asleep to her nursing rhymes in Malay. She called him Si Toetoet, a nickname (meaning 'snail' in Malay and Sundanese).

Ducroo himself was an '*Indische jongen*' (an Indies boy), which left open the option both of denial or affirmation that he was of mixed origins, and emphasized that he was culturally rooted in the Indies, but as a colonial patrician, as he was certainly not an Indo (lower class mestizo). Here we have a central point of comparison, between Brazil and Creole settler society in the Dutch East Indies. Here we have a class difference, which is, however, framed in terms of complexion, as wealth and complexion *are* highly related. It is class, education and complexion that separate the Creoles from the Indos, but they share a cultural domain. Colonial boundaries were extremely situational as Stoler rightfully argues.[30] Ducroo was not supposed to talk to the neighbouring Mollerbeek children or the children of their other Indo neighbours, the Leerkerks, because they were both from 'half-caste families'. Yet, these boys introduce Ducroo to Indies songs and native opera (*bangsawan*). Moreover, even Ducroo's mother enjoyed the *krontjongmuziek* of Portuguese origin played and sung by those families. It has some resemblances, and also some shared origins, with Portuguese *fado* music.

THE MOMENT OF ESTRANGEMENT

Children did not necessarily encounter racial barriers in the streets or in the countryside, certainly not in the first decade of the twentieth century. Some of Du Perron's most interesting characters are Ducroo's 'Native' playmates and childhood friends, of which he had quite a few. He was often the only European child around where his family lived, as in Balekambang, for instance. There is, for instance, Mahmoed. He knew Dutch, something uncommon among 'Natives' in the first decade of the twentieth century. He would read Ducroo's (Dutch) books and play with Ducroo's urban European friends when these came over to Ducroo's home. At the beginning this friendship sounds very much like the ones depicted in the novels of Freyre's contemporary and friend (and a sugar estate *casa-grande* scion), José Lins do Rego.[31] As a rule neither in Java nor in the Nordeste did these friendships last into adolescence. In Lins do Rego's novel, *Doidinho,* the young white master – called *sinhô*, a cognate of the Indies word of Portuguese origin *sinjo*[32] – usually ends up in the city. His former playmate however stays behind in the countryside.

Extinguishing friendships is what we expect, but in Du Perron's novel the breach is sharp, meaningfully foreshadowing the end of colonialism. Mahmoed turns into a complete stranger. He learned to pray in Arabic at the school for natives and became a pious Muslim.[33] Ducroo becomes to Mahmoed just a *blanda* or a Dutch (Christian) white man. Enraged by this transformation that he can neither understand nor accept, Ducroo ends up slapping Mahmoed in the face. It is the end of their friendship. Whereas in the Nordeste settings of Lins do Rego's novels the friendship between the white and non-white boys simply fades away as both grow up, the rupture in the Indies literature is dramatic and violent. It is, in fact, a literary trope, for instance returning in another, postcolonial, novel by the Dutch and Indies born Hella S. Haasse, *Oeroeg:* the intimacy of childhood is followed by estrangement and even a violent encounter, in adolescence.[34] For Haasse, the personal drama is contextualized by the estrangement of the colonial wars of 1945–9, and Du Perron's account is foreshadowing it. After his return to the Indies in 1936, Du Perron experiences that there is no way to cross the divide again. He realizes that the planter's son and the Indonesian nationalist are enemies, and that there is no reason to be sentimental or to moralize about it.[35]

Freyre and Du Perron take stock of a society that is bound together by violence. It is personalized in the omnipotence of the Roman-style *pater familias* who rules over the life and death of his family and his subjects. It is mitigated in the immediate vicinity of Batavia – and the colonial government was indeed trying to curb the power of the landowners – but in Freyre's book it is present in its full cruelty. The patriarch would take the life of a slave or of his own eldest son, if it was in the interest of his complete authority over the *casa-grande*.[36] In *Het Land van Herkomst*, violence presents itself as a daily routine of late colonial life. Father Ducroo is a patriarch in his own right, physically abusing his servants inside and outside the big house. Naturally enough, Ducroo father would use physical violence against Ducroo child, until the latter became an adult facing his father as an equal. Being a physically strong man was practically a requisite in many spheres of Indies life, whether in the school or the factory yard. Also, the fear of assault, robbery and murder was omnipresent for the Ducroo family too. Gangs were rooming the Batavia Ommelanden in these years. There was a colonial fascination with accounts of violence – say, murders. At times 'respect' from 'Natives' and others could only be had, according to colonial wisdom, through hitting people. Ducroo mentions several such instances, from his father's and his own experience. It was rather usual to carry a small revolver when walking around in native neighbourhoods, and these weapons were often advertised in the newspapers. It is only later on, after having found a relatively safe job as an archivist of the colonial government, that Du Perron sublimates this culture of violence into his polemics against the notorious colonial fascist-leaning journalist H.C. Zentgraaff, a former colonial army sergeant, which have become part of the Indies press history as *D'Artagnan contra Fuselier*.[37]

Du Perron carefully picked his enemy, as he had already carefully selected his characters to represent the culture of violence of colonial society. Ducroo's 'hero' – Eelco – is here a quintessential Freyrean character. He is described as having 'Indies blood and yet as being almost entirely white', feeling 'he was as comfortable among the daughters of the Bandung bourgeoisie on the dance floor of the [European] club as in the cheapest native brothel.' Again it is important to note how Du Perron constructs these figures, as he constructs for example another schoolmate, a strong fighter. This Arthur Hille went to study at the Military Academy in Breda (in the Netherlands) and he was an officer in the Aceh war, where he killed many natives. There is a detailed description of Arthur's gruesome war experiences in a conversation with Ducroo during a train ride in the Netherlands.[38] In fact, when Arthur embarked for the Netherlands, the Aceh War had been declared over for more than a decade.

What does Du Perron want to explain – apart from possible latent homosexual feelings – with these two male characters? As regards Arthur Hille, he writes in the thirties:

> Now that I have spoken again with Arthur Hiller I realise how small a place I have given him in my Indies memories. I also know why: from an intellectual point of view this friendship seems almost shameful; that I was almost proud of it seems unexplainable, and so on. As I talk now about the idiots (*abrutis*) with a Nazi uniform, how is that consistent with my old admiration for Arthur Hille, who could perhaps have been a beautiful SA leader? But it is not a question of glossing over the contradictions here but rather explaining them, or, if that is not possible, then just letting them exist in all their down-to-earthness [*in alle nuchterheid*]. Above all, you can only with difficulty be consistent, exactly because you are an intellectual.[39]

Ducroo is therefore fully aware of his attraction for white-looking violent Creole bullies who beat up and even kill natives. He is also aware of the contradiction that it brings into his account of the life of an intellectual. He solves this ambiguity and contradiction in an ingenious way: by letting them stand 'in all their down-to-earthness'.[40] What in Europe is unacceptable to him (a Nazi idiot) is in the Indies part of a colonial culture of violence. He sees it as inescapably there and as part of the Creole society where he grew up.

Thus we can relate Du Perron's *mise en valeur* of colonial violence to Freyre's contention that the colonial encounter between European and Indian and slave in Brazil was, despite the openly acknowledged violence, also harmonious. In fact, it is in their open acknowledgement of violence coupled to their construction of an identity linked to that violence – but not entirely subsumed by it – that the narratives of both authors come close to each other. In Freyre's narrative violence is part and parcel of Brazilian life during the era of slavery. Slavery itself is a 'necessary evil' if the country was to be settled at all, the Portuguese being so few and Indians so inadequate as labour force. Freyre in fact placed himself at the very centre of a long and important debate with roots in the nineteenth century. This debate focussed on discussions about the nature of Brazil through discussions about the racial and ethnic groups that would have shaped the nation, namely, Indians, Africans and Portuguese.[41] Brazil was believed by many to have no proper history. To counter that perception, Freyre shows that Brazil's history begins with the history of the Iberian peninsula (and its contacts with Africa, especially North Africa).[42] The same principle that obtained in peninsular history – the integration of 'antagonistic elements', that is, Moors, Jews and Christians – also obtains overseas, according to him. There was a 'world created by the Portuguese', as in the title of one of his famous works.[43] In this world the segregation and racism common to former English and Dutch colonies such as the US or South Africa was not present. Gilberto did not argue that Brazil had a political democracy; in fact, Brazil's uniqueness rested, for him, on a democracy that he claimed was 'social' or 'racial' (hence the famous phrase coined by him to describe Brazil, *democracia racial*). A democracy of ethnic contact and miscegenation, a democracy that Brazil could offer to a world ravaged by fascism, nazism, segregationism and colonialism.

Freyre therefore uncovers the history of slavery and appropriates it for his grand design of the Brazilian nation. His account is historically well informed by contemporary standards and deals skilfully and in rich detail with the entire gamut of relations between masters and slaves. From the history of slavery and colonialism he constructs a narrative about a nation, which partly reverses its gruesome past into a new superior existence. Yet his relationship with that violent past remains extremely ambiguous. His major narrative device here is, once established that violence was routine and inescapable in a slave society, to concentrate on the many links that brought together masters and slaves in the various spheres of life.[44] And the narrative point that he makes time and again, if not ad nauseam, is that the supposed lack of deep-seated racial prejudice among the Portuguese enabled them to cross the bridge between themselves and alterity.

THE DOMAIN OF SEXUALITY

It is therefore in the realm of sexuality that Freyre brings his Hegelian dialectics between master and slave to its most radical consequence. Slavery was a 'great exciter of sensuality' and he does not mince words, or waste any moral judgements, about the exact character of it. Brazilian boys and adolescents experienced 'sexual super-excitation'. For him 'there is no slavery without sexual depravation' and sadism and masochism of both white and black were quite common. The little white *sinhô* employs slave boys as his play beasts and has his first sexual experiences with slave boys and girls (and animals). He relishes torturing them, just as his parents relish torturing their own slaves. Out of five chapters, two are entirely devoted to 'The black slave in the sexual and family life of the Brazilian.' The gruesome character of sexual abuse, rape, illegitimacy, torture, incest, and so forth, made the oppressor addicted to his oppressive practices.

Sexuality is central to Du Perron's narrative as well and shocked his colonial contemporaries. His account has however an ambiguity that is often missing in Freyre's at times rather mechanistic descriptions. Du Perron has not yet taken a position towards the Indonesian nation in the making, although he already felt himself dislocated in metropolitan Europe. Freyre was steeped in his soil embellishing an identity that he somehow already has, rather than trying to reach out or to grapple with other identities. He is much less of a diasporic character or in-between intellectual than Du Perron. The latter is grappling with contradictions more than Freyre is in his grand historical canvas. In fact, during his Indies years, only once does Ducroo meet a female companion that he finds fully to his liking. That is An who, like him, is of mixed descent but has not been legally recognized as a European. Prostitution might have been the only way for her to survive as she really had fallen in between. She is intelligent and graceful as the image of a European courtesan. Ducroo can have an intelligent conversation with her and regard her as an equal, as a veritable companion – in fact, a kind of companionship that he has so far only experienced with males:

> Our greatest, and my only, girl friend in this debauchery was a half-caste girl that however passed as a Native . . . Her name was Onnie, and she was called An. She said that she was 19 and perhaps she was 24; long, straight, with a sharp profile for which she obviously had to thank her European father, but that gave her an Arab character. She was different from all others . . . She was after all a prostitute just as the others, but she did not allow herself to be paid by Europeans to whom she felt attracted . . . An said right away that she felt attracted to us in a friendly way exactly because of her European blood; she had been married a couple of times with a Native, but had also been with a planter for a time as a concubine (njai); she was so open-minded that she even went with Chinese, but these had to pay more . . . An was a courtesan of importance, an importance that the Sundanese never doubted.[45]

To underscore his message about her grace he compares her favourably with expensive French prostitutes, 'only for wealthy clients', but who were probably from a 'fourth rate' Marseilles brothel. A place to which he later, on his first trip to Europe, made a rather disappointing visit. On his way to a new life in Europe, Ducroo shows an American on his boat a picture of An. The American confesses that An looks much better than the *njai* that he has just left behind in Sumatra. Later, in Paris, Ducroo has a picture of An made into a drawing and sent to her.

These details – in the middle of shocking facts about brothels and planters leaving their concubines behind – are important, as they set a counterpoint to the contemporary colonial opinions. In the Indies, Ducroo – and his male friends – considered the idea of keeping a *njai* – a concubine, euphemistically called a *huishoudster* or native 'housekeeper' in the colonial society – disgusting. That was so even though neither of his parents would have raised an eyebrow had he taken in a *njai*, and even though more than one Native woman practically offered herself to him to become one (as it was an economically and socially advantageous arrangement for many poor women). His own older half-brother, Otto, had a *njai*, like most white European Indies bachelors. But Du Perron went along with the dominant current in (European) society that considered it degrading, which has everything to do with the romantic version of love that wanted sexual partners to be spiritual partners. But by narrating his romance with An, and placing her above the white metropolitan courtesans in sophistication, he somehow turns around colonial prejudice – or rather, reconstructs colonial society through a gender-related narrative device.

The poignant politics of gender and race, given additional drama through the rather arbitrary colonial racial categories, are therefore rendered in much more moving detail here than in Freyre's work. There is another Indo, Baur, to whom Du Perron devotes almost an entire chapter. Now, 'Baur' is actually Malay for 'mixed'. When he was about ten, Ducroo found himself living with his parents in Kampoeng Melajoe ('Malay Quarter') just outside Meester Cornelis in Batavia, the colonial capital. Ducroo's parents had no objection to him playing with native children, but they very much objected to him keeping company with the 'half-castes' (*halfbloeds*) in his neighbourhood (in case they might 'contaminate' him), and so they decided to send him to a Catholic school in the centre of town.[46] Eventually, however, he ends up going to the neighbourhood school instead. There he meets up with the half-caste Baur. He tells us that at the age of fourteen Baur already looked like a man, and that people said that he had a big one: he let other people look at it if they wanted to. Eventually, Baur's European father chases him out of the house and he comes to live with the Ducroo's. Later, Baur's expenses at the Ducroo's are paid for by a European homosexual architect who was interested in him. Baur has a violent temper and is a violent young man. Years later, Baur is married and has children, and lives in a small house across the street from the Ducroo's, 'completely one of the many Indo's that go to an office and about whom no one talks.'

Ducroo again brings out the other silences: the self-doubt, the hesitations, the prejudice and the inner fantasies. Also, the contours of colonial prejudice – gender and race prejudice – are somehow much sharper. In Freyre, it is as if they were sublimated into the grand historical narrative that he constructs.

BRAZIL: EMPIRE AND REPUBLIC

When slavery ended in 1888, so did the Empire of Slavery. As Carvalho stresses, the coming of the Republic was not a popular movement, neither did it bring about a major division and upheaval among the elite.[47] Yet, it threw up the question – already present in imperial times – about the nature of the Brazilian people and nation. At the time, nobody believed Brazil had an identity of its own that could imbue its citizens with a sense of pride. According to Eurocentric ideas imbibed by the local elite through its Europe-oriented upbringing, Brazil was a mestizo nation in the tropics, with a deficit in 'civilization'. In the last decades of the nineteenth and the first decades of the twentieth centuries views on miscegenation varied enormously, ranging from straightforward rejection to hesitant acceptance (some times within the work of the very same thinker or politician).[48] Being Europe-derived and therefore prestigious, 'race' theories of the time could not possibly be entirely rejected by the local elite;[49] however, due to the different local reality, nor could they be warmly embraced either. Slowly, a positive image of the mestizo nation emerged and Freyre's work was fundamental in this respect. It represented a major contribution towards building and consolidating a positive view of the nation that became acceptable both internally and internationally.[50] His ideas were hardly original, but he so masterly forged them into a novel framework that they acquired a lasting appeal. He also reworked and continued – albeit in a different way and in a different context – the imperial tradition that had been so important in late colonial times and in the nineteenth century. Furthermore, he developed a view of 'race relations' that would become fairly dominant in elite circles (and outside of them). And, finally, he translated colonial and imperial traditions into a powerful postcolonial discourse that has left an imprint on the Brazilian imagination to this day.

'HONETTE HOMME'

There was no society, which could be explained in a positive way by Du Perron. The only element he could explain as honest and true was the simple mestizo, who stood where he or she stood. This was heavily intertwined with his literary programme; namely, to be as uncomplicated as possible, an *honette homme,* the essence of which to him was to lead the uncomplicated life of an Indo. Moreover, Ducroo claims not to be interested in politics at all, but Du Perron is, albeit in his own detached intellectual way. In his 15 years in Europe, Du Perron has become someone else as Ducroo.

It is Ducroo, or the young Du Perron, who starts his working career at the most hideous colonial newspaper of Batavia. He attends a native political meeting (carrying a hidden revolver with him that he also employs in his forays into native quarters in search of prostitutes). Famous speakers are there, but he is not interested.[51] He confesses that his opinion on 'natives' is that of other colonials:

> Of course, there were still the politics, but it seemed to me in advance out of the question that I would ever understand it. I had accepted the political opinion of De Nieuwsbode [*Het Nieuws van den Dag voor Nederlands-Indië*, where he worked in 1919] just as that of my father and every other ordinary Dutch citizen in Indië: a rebellious [*opstandige*] Javanese was naturally our enemy. Not that people like my father thought that the Javanese were wrong; on the contrary, to acknowledge among each other that the [Dutch East India] Company officials had of course been robbers counted as evidence of intellectual freedom, just as the fact that we had as yet no business being in Java; once that said, you could, with the greatest indignation, take action against any native that did not humbly stoop before our superiority.[52]

Ducroo goes on to say:

> . . . I thought that the whole political part did not concern me at all, and if the Javanese got as far as murdering us Europeans, they would do so without distinctions: it was therefore a matter of resisting as far as possible without philosophy.[53]

The passages above create a huge divide between Du Perron's narrative and Freyre's. In Du Perron's text, Indië is recollected in many different ways – nostalgically, detachedly, passionately, and cynically – at different points. At the end of his book, writing in June 1935 in Paris, watching the march of Nazism next door in Germany, in a time full of foreboding, Ducroo remarks:

> I can imagine going back to the country of origin, not only to be wiped out by the 'daggers [krissen] of freedom'. I can also renounce that past and consider that I will never leave this place, but will instead drift through the dangers with what is strongest in my life . . . After all the probing, I can see only one wisdom: as long as you live, you should live according to your own nature and as if you still had a good deal of scope ahead of you, with all the curiosity and hope with which you are laden, but also with an adequate quantum of pessimism so that we can reconcile ourselves in one minute with the end of everything that makes our life possible, possible in every meaning.[54]

Even taking into account that Ducroo is talking from Europe in 1935, where gruesome events were happening or about to happen, the tone is incredibly pessimistic (the chapter is appropriately called 'For Pessimists'). It is precisely this pessimism and the cynicism of the passages quoted before that are lacking in Freyre's account. It is as if Ducroo is caught between two gruesome worlds: one in which the German airforce may flatten Paris by bombing or one in which he will be killed in 'the country of origin' by the daggers of the 'rebellious Javanese'.

This is Du Perron – to whom André Malraux dedicated his *Condition Humaine* – when he returned to his country of birth in 1936.[55] His reputation as a literary figure has been established, and he easily makes new friends. They all belonged, without exception, to the left fringe of European colonial society – later on he will make Indonesian friends as well. His friends find a job for him at the Landsarchief in Batavia. In addition, there is his literary production, on Multatuli and on the *belles lettres* of those who served under the East Indies company in the seventeenth and eighteenth centuries. But most important will be his work for *Kritiek en Opbouw*, a leftist journal to which both Indonesian and Dutch authors would contribute, and which soon becomes the target of colonial reactionaries.

Du Perron becomes the sympathetic spectator of the emerging Indonesian nation, a few years after Sukarno's finest days aroused a whole generation of young Indonesians. It is about this 'romantic nationalism' that he writes in his preface to the novel of Soewarsih Djojopoespito, *Buiten het gareel* (*Out of Order*). It is a preface to an autobiography of a female nationalist, in which he admires the sacrifice of many of her generation who quitted their easy government jobs to teach at 'wild schools' and educate the rising Indonesian nation. Du Perron points to two main issues, namely female equality and the role of Western education.[56] But his position is more than that of a spectator, as he addresses the Dutch readership of a book written in Dutch, trying to relate to the vantagepoint of its readership and thus positioning himself as an intermediary. Even the appeal by Sutan Sjahrir, one of the most respected leaders of the Indonesian nationalist movement, that he should stay in Indonesia is politely though firmly rejected by Du Perron. This *colonial* Indonesia is not his country any more and the cultural future of Indonesia, let alone the political future, should be in the hands of Indonesians, Du Perron writes in August 1939 in his farewell letter addressed to Sjahrir.[57]

Whereas Du Perron takes on a new role, Freyre gets firmly entrenched in his own *casa-grande,* as the impressive photograph right at the beginning of his book abundantly shows. Let us go back to the picture of Freyre standing at the foot of the stairs in front of his stately *casa-grande*.[58] We could read many things into this photograph. It strikes us as an almost arrogant picture: Freyre seems to be saying 'I am here', 'I am part and parcel of this' and even 'I am entitled to it.' His pose in the photograph is almost heroic: we might venture that it depicts the quintessential patriarch. In fact, we could say that it transforms the entire book from historical and sociological masterpiece into something much closer to autobiography by powerfully inserting the author into his own text. A wholly different reading of the book is made possible by the photograph: it not only asserts authorship but also, importantly, shows the author as the very embodiment of patriarchal society. In fact, we could say that Freyre is even more enmeshed in his own patriarchal society in his sociological study than Du Perron is in the Indies society described in his purported autobiography (for Ducroo does reveal at times a cynical detachment that is almost foreign to Freyre's narrative self). The mode of enmeshment, though, is different in both cases, and not only because one text is purportedly a scientific study and the other purportedly an autobiographical novel.[59]

Freyre inserts himself – and his text and his country – in an imperial lineage. He is himself part and parcel of the great Portuguese effort unfolding in four continents from the sixteenth century on. As he stands looking ahead of him – into the future perhaps, into the history yet to unfold – at the foot of the stairs leading to his grand house, he is somehow the direct descendant of the heroic sixteenth century Lusitanian navigators. The photograph on the next page is of an older, somewhat run-down, shoddy and slightly sagging *casa-grande*. Freyre's own *casa-grande* stands out in a good light against its more ancient ancestor: it is recognizably a *casa-grande*, and yet it seems new and quite solid. Its stateliness almost glows in the photograph: it is definitely not the past, as the following photograph, but the present and the future. Freyre is one with it, almost as if he were the main statue standing guard over the place. Freyre's text is so powerful because it re-appropriates the past – the Portuguese past, both metropolitan and colonial – and turns it into a Brazilian postcolonial present and future. As Veloso and Madeira point out, his aim is to reinvent a history marked by a past that was already strongly *national*.[60] In fact, Freyre's approach is almost revolutionary here: he appropriates the imperial past for the former colony. The colony becomes the empire, and the roles of metropolis and colony have become reversed, through the establishment of a continent-sized nation in the tropics (an 'American Russia' or a 'tropical China', to use but two names that he gave to Brazil at one point or another).[61] It is Brazil that has become the true imperial inheritor of Lusitanian greatness.[62] Freyre's counterparts of Du Perron's *abrutis* or 'Nazis' are therefore actually turned into heroes, and the violence of colonial and postcolonial history is sublimated in complex and multifarious ways into glorious imperial-like nationhood. The descendant of slave-owning 'patriarchal' families transmogrifies himself into a self-styled intellectual-patriarch living in his own *casa-grande*.

Now, Du Perron's mode of appropriation of the past is, by comparison, quite peculiar. He has no imperial past to be reappropriated, as in his view the Dutch East India Company officials, who had founded the colony back in the seventeenth century, had been robbers; their descendants in Java, three centuries on, still had no business being there. 'The Country of Origin' is therefore by definition somebody else's country. How symbolic is his stint at Gedong Menu, the house of his birth for a few weeks in 1939, no longer his family property. He can just rent two rooms for himself, his wife and son.[63] A less Freyrean imagining of nationhood is hardly possible. The Hollander and the 'Rebellious' Javanese are forever foreign to each other, no matter how long they have lived together, and no matter how much Du Perron becomes befriended with some leading Indonesian nationalists. The colonial reality of mixing and living together – so powerfully and poignantly depicted in the pages of *Het Land van Herkomst* – is like a parallel story that gives the lie to this way of imagining nationhood. The big question here – which will necessarily remain unanswered – goes to the heart of the Dutch colonial experience in Java. If there are important points of contact between the way Freyre and Du Perron both (re) construct their colonial pasts – and we believe that we have shown that there are – then why is it that in the Dutch case the colonial past eventually became *tempo doeloe*, the 'old times', a lost time to be recollected in the comfort of the distant former metropolis by former colonials and their metropolitan peers, while the former colony reconstructed its own past (and present and future) out of materials that were not imperial and much less recognizably Dutch?

Freyre's narrative easily jumps over any discontinuities between empire and colony, Europe and South America (and Africa and Asia), colony and postcolony. The notion that Freyre keeps at bay as it would destroy his entire narrative edifice is that Brazil is very much a creation of its own and owes little to Portuguese colonialism. This would indeed make the Portuguese an alterity, the Other, bring them in the same position as the Dutch had in the emergence of Indonesian nationalism. Instead, Freyre, insists on the Portuguese ability to 'dissolve' into the non-white populace. Of course, Java is here a wholly different imaginative territory: after all, powerful local kingdoms of precolonial origin, with large populations, remained until the end of the Java War in 1830 (and continued to exist afterwards there and throughout the archipelago), whereas Brazil was very much a settlement colony, its (now comparatively tiny) Indian population notwithstanding. Nonetheless, Java (and even more so Indonesia) is all the same a colonial construct/construction. The comparative deletion of the Indies past in Java, and its transfer to the metropolitan imaginative space, remains a complex issue to be tackled comparatively. Here it must be enough to point out that it would be too easy to attribute the difference to the different histories of Java and Brazil; the (post) colonial imaginaire through which those histories are or were constructed also needs to be included. Reading Du Perron and Freyre comparatively, it is difficult to avoid the impression that it could all have been different – namely, differently imagined. This is indeed one of the uneasy silences, leaving space for very different readings and projects, for an inclusion of creole/mestizo identity in the emerging Indonesian nationhood on the one hand and a black Brazilian identity not subsumed by the grand project of 'racial democracy' on the other.

NOTES

1. Ann Laura Stoler, *Race and the Education of Desire. Foucault's History of Sexuality and the Colonial Order of Things* (Durham, 1995), p. 11.
2. José Murilo de Carvalho, 'Brasil: Nações Imaginadas', in *Pontos e Bordados. Ensaios de História e Política* (Belo Horizonte, 1999), p. 233.
3. Roderick J. Barman, *The Making of Brazil* (Stanford, 1988), p. 178.
4. Lilia Schwarcz, *As Barbas do Imperador: D. Pedro II, um monarca nos trópicos* (São Paulo, 1998).
5. Ulbe Bosma and Remco Raben, *De oude Indische wereld 1500-1920* (Amsterdam, 2003).
6. Kees Snoek, *E. du Perron. Het leven van een smalle* mens (Amsterdam, 2005); Kees Snoek, *De Indische jaren van E. du Perron* (Amsterdam, 1990).
7. See the account of his trip in Gilberto Freyre, *Aventura e rotina. Sugestões de uma viagem à procura das constantes portuguesas de caráter e ação* (Rio de Janeiro, 1953).
8. Carlos Henrique Siqueira, Universidade de Brasília, personal communication, 19 December 2003. For Freyre's ambiguous connection to Boasian anthropology, see Luiz Costa Lima, 'A Versão Solar do Patriarcalismo: *Casa-Grande e Senzala*', in Luiz Costa Lima, *A Aguarrás do Tempo. Estudos sobre a narrative* (Rio de Janeiro, 1989), pp. 198–210.
9. About his links to the Brazilian dictatorship, see the article by Mário César Carvalho, 'Céu e inferno de Gilberto Freyre' in *Folha de São Paulo*, Sunday supplement, *Mais!*, 12 March 2000 (a special issue devoted to a revaluation of Freyre's work). A partial result of his collaboration with and sympathy for the Salazar dictatorship is the official bilingual publication issued by the government body in charge of studying colonial affairs: Gilberto Freyre, *Integração portuguesa nos trópicos/Portuguese Integration in the Tropics* (r, Vila Nova de Famalicão, 1958).
10. These works are Freyre's *Casa-Grande e Senzala* and E. Du Perron's *Het land van herkomst*, first published respectively in 1933 and 1935. Freyre' s work is part of a trilogy, whose two other volumes are *Sobrados e Mucambos* (dealing with imperial Brazil, first published in 1936) and *Ordem e Progresso* (about republican Brazil, first published in 1959). *Casa-Grande e Senzala* is however by far his best known work, particularly outside of Brazil.
11. Quoted in Mariza Veloso and Angélica Madeira, *Leituras brasileiras. Itinerários no pensamento social e na literatura* (Rio and São Paulo, 1999), p. 152.
12. 'Uma história da intimidade', in *Mais!* Supplement, *Folha de São Paulo*, 12 March 2000, p. 15.
13. Quoted in Mariza Veloso and Angélica Madeira, *Leituras brasileiras*, p. 142.
14. Evaldo Cabral de Mello, 'O ovo de Colombo gilbertiano' in *Mais!, Folha de São Paulo*, 12 March 2000, p. 13. Another observer, Luiz Costa Lima, also points out the importance of the private life (the 'patriarchal family') in Freyre's narrative: 'A Visão solar do patriarcalismo', pp. 228 ff.
15. E. du Perron, *De smalle mens* (Amsterdam, 1934).
16. Leo Spitzer, *Lives in Between: Assimilation and Marginality in Austria, Brazil, West Africa, 1780–1945* (Cambridge University Press, 1989).
17. For the social and historical context in which Gilberto wrote, see 'Gilberto Freyre: uma leitura crítica' in Veloso and Madeira, *Leituras brasileiras,* pp. 136–61.

18. Gilberto Freyre, *Casa-Grande e Senzala. Formação da Família Brasileira sob o regime da Economia Patriarcal* [*Casa-Grande and Senzala: Formation of the Brazilian Family under the Regime of the Patriarchal Economy*] (Rio de Janeiro, 1984), p. 283.

19. Kees Snoek, *Manhafte heren en rijke erfdochters. Het voorgeslacht van E. Du Perron op Java* (KITLV Press, Leiden, 2003), p. 9.

20. E. Du Perron, *Het land van herkomst* (G. A. van Oorschot. Amsterdam, 1997), pp. 30–1. Except where indicated, all translations from the Dutch and Portuguese are our own.

21. *Bataviaasch Nieuwsblad*, 24 May 1930.

22. Snoek, *De Indische jaren van E. du Perron*, p. 49; Kees Snoek, *Manhafte heren en rijke erfdochters.* p. 33.

23. Du Perron, *Land van Herkomst*, p. 52

24. Snoek, *De Indische jaren van E. du Perron*, p. 30.

25. Du Perron, *Land van Herkomst*, p. 85

26. Du Perron's father owned Maatschappij tot exploitatie van de Gedong and the Mercurius real estate agency.

27. See the 1821 drawing from a book by an English traveller on p. liii; the photograph on p. xciv; a Dutchman's seventeenth-century drawing on p. 95; a simple drawing on p. 243 and more drawings on pp. 288, 295, 303, 322, 330, 339, 353, etc.

28. Freyre, *Casa-Grande*, p. 91.

29. Especially in his later work, as in *Casa-Grande e Senzala*, it is rather a question of Portugal and Brazil only. See for instance his *Aventura e rotina*.

30. Ann Laura Stoler and Frederick Cooper, 'Between Metropole and Colony' in Ann Laura Stoler and Frederick Cooper (eds), *Tensions of Empire: colonial cultures in a bourgeois world* (Berkeley, 1997), pp. 10 and 16.

31. See for instance his *Doidinho*.

32. Even the pronunciation is similar, except that the Portuguese *ô* is a long vowel. *Sinhô* is the white (Creole) master, whereas *sinjo* is a Creole man.

33. *Pesantren* or Islamic schools were (and are) very common in Java.

34. Hella S. Haasse, *Oeroeg* (Amsterdam, 1948).

35. Kees Snoek, *De Indische jaren van E. Du Perron.*

36. For the complexities of Freyre's depiction of violence, see Ricardo Benzaquen de Araújo, *Guerra e paz: Casa-Grande e Senzala e a obra de Gilberto Freyre nos anos 30* (Rio de Janeiro, 1994). Araújo argues that Freyre never quite depicted the *casa-grande* as paradise, as many of his critics posited. Namely, he had a complex (and perhaps highly ambiguous) view of colonial violence. Araújo's is a major study of the book.

37. J.W.H. Veenstra, *D'Artagnan tegen Jan Fuselier; E. du Perron als Indisch polemist* (Amsterdam, 1962).

38. There is in fact a short chapter devoted to Hille, ch. XXV ('Dubbelportret van Arthur Hille'), pp. 477–8.

39. Du Perron, *Land van Herkomst*, p. 303.

40. Compare this attitude with that of Gilberto as highlighted below (see also note 57 below).

41. See the introduction by Omar Thomaz to Gilberto's *Interpretação do Brasil* (Cia das Letras, São Paulo, 2001), p. 11.

42. *Leituras brasileiras*, pp. 147–8.

43. *O mundo que o português criou. Aspectos das relações sociais e da cultura do Brasil com Portugal e as colônias portuguesas* (Rio, 1940).

44. See Araújo, who, to counter critics who believe that Gilberto depicted slaveholding Brazil as paradise, mentions a *Jardim dos Suplícios* or 'Garden of Pains' as a metaphor for Gilberto's depiction of Brazilian society and its violence (*Guerra e Paz,* pp. 48–57). Costa Lima also shows that concentrating on the intimate life of the 'patriarchal family' and its *plasticidade* ('plasticity' or flexibility) was Gilberto's main narrative device to 'soften' antagonisms inherent to a slave society (*A Aguarrás do Tempo*, p. 233).

45. Du Perron, *Land van Herkomst*, 279.

46. 'Contaminated' stands for '*besmet*' here, which also means 'infected'.

47. 'Brasil: Nações Imaginadas', p. 249.

48. 'Brasil: Nações Imaginadas', p. 251. Carvalho mentions Sílvio Romero's work as an example of this huge variation of opinion within the work of the same author.

49. Lilia Schwarcz, *O Espetáculo das Raças: Cientistas, Instituições e Questão Racial no Brasil, 1870–1930* (São Paulo, 1993).

50. In the words of a leading historian from Pernambuco, what Freyre did was to change miscegenation from a disadvantage into an advantage. See Evaldo Cabral de Mello, 'O ovo de Colombo gilbertiano' in *Mais!, Folha de São Paulo*, 12 March 2000, p. 13.

51. Page 271. The speakers are Abdoel Moeïs and Dr Tjipto Mangoenkoesoemo. Both were famous Javanese nationalists.

52. Du Perron, *Land van herkomst,* pp. 270–1.

53. Du Perron, *Land van herkomst,* p. 271.

54. Du Perron, *Land van herkomst,* p. 437.

55. Decades later Malraux would also write the preface to the French translation of Du Perron's book: *Le pays d'origine* (Paris, 1980).

56. E. Du Perron, 'Inleiding' (Preface) in Soewarsih Djojopoespito, *Buiten het gareel: Indonesische roman; Met een inleiding van E. Du Perron* (Amsterdam, 1947) pp. 5–10.

57. E .du Perron, P.P.C Brief aan een Indonesiër. *Kritiek en Opbouw* 16 August 1939. See also Snoek, *E. du Perron, het leven van een smalle mens*, pp. 942–3.

58. It now houses the Fundação Gilberto Freyre in Recife.

59. See also: Araújo, *Guerra e Paz*, p. 201.

60. Veloso and Madeira, *Leituras* brasileiras, p. 147.

61. Gilberto Freyre, *China Tropical* (Brasília, 2003).

62. In fact, Lusitanian *and* Iberian greatness: for the complexities of his interest in *hispanismo* and his early admiration for the Soviet Union (later followed by disappointment), see Omar Thomaz's preface in Freyre's *Interpretação do Brasil*, pp. 24–32. In fact, Gilberto seems to have been very attracted to several countries that had an imperial past.

63. Snoek, *E. du Perron, het leven van een smalle mens,* p. 897.

FINDING A MATE IN LATE TSARIST RUSSIA

THE EVIDENCE FROM MARRIAGE ADVERTISEMENTS

Stephen Lovell
King's College London

ABSTRACT This article examines a hitherto unstudied source – the marriage newspapers of late tsarist Russia – for the light it can shed on two important but elusive subjects for historical inquiry. First, the history of marriage in an era of astonishingly rapid social and economic change. Second, the history of social identities. It is argued that the small and apparently trivial texts of marriage advertisements offer a rare opportunity to see the language of social description in cultural practice – to discover, in other words, how the various labels of class, estate, occupation and status acquired meaning in people's everyday lives and discourse.

Keywords: Russia, marriage, newspapers, advertising, gender

In *The Philosophy of Money*, his monumental inquiry into the implications of monetarization for human society and relationships, Georg Simmel reflected on the predicament of men and women seeking a marriage partner in modern society. Choice and autonomy did not seem to make the process easier or more satisfactory. As people became more individualized, and so less inclined to stay inside the protective cocoon of custom and ritual, they made themselves less likely to find an appropriate match in the (equally individualized) population of the opposite sex. Perversely, as society became ever more commodified, the most powerful commodity of all – money – was losing its value as the arbiter of a prospective partner's marital suitability: men and women in search of companionate marriages required a range of less quantitative indicators.

Simmel's view of marriage in modernity now sounds rather familiar. It has been echoed by many sociologists in the last hundred years. Anthony Giddens has written of the ways in which the modern age transferred romance from an otherworldly domain of myth and fiction to the sphere of individual preoccupations and expectations. In the eighteenth century, he implies, people imagined romantic love, whereas in the nineteenth they could hope to act it out.[1] Efforts have been made to provide an ever-more refined periodization: to trace the shifts and mutations in modern expectations of love through its Victorian 'spiritualization' and postwar 'eroticization'.[2] The very broad outlines of the intimate history of modern Europe have emerged clearly

Address for correspondence: Dr Stephen Lovell, Reader in Modern European History, Department of History, King's College, Strand, London, WC2R 2LS. E-mail: stephen.lovell@kcl.ac.uk

enough: from the mid-nineteenth century onwards, at different rates in different societies and social milieus, love came increasingly to be promoted as a prerequisite for the legal relationship of marriage. It is equally clear that this development has not always simplified the business of contracting matrimony.

Simmel did, however, mention a practical way in which the time and trouble of finding a mate might be alleviated. By placing an advertisement, he suggested, people could hugely expand their field of candidates and substantially increase their chances of success. Marriage ads were the most rational way of distributing a society's amorous resources: after all, a perfect match existed for everyone, if only he or she could be tracked down. Simmel regretted that precisely those people who would benefit most from placing and reading marriage advertisements were most liable to shun and disparage this form of communication. The problem was that human beings were unable to describe themselves adequately in a few dozen words and could not avoid focusing on easily measurable attributes. In the first instance, that meant money (or lack of it), and this materialistic directness conflicted with the love-match ethos of the times. The middle class wanted intimacy and self-fulfilment and did not appreciate being reminded of the monetary bottom line.[3]

Shortly after Simmel published the first edition of his work in 1900, marriage advertisements appeared, and enjoyed a brief heyday, in imperial Russia. This was a place very different from the one envisaged in the German sociologist's thought experiments. It certainly was not 'middle class' in any then or subsequently conventional sense of that term. It did not contain a stable core of 'bourgeois' values; wealth and social status could not be said to have struck up a harmonious and mutually beneficial relationship. Rather, this was a society in alarming upheaval, whose political order had just been shaken to its foundations in the 1905 Revolution. Nor was it clear that Russia had advanced very far along the road of the individualized modern subject. Old-style matchmakers were still a feature of urban existence, and patriarchy remained the norm in family life. All in all, it was not clear that the genre of marriage advertisement would work in Russia. Such a depersonalized form of communication was surely likely to suffer from a greater than average stigma in a still undermodernized society,[4] and there was no guarantee that even those men and women brave or desperate enough to send in their copy would be able to find appropriate and effective words to describe themselves and their conjugal requirements.

In this article, then, I wish to consider the corpus of 'marriage newspapers' (*brachnye gazety*) for the evidence they can provide on the institution of marriage in the early twentieth century. Before I do so, however, the status of this evidence requires careful consideration. Readers might well object that these newspapers form a trivial and profoundly unrepresentative source base.[5]

I do not think that marriage adverts are trivial – after all, especially in an era when the genre was not well established, they often involved people putting their sense of decorum aside and their selves and future happiness on the line – but I happily agree that they are unrepresentative. It is unlikely that more than a few hundred people were placing such advertisements at any given time. They tended to be disproportionately urban, educated and male.

However, if we accept that everyday life is a legitimate subject for historical research, it is hard to imagine a set of sources that would not be unrepresentative. This goes especially for the history of intimate relations between the sexes. These relations are passed over in silence as embarrassing or unworthy of mention or they leave traces in normative materials or they are heavily refracted in narratives of one kind or another.[6] To be sure, we can also make use of a small number of fascinating and self-revelatory memoirs and diaries, but these are no more 'representative' than any other kind of source.

Like several other historians, I contend that the proliferating print media and other cultural industries of late tsarist Russia can offer exceptional insights into processes of social diversification and identity formation.[7] Whether in popular stories, newspapers or advice books, this was a society that was describing, depicting and imagining itself much more intensively and extensively than had previously been the case. If we want to hear the voices of the many subjects of the Russian empire who did not write memoirs or leave documentary legacies, we have no better option than to turn to publications that, while they were not authored by the voiceless majority, did at least have to address their concerns directly (in order to induce readers to part with their kopecks and roubles).

The further advantage of the matrimonial newspaper as an object of study is that we do not have to limit ourselves to intuiting the values of the reading public from material written on its behalf. Members of this public were themselves co-authors, providing through their advertisements anywhere from one-quarter to four-fifths of the copy. Each issue of a matrimonial newspaper contains dozens of short exercises in self-fashioning. The genre of marriage advertisement thus has much to offer the burgeoning sub-field of the history of the Russian self: it is more socially inclusive and less fragmented than the corpus of full-scale memoirs that has come down to us, yet it is also less indirect than much of the evidence adduced in wider-ranging investigations.[8]

Yet marriage advertisements do nonetheless raise problems for a historian interested in composing a judicious account of the past. Perhaps the most fundamental of these is the fact that people placing such advertisements are likely to be out of the social mainstream. After all, the vast majority of couples in early twentieth-century Russia (and in Europe as a whole) were formed without resorting to public communication of this kind.

It is undoubtedly the case, as research into marriage advertisements and lonely hearts in other cultures has shown, that men and (especially) women who resort to such a method tend to be socially marginal.[9] For one reason or another, they cannot find a match through the usual channels (family, kin, social networks). But how many people in the cities of late imperial Russia were *not* in some sense marginal? As many scholars have now shown, this was a society where class, occupation, nationality, culture, wealth and social estate jostled with each other for primacy. Whether we focus on the educated elite or on the urban lower orders, we look in vain for stable identities or hierarchies of status. As Lev Tolstoy tells us in the twelfth chapter of Part I of *Anna Karenina*, finding a suitable match for a daughter was not a straightforward matter even for the tightly woven clans of the Moscow aristocracy, and even as early as the 1870s: Princess

Shcherbatskaia, who remembers her own marriage thirty years earlier as being regulated entirely by custom, admits to herself that she has no idea how parents give their daughters away these days – and cannot find anyone to tell her. The predicament of those of less elevated social station can best be suggested statistically. At the end of the nineteenth century, only 4 per cent of men and 5 per cent of women in European Russia in their late forties had never married, so matrimony was still overwhelmingly the social and cultural norm. But the great majority of urban people in the empire were a long way off their forties: more than 60 per cent of them were below thirty. And, as young people flooded into the cities, they usually had to cope not only with social and geographical dislocation but also with a substantial imbalance between the sexes: men significantly outnumbered women, especially in the 'marriageable' age range of between twenty and thirty years. The result was that, according to the 1897 census, 584 out of every 1,000 urban men were unmarried.[10]

Historians can quickly agree that millions of urban people in late imperial Russia were forced to question and redefine the social location in which they had been born. The problem, however, is to find a way of discussing social identities that does not make them seem nebulous: to show complexity and fluidity in action rather than simply asserting their existence. In this light, marriage advertisements make for an unusually informative source, as they contain a high density of identity affirmations. With only a few dozen words (often less) at their disposal, advertisers were forced to home in on those attributes they considered especially important or desirable. There is perhaps no other kind of material where words like 'member of the intelligentsia' (*intelligent*), 'nobleman' (*dvorianin*) and 'widow' (*vdova*) occur with such incessancy – or where the interdependence of social and cultural history is so manifest.

Marriage advertisements may be an expression of the subject's most deeply felt desires, fears and aspirations but, after reading hundreds of these small texts, one is struck as much by their basic homogeneity than by the distinctive personalities of their authors. A marriage ad is not a direct emanation of the individual spirit but a convention-ridden genre. Although some such items in late tsarist Russia were extraordinarily long, discursive and informative, many others were laconic and even tight-lipped. What emerges from this material is a sense of the prevailing values of a society: notions of the ideal wife and the ideal husband, hierarchies of status, the balance between materialistic and affective dimensions of marriage. By attending to these matters we can make some suggestions, however tentative, regarding the effects of social change on intimate life. Change is notoriously difficult to disentangle from continuity in the history of the family.[11] Perhaps our best hope of doing so is to look at new forms of cultural expression at times of socio-economic transformation.[12] In Russia's marriage newspapers thousands of people, both men and women, many of whom had changed their social position between childhood and adulthood, suddenly had the chance to put into printed words who they were and whom their potential spouse should be.[13] It is worth investigating what they made of this opportunity.

COURTSHIP AND MARRIAGE IN NINETEENTH-CENTURY RUSSIA: WHAT DO WE KNOW ALREADY?

Like so many other areas of social history, marriage shows up in the documentary record mainly when it goes wrong or comes under strain. The most impressive existing studies of the institution of marriage in imperial Russia are concerned largely with legislation concerning divorce, family life and property. Gregory Freeze shows that Russia was the reverse of secularizing trends found in much of nineteenth-century Europe. From the second half of the eighteenth century onwards, the Orthodox Church set about establishing 'a marital order of a rigidity unknown elsewhere in Europe'.[14] Bolstered by its doctrine of the indelibility of sacraments, the Church was able to enforce a minuscule divorce rate: an annual average of 58 for the whole of the Russian empire between 1836 and 1860. Syphilis and physical abuse were not considered grounds for divorce. In addition, the cards were stacked against annulment in all kinds of ways. Male sexual incapacity was deemed proven only after three years, and women had to undergo a humiliating medical examination to prove their virginity. As William G. Wagner has subsequently shown in absorbing detail, the pressure built for a liberalization of divorce and family law in the decades following Emancipation. Liberal jurists and conservative hierarchs struggled for the right to set the tone of the institution of marriage. By the turn of the century, although the Orthodox Church fought a determined rearguard action, the liberals could reflect on some tangible successes. Divorce became noticeably more frequent in St Petersburg and Moscow from the 1890s onwards, and in 1904 the Holy Synod relaxed its rules on divorce.[15] Still more recently, Barbara Engel has reminded us that lawyers and churchmen had to reckon with a third party in the legal regulation of marriage: the tsarist state. In a study of more than 2,000 cases from the archive of the Imperial Chancellery for Receipt of Petitions, Engel has shown that chancellery officials sometimes did more than liberal jurists to improve the married lot of women, and that they too had an interest in marital reform.[16] Yet, as Simon Dixon has also pointed out, marriage remained a fiercely contested institution to the very end of the tsarist period: the Orthodox Church if anything intensified its efforts to counteract liberal trends, especially in areas where such developments posed a serious challenge to its authority and social impact.[17]

This body of work is illuminating on marriage as a legal institution, but it cannot be expected to shed much light on the meaning and practice of marriage in different sections of Russian society. It necessarily leaves unexplored the question of what people were looking for in a marriage partner, and how they went about finding one.

The only English-language social history of marriage in any part of the Russian empire is ChaeRan Freeze's excellent study of Jewish marriage and divorce in the Ukrainian and Lithuanian provinces.[18] The story Freeze tells can be accommodated under the broad conceptual umbrella of 'modernization'. Average marriage age rose steadily for the Jewish population in the second half of the nineteenth century; over the same period, moreover, Russia's Jews went from being the most fertile religious group in the empire to the second least fertile. The ideal of the companionate marriage strengthened as the role of matchmakers in marriage negotiations weakened. The scope for affective ties between young men and women increased, as did publicly expressed concerns about the decline of the family and the real incidence of marital breakdown. Exceptionally, however, the Jewish divorce rate did not rise in line with the liberalization of marriage: partly because there were powerful economic disincentives to initiate the legal dissolution of the family, partly because men and women tended to be older when they entered the marital relationship, but also, paradoxically, because of the decline of 'traditional' rabbinical authority (which made formal dissolution harder to achieve in practical terms).

Besides the illuminating, but also somewhat anomalous, case of the Jewish population, the scholarly literature does not have too much to say on the social history of marriage in the Russian empire. Until recently, the study of marriage in its everyday aspects was largely the province of Soviet ethnography, which always devoted most attention to rural society and to the unchanging features of its rituals and practices. The urban environment rarely received a mention; issues of social differentiation and intermarriage between classes or estates were almost never considered. A shining exception is G.V. Zhirnova's study of four provincial towns (Kaluga, Elets, Efremov and Kozel'sk) from the late nineteenth century onwards.[19] Using a combination of contemporary documents (marriage registers, contracts and dowry inventories), questionnaires, and interviews (conducted with very elderly people in the 1970s), Zhirnova did much to reconstruct the range of marriage choices open to the inhabitants of these ethnically Russian towns in the region south of Moscow. She found clear evidence of change over time. In the 1870s marriages tended strongly to occur within a single social estate. Especially in the merchantry and the nobility, exceptions to this rule were few indeed. Even within the fluid *meshchanstvo* (non-noble townspeople), estate purity was maintained in about 80 per cent of cases. By 1917, however, the situation had changed radically. Now about 60 per cent of marriages in Efremov were socially mixed; it was only within the nobility that estate purity was still largely the norm. In the early twentieth century mutually advantageous marriages were contracted between the *meshchanstvo* and the peasantry. Similarly, many merchants liked the idea of social mobility through marriage with the nobility. Although scruples concerning social status persisted, enough nobles had fallen on hard times to make noble-merchant intermarriage a recognized phenomenon.

All the same, the patterns of marriage behaviour continued to vary from one social group to another. The age of marriage tended to be higher in the town than in the village, but was strongly differentiated according to class and occupation. Young men from the *meshchanstvo* tended to marry in their early twenties (that is to say, as soon as they had acquired a trade). Their brides were on average two or three years younger. In the merchantry the age gap was much greater, as men needed to wait longer before they had built up a business robust enough to support a family. Nobles, similarly, tended to wait until they had advanced to a reasonable rank in service or inherited their portion of the family wealth.

Courting rituals also varied according to estate. In the *meshchanstvo*, six or seven couples might congregate for an evening at weekends to sing songs and play games. These occasions usually came to an end around eleven, and each young man would try to accompany home the woman who had taken his fancy. A higher class approach was to organize parties for young people on a birthday or name day. Here there might be piano or dancing. A still grander option was the ball. But for lower strata, the street was always the best place to meet members of the opposite sex. It was rivalled only by the church, which in some localities became notorious as a place for sizing up potential brides and initiating acquaintance with them. Priests sometimes delivered special sermons to warn that church should not be a place for the amorous rendez-vous.

But, of course, sweet nothings under the church candles were not the main way that marriages were concluded. These were business transactions as much as anything. They were sometimes preceded by conspicuous displays of wealth: marriageable merchant girls were, for example, exhibited as part of a train of sleighs that was decked out with carpets and velvet cushions and headed by the paterfamilias. Most of all, however, the material aspects of marriage required negotiation, often on the basis of a dowry inventory drawn up by the bride's father. Establishing contact between the families was by no means a simple matter and usually entailed an intermediary. In the eighteenth and nineteenth centuries the role of matchmaker (*svakha*) expanded so significantly that it became an unquestioned social institution for the wealthier strata of provincial towns. This function was performed by energetic and well-connected women in middle and old age from the *meshchanstvo* and the merchantry. Zhirnova makes the case that matchmakers, by the early twentieth century, were viewed almost as a distinct professional group. The matchmakers gathered information on the bride's family from all available sources: servants, dependants, even caretakers and supervisors of the building or courtyard where the family resided. They usually charged a fee of between ten and twenty-five roubles.[20]

Further localized studies of marriage would be valuable and interesting (even if it is now too late for the oral history Zhirnova conducted in the 1970s). In this article, however, I want to review some of the published and (at least in principle) more widely circulating evidence on attitudes to marriage and courtship. To be sure, this material is at a greater remove from everyday life than dowry records and marriage registers but it has at least some compensating advantages. Russia had a publishing industry that grew substantially in the first half of the nineteenth century and explosively in the last third. Many of the books and periodicals it produced were designed to achieve commercial success by exploiting the tastes, concerns and anxieties of the reading public. As with any rapidly modernizing print culture, relations between the sexes were an area of special concentration.[21]

If we want to explore attitudes to marriage at the end of the tsarist era, etiquette books are among our most eloquent (not to say prolix) sources.[22] Advice literature has always been full of tips on how to find a spouse (mostly a wife, as men were assumed to exercise most agency and discretion in these matters). In the eighteenth-century early days of the genre in Russia, the issue was generally that of choosing a wife wisely: reaching a careful assessment of her good sense, intelligence and morals, and not being distracted by looks or wealth.[23] Then, when sensibility became the order of the day, instructions for putative lovers became abstract and verbose.[24] The genre received an injection of drawing-room *savoir-faire* in the 1830s. One work of 1840 gave an entire choreography of seduction as it detailed the successive stages of intimacy that were made possible by various ballroom dances. By the third figure of the quadrille, all commonplaces were already redundant; in the fourth, the two hearts resolved their fate; the fifth fanned the 'pink flame of love'; while the sixth was 'like the victory celebration after a war'.[25]

The pace of publication in this area increased greatly in the 1850s and 1860s. The advice handed out was mostly pragmatic. Given that young people were susceptible to the charms of just about anyone of the opposite sex, they should wait a little before marrying, or at least follow their parents' advice. Men should not try to marry into a family more prestigious than their own: it was best to go for a large family of equal status. Wives had to be younger than husbands; husbands had to be able to provide materially for wives (reliance on a wife's fortune was humiliating for a man and, in the long run, was sure to undermine a marriage). Brunettes were capable and dependable and to be preferred if a man wanted assistance in his career. A beautiful face was quick to attract but also quick to fade. It was best to seek a golden mean between beauty and ugliness. Men should be vigilant with regard to women's character flaws. Lengthy observation was advisable before marriage: women were good at concealing their faults. It was also important to choose a healthy woman: a good idea was to watch how thoroughly she chewed her food and whether she walked with a firm step. For their part, men should look after their appearance, be natural and polite in manner, and take care to be pleasant to the woman's family. In return they should expect a lifetime's gratitude from their wife.[26]

Advice literature from the more liberal era of the Great Reforms suggests, then, that marriage seekers (primarily men) were viewed as independent agents who needed to acquire as much information and expertise as possible in order to make a rational choice. Over the next few decades the formula did not undergo any radical change. Perhaps the most noteworthy development was the fact that advice literature tended to become more even-handed in its treatment of the sexes: it might even seriously entertain the idea that women too had a role to play in selecting their marriage partner.[27]

Another notable feature of advice literature on courtship and marriage was its growing emphasis on love as a trigger for conjugal union. The genre most intensively concerned with helping true feeling to develop was the letter-writing manual (pis'movnik). Of course, such books were not an invention of the late nineteenth century.[28] This was, however, the first time that printing technology and the market allowed them to aim for a mass urban audience. The readers of the 1860s or the 1890s were not those of the 1800s and they seemed to require a little preliminary persuasion that the letter-writing manual was not an anachronism. The epistolary genre, they were told, still played a critical role in arousing the feelings of a potential spouse. Lovers tended to 'read one and the same letter a countless number of times, searching to find in it what it sometimes does not contain. The external gloss of a letter and a striking phrase act like electricity on the nerves of exalted natures.'[29] Compilations of letters offered a range of models according to the relative material positions of author and addressee. A rich man, for example, was recommended to declare that 'I cut across the customs of society. My relatives have long been suggesting to me a bride from a rich family, placing the emphasis on commercial calculation.'[30]

Advice books also offered guidance on spoken communication. In order to make a pleasant impression in society, young men should not talk too much, keep language simple if they were to discourse on specialized subjects, avoid entering heated arguments and never engage in flattery. Recommended phrases were perhaps less practical. A good line on entering the home of acquaintances was reckoned to be: 'I have long wanted to visit, but I have been held back by obstacles; now I am completely free and have come to visit.' On entering a house for the first time: 'I am very pleased to meet you. I consider the present day the most pleasant of my life, because I have had the opportunity and the pleasure of making your acquaintance.'[31]

We will probably never know whether any readers ever tried out these stilted phrases, or what kind of reception they met. It is hard to avoid the conclusion that advice literature was a long way from representing the vanguard of changing social mores. Many of the late imperial conduct guides – and especially the *pis'movniki* – were remarkable not for the advice they dispensed but for the extent to which they borrowed wholesale from earlier publications of the same kind. The author-compilers of these books seem to have taken rather little account of the enormous social change occurring before their eyes. Letters first published in the 1860s or earlier were readily recycled in the early twentieth century.[32]

Content analysis of the *pis'movniki* does not need to be pushed too far, however. Model letters were by no means the only relevant material for would-be lovers. The often arch and pious recommendations of traditional advice literature were increasingly being supplemented by more irreverent and jokey material on relations between the sexes.[33] The early twentieth century even saw a lurch towards more speculative approaches drawing on 'magical' seduction techniques.[34] Advice literature of all its various kinds – from conservative letter-writing manuals to racy recommendations for aspiring Don Juans – indicates the extent to which relations between the sexes had become an area of preoccupation and independent reflection for hundreds of thousands of Russian urbanites.

What we have from the various sources I have reviewed in this section – the legislation and institutions analysed by Freeze, Wagner and Engel, the provincial everydayness of Zhirnova, and the commercialized commonplaces of advice literature – is varied, but mostly complementary, evidence of shifts in attitude. Marriage, to be sure, was still a primarily social institution and courtship was still largely governed by convention, but individual marriage-seekers had more elaborate decisions to make about how to go about finding a partner – and how to make themselves appealing to that partner. I now turn to what was sold as the most direct path through the labyrinth of social convention to the goal of happy and advantageous matrimony: the marriage advertisement.

THE MARRIAGE NEWSPAPERS

Newspaper advertisements offered a powerful form of communication in late imperial Russia, and not only in Russia. Across Europe, they became much more visually appealing and striking towards the end of the nineteenth century as printing technology improved in quality and came down in price. There is strong contemporary evidence that advertisements were a major attraction for newspaper consumers, being read not only for information but also for entertainment.[35] The techniques of advertising were now a matter of interest for market actors of many different kinds; they were subjected to elaborate analysis in instructional literature that increasingly found its way to Europe from North America.[36]

Advertising gained a position of great prominence on the pages of Russia's wide-circulation newspapers from the late nineteenth century onwards. The densely printed pages of *Novoe vremia*, for example, were flooded with literally hundreds (sometimes thousands) of advertisements per issue, mainly from job seekers. Most concerned domestic employment, but some were distinctly white-collar (office-clerk, engineer, bailiff on an estate). After the 1905 Revolution newspapers were less restricted in the material they carried, and a new category of more personal, not to say sexual, advertisements emerged. To be sure, there was nothing that would count as explicit by twenty-first century standards but offers of service from nude models and masseuses did not leave a huge amount unsaid.[37] Another result of the loosening of inhibitions after 1905 was a franker approach to marriage. Divorce lawyers advertised their services before 1905, but they became more numerous and more direct in their sales pitch in the second half of the decade. Matchmakers (*svakhi*) and 'intermediaries' (*posrednitsy*) also used the major newspapers for self-publicity. And people who wanted to manage without such specialized assistance began to appeal directly for a marriage partner. By January 1906 *Novoe vremia* regularly carried about twenty individual marriage advertisements per issue.[38]

The marriage advertisement flourished especially in publications specially dedicated to matrimonial and conjugal matters. These appeared in several widely dispersed areas of the Russian empire: Odessa, Piatigorsk, Tiflis, Tomsk, Riga, as well as Moscow and St Petersburg.[39] The longest running of them was the Moscow *Brachnaia gazeta* (hereafter *BG*), which came out continuously from September 1906 to June 1918 and claimed (apparently with justification) to be the progenitor of all the others. It also alleged (again, it seems, with justification) that other publications had not only borrowed its pioneering format but also stolen many of the articles, and even the individual advertisements, that it published. The editors of *BG* maintained that its rivals, whatever unprincipled tactics they adopted, could not match it for its distribution network or for its reputation in 'the intelligentsia circles of the capital and the provinces'.[40]

This reputation is hard to gauge with any certainty. In the absence of an archive, the only information we have is that provided on the pages of the newspaper itself. Naturally, the editors had a hard commercial interest in exaggerating the size of their circulation and their postbag. In July 1911 they claimed to have brought about thousands of successful marriages and to have received thousands of grateful letters from members of happy couples.[41] In 1909 they boasted of a well-developed distribution system stretching all the way to the Far East: the paper was said to have a few thousand readers in Bulgaria and Serbia, subscribers in London, Paris, Berlin, and America, and an estimated readership of a few hundred thousand (assuming each copy was read by five to ten people).[42] At the start of the following year they claimed, more plausibly, a circulation of 10,000 per issue and an annual total of 4,000 ads.[43]

Perhaps the strongest evidence for the success of *BG* is its relative longevity. At a time when newspapers appeared and vanished in a flash, and when *BG*'s direct competitors would typically last no more than a year or two, the Moscow paper continued uninterrupted publication for nearly twelve years, through a world war and two further revolutions. The number of ads soon grew to as many as fifty per issue. The paper then extended to six pages in November 1909 and accommodated as many as ninety ads per issue. After the outbreak of the First World War, *BG* was reduced to two pages due to paper shortages. The number of ads it ran briefly fell to thirty-five to forty, but by autumn 1914 it had recovered to about seventy per issue. Before long the ads were crowding out the articles. In July 1916 the paper size was reduced, but again the number of ads remained buoyant or even increased.

This publication proudly announced its foreign pedigree from the first issue (of September 1906): it was following the 'Western European model'.[44] Its aim was to make acceptable marriage 'by advertisement' (*po ob''iavleniiu*), a method of contracting matrimony that had been 'recognized by public opinion in America, England and Germany'.[45] Its civilizing mission was unambiguous and restated regularly over the decade of the paper's existence: 'By penetrating the far reaches and wild areas that are so abundant in our immense motherland, our publication serves everyone as a bright lodestar leading to peaceful family happiness, it makes people part of the cultural life of the cities, and it brings together people who are sometimes on opposite sides of the world to enjoy a warm, cosy corner of personal happiness'.[46]

The paper was to include, besides the ads themselves, heavyweight articles on marriage, descriptions of wedding rituals in other countries, updates on the 'woman question', stories, poems, jokes and cartoons. Setting itself up as a solemn upholder of the institution of marriage, *BG* regularly lamented the assault of 'pornography' in contemporary Russian culture. Periodically quoting Simmel to bolster its authority, it recommended advertisements as an efficient way of expanding one's field of acquaintances and of overcoming the loneliness and isolation to which many young people were prone in modern cities. The very first issue included a mock letter of complaint from a Moscow matchmaker, who protested that the paper would put her out of business. In a less lighthearted vein, the paper would regularly warn readers to beware of matchmakers – of both the traditional and modern entrepreneurial varieties.[47]

The paper professed a modern and liberal view of marriage issues. It kept up a regular commentary on the tortuous progress of divorce law in theory and practice and always remained sympathetic to liberalization. It also repeatedly endorsed the women's emancipation movement, and treated patriarchy as a dirty word. *BG* acknowledged that Russia was falling victim to the inexorable effects of capitalism: the divorce rate was rising, the marriage rate was falling, birth control was now more widely practised. But moralizing was no solution to these woes. The traditional certainties of arranged marriage did not provide a satisfactory alternative.[48]

Marriages by advertisement, the editors claimed, were a perfect middle ground between *coup de foudre* and convention. Such unions were in general happier and more stable than matches arranged by family or immediate circle and they were also a better bet than the marriages young people stumbled into without due consideration. The editors took care to steer a middle path in their discussion of the marriage advertisement. On the one hand, they argued, ads gave the opportunity to express individual requirements more precisely and to obtain detailed preliminary information about potential partners. Yet, on the other hand, this was no place for naked materialism: marriage should not become a 'commercial deal'.[49]

From time to time *BG* exposed its guiding principles to scrutiny by questionnaire. On one occasion it invited readers to reflect on the meaning of marriage. The results were not entirely as expected or desired. Clearly, not all respondents had treated the exercise with due seriousness: the editor remarked that 'not all replies were sufficiently thought through.' But above all the letters laid bare class differences. Of 109 replies, sixty-nine came from members of the intelligentsia (which probably meant higher or at least complete secondary education). Fifty-seven of these *intelligenty* wrote that marriage had to be based on love. A rather different view of matrimony was presented by the forty respondents classified as 'toilers' (*truzhenniki*): twenty-two of these stated that women had to bring to marriage some kind of dowry or else the capacity to work productively with her husband.[50] More jarring were the overwhelmingly negative or facetious replies that the paper received to the direct question 'What Is Marriage?'. Definitions included the following: 'love on trial at a military field tribunal', 'the beginning of the end', 'a lottery with a prize that no one ever wins', 'love's tomb', 'a scorpion that kills personal initiative'.[51] When invited to give their opinion on serious current issues, however, readers were shown to take up the same moderate liberal position as the editors. On the big question of whether civil or church ceremonies should be preferred, seventy-two out of 109 readers averred that it was time to stop disapproving of civil weddings. An even larger proportion (eighty-eight), however, felt that civil weddings should not necessarily be seen as superior to the church rites.[52]

The paper's *raison d'être,* however, lay not in articles or questionnaires but in the advertisements themselves. Most of these were between two and six lines long, with the first word or phrase typographically highlighted. A very few of the ads were so outlandish in their tone or in the information they provided that they may well have been the work of practical jokers. The vast majority, however, were entirely plausible. It is likely that, despite the best efforts of the editors, a few were sent in by conmen (or conwomen) but I have no corroborating evidence of this in my wider reading of the contemporary press. In any case, an advertisement does not lose its value as an expression of cultural and social norms just because its author's intentions are dishonourable.

Certainly, few of the ads read like the work of a conman. There was the occasional bounder who made astonishingly little effort to disguise the fact: 'URGENTLY, because my leave is coming to an end, I need a matchmaker or a bride. My requirements are as follows: a lady or widow of 25–30, not ugly, well brought up or educated, a good person. I need 5,000 to pay off a debt, and the remaining capital should not be less than 1,000, of which half should stay untouched and be spent only on the mutual agreement of husband and wife, but in the case of adultery by the wife pass to the husband after divorce. I am a cavalry officer, good-looking, energetic, with a good name. Would like to remain in the regiment, but if the wife desires I can transfer to another form of service . . . Will be a faithful husband as long as the wife is a good person.'[53] Occasionally one finds raffish declarations like the following: '30 YEARS OLD, brown hair, average height, have 20,000 per annum, would like to meet pretty woman. To go to the theatre, take a spin out of town on a fine frosty night and then warm up with a glass of wine' (*BG* 46 [1907]: 1). Much more common, however, was the down-to-earth approach: 'LONELY MAN, widower completely on his own, 42, has business in guberniia capital, earns 800–1,000 per annum. Totally sober, good-natured, educated, seeks wife to be friend, household manager and assistant, 25–35, average height, not fat, not thin and not ugly, a totally decent person' (*BG* 51 [1907]: 4). Or, even more to the point: 'WORKER, alone, bachelor, sober, decent, 42 years old, with a physical defect, right eye is 2/3 blind – but face not deformed, self-educated [*samorazvityi*], have been to West for scientific purpose, have studied agriculture, now involved in agriculture; have property of 500 rubles and 8 desiatinas of land' (*BG* 1 [1914]: 4).

Self-professed 'workers' (*rabochie*) were rare visitors on the pages of *BG*: their work regime and homosocial environment surely made such a form of communication unnecessary, ineffective or simply inconceivable (not to mention prohibitively expensive).[54] But people who declared themselves as 'toilers' (*truzhenniki*) – whose social identity depended on the laborious exercise of (primarily manual) skills – always had a place in these columns, even if they were comfortably outnumbered by *intelligenty*. The corpus of advertisements is notable for a social inclusivity rarely associated with late imperial society: authors ranged from seamstresses to wealthy or titled noblemen, while the middle ground between these extremes became ever more richly populated with civil servants, railway engineers, pharmacists, accountants, businessmen, army officers, and many others. By the mid-1910s, a number of strikingly modern professions and identity affirmations were featured in the highlighted phrases: 'theatre director', 'photographer', 'sportswoman', 'vegetarian theosophist', to name but a handful. In other words, professional and other non-hereditary identities became somewhat more salient over the years. (The ads are otherwise remarkable for how little they reflect the social and political upheaval of the times: the First World War brought a handful of wounded officers to the pages of *BG*, but little else.)

These columns also showed significant diversity in age: *BG* was not the exclusive preserve of no-longer-young women and lonely widowers. Some authors (especially women) were striking for their extreme youth and their not inconsiderable social or economic status: 'A YOUNG PERSON of the merchant estate (19 years old), *intelligentny*, with dowry of 15 thousand, desires to marry a young man in permanent well-paid employment. Only serious offers (with photograph enclosed)' (*BG* 1 [1906]: 1).

Another immediate impression one gains from reading the full run of *BG* is that the paper justified its pretensions to be a national – even international – publication. Only a minority of authors revealed their place of residence, but those that did came from all over the Russian empire. A respectable minority, moreover, were foreigners (mostly French, German or Polish), and a few of these wrote in their native language.[55] The paper thus gave evidence of fulfilling one of its most important missions: to reach out to the provinces and help geographically dislocated readers to find each other.

The authors also amply bore out the paper's main rationale: to provide a virtual meeting place for individuals, mainly young, who found themselves without adequate social networks. Many of the ads alluded to this kind of predicament, and some drew attention to it. 'I AM BORED', 'DYING OF BOREDOM' or 'MINUTES OF SOLITUDE LIE HEAVY' were quite standard headlines. A less despondent alternative was to strike an impassioned tone: 'WHO WILL RESPOND to my advertisement? A young man, disenchanted with life, 23 years old, *intelligentny* (completed gimnaziia), comfortably off (2,000 annual income), wishes to find a suitable pairing with the aim of marriage. He dreams of a beautiful brunette, healthy, high-spirited, *intelligentny*, placid, who might restore his faith in people' (*BG* 1 [1906]: 4). A popular option was to find literary analogies. One favourite character was Chekhov's Masha, but the clear leaders were Tat'iana Larina and Evgenii Onegin:

> ONEGIN, having parted from Tat'iana Gremina, is still in the grip of ennui. He cannot hope for a Lenskii to introduce him to the charming Larin family; he will have to take action himself. He is choosing a contemporary method – publication – which he has reason to think will bring success. He once more longs to meet a Tat'iana. He promises the woman who is the prototype of Pushkin's heroine, or at least not too dissimilar, not to give her lectures or to crush the poor girl by saying that 'he's not made for happiness'. (*BG 3* [1906], 4)

(According to the editors, this letter had received ten replies by the following week.)

The surest way to characterize Russia's matrimonial advertisements, however, is statistically. In what follows I draw on a database of 352 marriage ads from *Brachnaia gazeta* in 1908, including all marriage ads contained in a total of nine issues. My method was to take every fifth issue so as to reduce the chances of using repeated adverts. The only kind of material I excluded was adverts from matchmakers offering their services: there were typically a handful of these in each issue.

What generalizations does a statistical analysis permit us to make? First of all, just over two-thirds (238) of the authors were male. Of these, 207 appealed directly for a bride, while the rest (thirty-one) requested the services of a matchmaker. The high representation of men is what one might expect: in Russia, as in all other cultures known to me, it was more culturally acceptable for men to take the initiative in matters of this kind. Men had more to gain, and women more to lose, from the public matrimonial arena.

Another indication of men's position of strength was how uninformative they could evidently afford to make their advertisements. Of the sample of 238, more than half made no reference to their appearance or to other qualities of any kind (152 and 131, respectively). This reticence extended even to matters of more immediate practical significance. A strong majority of the men (141) gave no indication of the state of their finances, while a strong minority (111) made no reference to their profession or social status. To the extent that such information was provided, it tends to bear out the hypothesis that *BG* catered primarily to a weakly structured late-imperial middle class where the language of hereditary estate was challenged – and tended gradually to be displaced – by that of profession and occupation. Sixteen of the men in my sample identified themselves as some kind of noble (*dvorianin*), while thirty-eight mentioned paid employment (*sluzhba*), either in the civil service or in private enterprise. Nine declared themselves to be officers, six were engineers, two were merchants, but thirteen were students. Religion and nationality, however, figured barely at all: in only twenty-six cases were they mentioned.[56] There was only one piece of information that men were generally willing to volunteer: 119 gave an exact age and a further sixty gave some vaguer indication (for the most part 'young' or 'middle aged'). All in all, if we assume that male youth extended to the age of thirty, ninety-eight of the men could be called young, seventy-eight were middle-aged, and three identified themselves as 'old'.

Men were much more forthcoming, however, when it came to specifying their requirements in a woman. In particular, they were not coy about discussing money: 133 had financial demands of some kind. Many were seeking to ensure that the woman would bring an appropriate monetary contribution to the marriage but some were hoping for rather more than that. One subgenre of advertisement came from the hard-up young man (often a student or a southerner) looking for a materially advantageous match. Take for example the following: 'INTELLIGENTNY Petersburg student, of handsome appearance, wishes to enter the Conservatory and the Academy of Arts; he intends to marry a well-off (not less than 8,000 roubles per annum), interesting girl or widow aged 18–28' (*BG* 8 [1906]: 4). Another category was the advertisement placed by a man in need of start-up capital for some business venture. The advertisements placed in *BG*, then, bear out a common perception of the time that many young men were entering the fray with a surplus of education but a deficit of marketable skills. One plausible way out of this predicament was to find a wealthy woman – although, if the wealth turned out to be not quite as great as anticipated, that might cause great stress in a marriage.[57]

Financial means, however, were by no means all that men were looking for. Often tight-lipped when describing themselves, they became much more articulate when explaining the kind of woman they had in mind. Only twenty-four out of the sample of 238 mentioned failed to mention at least some qualities they considered important. A pleasing appearance was a prerequisite for many: forty-five men wanted a woman who was 'nice-looking' (*simpatichnaia*), 10 wanted a good figure (*stroinost'*). *Intelligentnost'* was the most widely esteemed of non-physical virtues: it was specified as desirable by forty-one men (including a few who planned to find their bride through a matchmaker). Youth was prized by sixteen, education by twenty-four, 'high spirits' (*veselost'*) by fourteen, 'kindness' by twenty-two, 'modesty' by eleven, health by fourteen, good morals by seven, brains by six. Seven alluded to the woman's previous experience with men: four declared magnanimously that her 'past' had no importance, or at least that they were willing to put it aside; three specified that they required a wife 'without a past' (*bez proshlogo*).

What of the 114 women in my sample? They were more self-revealing than the men. Nearly half (fifty-two) made some effort to describe their appearance; seventy-two mentioned other qualities, among which *intelligentnost'* again figured strongly (in twenty-seven cases). Even more significant was the extent to which women sought to emphasize their looks or personal qualities: forty-five put information of this kind in the highlighted phrase at the start of their ad. Women were more reticent, however, on money matters. Only thirty-seven made any mention of their financial situation, while even fewer (thirty-four) gave an indication of profession or social status (exactly half of these, moreover, had the status of 'widow'). As with the men, religion and nationality did not appear to be significant factors: they were mentioned by only twenty women. Age, however, was a different matter: forty women gave an exact age, and forty-nine more gave a less precise indication. If we take twenty-five as the upper limit of youth for women in late imperial Russia, then forty were young, forty-eight were middle-aged, and one was elderly.

Women were also capable, however, of formulating their own requirements. In just over half of cases (sixty) these requirements had a financial dimension but a very large majority (102) expressed preferences of a non-material kind. Once again, *intelligentnost'* and cognate virtues came to the fore.

In general, then, the women who advertised in *BG* tended to conform to the definitions of the 'ideal wife' sent in (by men) in answer to a questionnaire in the early days of the paper. To find a good husband and to have a successful marriage, women needed to be feminine, well brought up, serious, healthy, caring, clean, playful, and – not least – they had to 'know the right moment to give way to their husband' (*BG* 6 [1906]: 3). Perhaps the closest to a standard short example of a woman's self-presentation would be the following: 'A YOUNG BRUNETTE (22 YEARS OLD), perfectly *intelligentny*, capable of deep feeling, would like to meet an interesting, comfortably off man (30–35 years old). If correspondence makes a good impression, I am prepared to marry' (*BG* 1 [1906]: 1). Much rarer were ads where the woman seemed to hold all the cards: 'ELDERLY BRUNETTE wishes to marry for a second time. Has means. Suitor should be no younger than 35' (*BG* 2 [1906]: 4).[58]

CONCLUSIONS

Do these marriage advertisements ultimately tell us anything that is worth knowing? After all, the conclusion that men called the shots – and that women had to make more effort to please – is hardly out of line with what one would expect. Patriarchy dies very hard – even in the more urbanized and adventurous sections of the population.

A closer look at the evidence, however, suggests that a few more nuanced conclusions are in order. Although women constituted a minority of the authors, this was not a small minority. If we reduce my sample of 352 to genuinely 'personal' ads – by excluding the thirty-one men who appealed for a matchmaker rather than directly for a bride – women made up well over a third of the authors.[59] This is surely a larger proportion than a reading of other sources – such as advice literature – would lead us to expect. The Russian case, moreover, needs to be distinguished from those of other modernizing countries – such as 1950s Egypt – where the women who featured in the matrimonial press mostly did not fit the standard marriageable profile (in particular, they tended to be older than convention allowed). In Russia, by contrast, young women constituted a strong minority of the sample.

What happens if we try out another comparative framework: if, instead of putting Russia alongside other late modernizers, we compare it with Western 'bourgeois' society? We find that it is everywhere traumatic for middle-class courtship to have to move to a more impersonal arena than the family. In Victorian and Edwardian England, for example, the family became stronger, not weaker, as an idea and an ideal – which only made the uncertainties and tribulations of courtship more disturbing to the public imagination.[60]

How did European middle classes counter the threats to marriage and other social institutions that arose in times that were ever more frequently characterized by contemporaries as 'modern'? On a public, discursive level they worked out a set of core values – and associated key words – that would tend to reduce the uncertainties of social interaction and to counter the vagaries of changing status. In England, for example, the middle classes adopted from the fashionable set 'a certain vacuous cosmopolitanism of expression that reduced all utterances to exaggerated clichés of praise or blame.'[61] Men and women who declared a fellow being to be 'terribly decent' or 'absolutely frightful' were above all sending out signals about their own linguistic and cultural competence.

Would-be middle-class Russians did not wait for upper-class vocabulary to percolate down to them. Instead, to a large extent, they invented their own. The ideal person was decent (*poriadochnyi*), interesting (*interesnyi*) and, most of all, educated, civilized and well-mannered (*intelligentny*). *Intelligentnost'* was clearly the closest to a core value held by the authors of marriage advertisements: it was mentioned by more than a third (121) of my sample.[62] 'Intelligentsia' was, however, a recent arrival in Russians' social and cultural lexicon: it first appeared in the 1860s, and does not seem to have been widely used in the 1880s or 1890s. In the early twentieth century, however, it came into its own but as a cultural and existential more than a political or socioeconomic descriptor.[63]

Most scholars tend, however, to emphasize the inadequacy of 'intelligentsia' as a social identity in this period. As Samuel Kassow, James West and Edith Clowes write in the best known work on the social 'middle' of late tsarist Russia, the intelligentsia carried within it 'a basic contradiction between self-interest and the common good'; its many failings were held to include 'lack of patriotism', 'intolerance' and 'failure to recognize the importance of the private life'.[64] While these may be appropriate conclusions to draw from some areas of public discourse (above all, those dominated by intellectuals), a study of marriage adverts suggests a different picture. For the authors and readers of these ads, *intelligentnost'* was an unproblematic and positively construed notion: the Russian version of middle-classness. Of course, it differed significantly from analogous social identities in England or the US – above all in the emphasis it placed on education and self-cultivation. But I would argue that this discrepancy was due not to any hegemony of Marx-reading intellectuals but rather to the fact that Russia was a large, multi-ethnic, multi-confessional, overwhelmingly rural empire where people with a complete secondary education were few, thinly spread, and often miserably isolated. Under these circumstances, 'culturedness' (in all senses) was bound to loom large as a criterion for desirability.

Marriage newspapers, then, offer a guide to the emerging ethos of the love match but also to a rapidly changing, but non-dysfunctional, language of social description and aspiration. They seem to have been a more productive meeting place for convention and individual desires than the normative literature on courtship, whose contents, by comparison, appear static and stylized (though certainly not without historical interest, if they are read in the right way). They also go some way towards resolving the contradiction Simmel identified between materialism and the companionate or romantic aspirations of modern marriage-seekers. In the everyday cultural practice of the matrimonial advertisement, affect and filthy lucre could strike up an effective, and often entirely harmonious, relationship. The public avowal of middle-class courtship was soon, in Soviet Russia, to become taboo, but it advanced a long way in the decade or so that it was permitted to flourish. As late as June 1918, in the last copy of *BG* that has come down to us, Muscovite young women could read ads such as the following: 'OWNER of factory (for several years) in Moscow, turnover up to 200,000 per annum, has capital and the rest, would like to find wife and life companion to help create a fine life based on mutual trust and love. My aim is marriage. I am 24, people say I'm interesting, with decent education' (*BG* 24 [1918]: 2).

ACKNOWLEDGEMENT

I am grateful to Catriona Kelly for her insightful comments on a draft of this article. Thanks also to audiences at the School of Historical Studies, University of Newcastle, the Faculty of Psychology, Russian State University for the Humanities, and the Annual Convention of the American Association for the Advancement of Slavic Studies (Salt Lake City, 2005).

NOTES

1. A. Giddens, *The Transformation of Intimacy: Sexuality, Love and Eroticism in Modern Societies* (Cambridge, 1992).
2. These terms are used in S. Seidman, *Romantic Longings: Love in America, 1830–1980* (New York, 1991).
3. G. Simmel, *The Philosophy of Money*, trans. T. Bottomore and D. Frisby (London, 1990), pp. 382–3.
4. For evidence of the poor reputation endured by matrimonial advertisements even in a society with a print culture as developed as England's, see H.G. Cocks, 'Peril in the Personals: The Dangers and Pleasures of Classified Advertising in Early Twentieth-century Britain', *Media History*, 10 (2004): 3–16. By 1900 there were about twenty-five matrimonial newspapers in England; readers could even consult a subgenre of advice literature on how to reply to such advertisements. This evidence of social acceptance did not, however, do much to forestall moral panic: a number of high-profile cases suggested

that the matrimonial newspapers were primarily a way for conmen and even killers to ensnare innocent young women.

5. Certainly, this has been the most common reaction I have encountered when describing this material to colleagues.

6. Normative materials – legal and medical – form the bedrock of Laura Engelstein, *The Keys to Happiness: Sex and the Search for Modernity in Fin-de-Siècle Russia* (Ithaca, 1992), which is probably the most widely cited work on sex and marriage in late-tsarist Russia.

7. The most significant titles in this vein include the following: J. Brooks, *When Russia Learned to Read: Literacy and Popular Literature, 1861–1917* (Princeton, 1985); L. McReynolds, *The News under Russia's Old Regime: The Development of a Mass-Circulation Press* (Princeton, 1991); C. Kelly, *Refining Russia: Advice Literature, Polite Culture, and Gender from Catherine to Yeltsin* (Oxford, 2001); L. McReynolds, *Russia at Play: Leisure Activities at the End of the Tsarist Era* (Ithaca, 2003).

8. For an interesting recent collection of statements on the subject, see L. Engelstein and S. Sandler (eds), *Self and Story in Russian History* (Ithaca, 2000).

9. J. Abu-Lughod and L. Amin, 'Egyptian Marriage Advertisements: Microcosm of a Changing Society', *Marriage and Family Living,* 23 (1961): 127–36; E. Bend, 'Marriage Offers in a Yiddish Newspaper – 1935 and 1950', *American Journal of Sociology*, 58 (1952): 60–6; C.B. Vedder, 'Lonely Hearts Clubs Viewed Sociologically', *Social Forces,* 30 (1951): 219–22.

10. Iu.A. Poliakov and V.B. Zhiromskaia (eds), *Naselenie Rossii v XX veke*, 1, (Moscow, 2000), pp. 32–6.

11. See for example T.K. Hareven, 'The History of the Family and the Complexity of Social Change', *American Historical Review*, 96 (1991): 95–124.

12. Similarly, 'tradition versus modernity' has served as the main interpretive framework and the rationale of several other studies in this area. See Abu-Lughod and Amin, 'Egyptian Marriage Advertisements'; Bend, 'Marriage Offers'; J. Kwong, 'Ideological Crisis among China's Youths: Values and Official Ideology', *British Journal of Sociology*, 45 (1994): 247–64, especially p. 258; G. Litton Fox, 'Love Match and Arranged Marriage in a Modernizing Nation: Mate Selection in Ankara, Turkey', *Journal of Marriage and the Family,* 37 (1975): 180–93.

13. A similar phenomenon, albeit on a much larger scale and technologically more advanced level, has occurred in post-Soviet Russia. For a glimpse of more recent partner-seeking practices, see S. Luehrmann, 'Mediated Marriage: Internet Matchmaking in Provincial Russia', *Europe-Asia Studies,* 56 (2004): 857–75.

14. G.L. Freeze, 'Bringing Order to the Russian Family: Marriage and Divorce in Imperial Russia, 1760–1860', *Journal of Modern History,* 62 (1990): 709–46, here p. 711. Freeze's view is that the early modern Church, while it had ambitions to control people's everyday lives in general and matrimonial behaviour in particular, lacked the institutional apparatus to do so. His interpretation has recently been challenged by Daniel Kaiser, who argues that the Church before the eighteenth century was much less impotent than Freeze assumes. See Kaiser's '"Whose Wife Will She Be at the Resurrection?" Marriage and Remarriage in Early Modern Russia', *Slavic Review,* 62 (2003): 303–23.

15. W.G. Wagner, *Marriage, Property and Law in Late Imperial Russia* (Oxford, 1994), especially chs 1 and 2.

16. B.A. Engel, 'In the Name of the Tsar: Competing Legalities and Marital Conflict in Late Imperial Russia', *Journal of Modern History,* 77 (2005): 70–96.

17. Dixon's case study focuses on Finland, a region where the incumbent bishop attempted to

clamp down hard on the mixed marriages that were depleting Orthodox congregations: see Dixon, 'Sergii (Stragorodskii) in the Russian Orthodox Diocese of Finland: Apostasy and Mixed Marriages, 1905–1917', *Slavonic and East European Review*, 82 (2004): 50–73.

18. C.Y. Freeze, *Jewish Marriage and Divorce in Imperial Russia* (Hanover, 2002).

19. G.V. Zhirnova, *Brak i svad'ba russkikh gorozhan v proshlom i nastoiashchem (po materialam gorodov srednei polosy RSFSR)* (Moscow, 1980).

20. See especially Zhirnova, *Brak i svad'ba*, pp. 36–7. Craftsmen and labourers did not tend to pay for this kind of service. They usually relied on a female relative on the paternal side. When they had found a suitable bride, it was important to test out her craft skills, as she would have to be a working partner. Nobles lay at the other extreme. Not willing to leave anything to chance, they drew up sometimes very detailed marriage contracts where the dowry was entered in meticulous detail.

21. A well-chosen sample of this material can be found in J. von Geldern and L. McReynolds (eds), *Entertaining Tsarist Russia: Tales, Songs, Plays, Movies, Jokes, Ads, and Images from Russian Urban Life 1779-1917* (Bloomington, 1998).

22. The definitive study of this genre is Kelly, *Refining Russia*.

23. *Nauka shchastlivym byt'*, trans. from German by Sergei Volchkov (St Petersburg, 1759), pp. 212–23.

24. *Liubovnaia shkola, ili Podrobnoe iz"iasnenie vsekh stepenei i tainstv liubovnoi nauki* (Moscow, 1791).

25. *Nauka liubvi: Sochinenie, pisannoe na poluchenie zvaniia Doktora liubvi* (St Petersburg, 1840), pp. 71–4.

26. Examples in this paragraph are mainly taken from *Iskusstvo byt' schastlivym v supruzheskoi zhizni i delat' bezoshibochnyi vybor muzha ili zheny, soobrazno razlichnym kharakteram, letam, naruzhnosti, polozheniiu v obshchestve i prochim obstoiatel'stvam* (Moscow, 1857). Similar are: *Retsepty k raspoznaniiu zhenshchin, osnovannye na pokazaniiakh liudei opytnykh i byvalykh* (Moscow, 1860); and *Net bolee neschastnykh brakov, ili Verneishii sposob sdelat'sia schastliveishim muzhem*, 2 edn (St Petersburg, 1862).

27. An early example of the even-handed approach is *Sekretnyi portfel' dlia muzhchin i zhenshchin, soderzhashchii v sebe chetyre roda zhiteiskikh neobkhodimostei* (Moscow, 1862). For a later example, see M.A. Khovanskii, *Zhenit'sia i vse taki byt' schastlivym: Nauka o supruzhestve, ego radostiakh i stradaniiakh* (St Petersburg, 1888).

28. The first such text published in Russia came in 1708; the first original Russian text was published in 1788. A bibliography of *pis'movniki* that draws on the major Russian library catalogues identifies 199 items appearing between 1708 and 1916. See A. Joukovskaia, 'La Naissance de l'épistolographie normative en Russie. Histoire des premiers manuels russes d'art épistolaire', *Cahiers du monde russe*, 40 (1999): 657–89.

29. *Tainyi drug vliublennykh, ili Amurnaia pochta* (Vil'na, 1894), p. 5.

30. M. Evstigneev, *Sbornik liubovnykh pisem dlia muzhchin i zhenshchin ili Pravila dlia vliublennykh kak pisat' nezhnye pis'ma* (Moscow, 1868), p. 27.

31. Evstigneev, *Sbornik liubovnykh pisem*, p. 105.

32. Svetlovskii, *Polnyi pis'movnik dlia vliublennykh*, 2 pts (Moscow, 1898–99); N. Volokitin, *Polnyi liubovnyi pis'movnik dlia molodykh liudei vsekh vozrastov, zhelaiushchikh oderzhat' pobedu nad zhenskim serdtsem* (St Petersburg, 1909); N.I. K-skii, *Nastol'naia kniga dlia molodykh liudei: Polnyi pis'movnik dlia vliublennykh* (Moscow, 1912); letters also to be found in *Vas vse poliubiat: Magicheskii sekret zastavit' v sebia vliubit'sia* (Moscow, 1914).

33. B.F. Zakharov, *Spravochnaia kniga dlia zhenikhov i nevest v stikhakh* (St Petersburg, 1876);

Vernoe sredstvo dlia molodykh oboego pola nravitsia [sic] *drug drugu ili Pokhozhdenie dvukh vliublennykh osob*, (Moscow, 1879); N.I. Krasovskii, *Shutki, zabavy i priiatnoe razvlechenie: Sovremennaia liubovnaia pochta* (Moscow, 1896).

34. *Vas vse poliubiat: Magicheskii sekret zastavit' v sebia vliubit'sia* (Moscow, 1914); B. Mufii, *Rukovodstvo k vyboru zhen s pribavleniem dobra i zla o zhenshchinakh (zhenshchinam eta kniga ne prodaetsia)* (Moscow, 1915); T. Maingardt, *Chary liubvi i liubovnoe koldovstvo* (Moscow, 1918). Morits Kastellian, *Tainy uspekha v liubvi Don-Zhuanov (Vas vse poliubiat)* (Moscow, 1918).

35. This point is made in Cocks, 'Peril in the Personals', p. 5.

36. For Russian examples, see S.Ia., *Ob"iavleniia i drugie sredstva reklamy: Zadachi reklamy, sostavlenie i rasprostranenie razlichnykh vidov ee* (Moscow, 1904), pp. 19–20. Further evidence of the prominence of advertising can be found in *Uchites' reklamirovat' u amerikantsev: Rukovodstvo po sostavleniiu reklam, katalogov, reklamnykh broshiur, po ustroistvu vitrin i vystavok* (Moscow, 1911).

37. Engelstein, *The Keys to Happiness*, pp. 360–7; B. Engel, *Women in Russia, 1700–2000*, (Cambridge, 2004), pp. 122–3.

38. I have also sampled *Peterburgskaia gazeta* and *Peterburgskii listok*. The latter contained a handful of marriage ads. The former carried ads for *posrednitsy* but I found no marriage ads.

39. Besides the Moscow *Brachnaia gazeta* I have read the following publications, which to my knowledge are all the marriage newspapers held in the Russian National Library in St Petersburg (although the list is far from exhaustive, as I have seen other such papers referred to by name in the contemporary press): *'Amur', literaturno-brachnaia gazeta* (Moscow), eight issues in 1908; *Literaturno-brachnaia gazeta* (Moscow), seven issues in 1909; *Brachnaia gazeta iuga Rossii* (Odessa), thirteen issues in 1910 (from the fifth issue onwards it changed its name to *Odesskaia i iuga Rossii brachnaia gazeta*); *Brachnaia gazeta iuga* (Odessa), ten issues, August-October 1910; *Brachnaia gazeta dlia vsekh* (St Petersburg), seven issues, January–February 1914; *Mezhdunarodnaia brachnaia gazeta* (Piatigorsk), six issues, 1911; *Sibirskaia brachnaia gazeta* (Tomsk), six issues, 1910; *Brachnyi vestnik* (Moscow), 1914–16, one issue per year; *Brachnyi soiuz* (Odessa), one issue in 1907; *Brachnaia gazeta* (Riga), two issues, 1910; *Brachnaia zhizn'* (Moscow), fourteen issues, 1909; *Moskovskaia brachnaia gazeta*, 1910–15, mostly one issue per year; *Muzhchina i zhenshchina* (Moscow), five issues, 1908; *Kavkazskaia brachnaia gazeta* (Tiflis), five issues, 1914; *Zakavkazskaia brachnaia gazeta* (Tiflis), eleven issues, 1914. It is unlikely that the library's holdings represent the full runs of any of these publications but it seems certain that none of them was as long-lived as *BG*.

40. 'Brachnaia Gazeta i podrazhaniia', *BG*, 21 (1909): 2. For one clear example of a steal from the Moscow paper, see 'Pervye brachnye ob"iavleniia v Evrope', *Zakavkazskaia brachnaia gazeta*, 10 (1914): 2 (compare with the article cited in n. 45 below). For evidence of cut-throat competition among provincial publications, see the editorial in *Kavkazskaia brachnaia gazeta*, 2 (1914): 1.

41. 'K nashemu izdaniiu', *BG* 28 (1911): 2.

42. 'Brachnaia gazeta i obshchestvennoe mnenie', *BG* 10 (1909): 2.

43. *BG* 1 (1910): 1. The number of ads is verifiable and correct.

44. *BG* 1 (1906): 1.

45. According to *BG*, marriage advertisements in newspapers first appeared in England in 1768 and in France in 1790: see 'Pervye brachnye ob"iavleniia v Evrope', *BG* 4 (1911): 2–3. The earliest evidence I have found is the following notice in *The Times*: 'In answer to several persons, whose advertisements we have refused, we state at once that we do not admit

advertisements which are called matrimonial advertisements. In general they are mere hoaxes, and, what is worse, are sent by procuresses and people of that class' (1 January 1831, p. 2).

46. *BG* 1 (1908): 1.

47. See, for example, the editorial warning at the top of the first page in *BG* 16 (1911). Of course, this stern disapproval of matchmakers did not prevent the editors from printing advertisements for their services.

48. Agro-kom, 'Krizis braka', *BG* 6 (1906): 3.

49. *BG* 6 (1906): 1–2.

50. *BG* 8 (1906): 3.

51. *BG* 7 (1907): 3.

52. *BG* 9 (1906).

53. *BG* 2 (1906): 1. References hereafter in-text. The words in upper case are those that are typographically highlighted in the original.

54. On working-class masculinity in this period, see S.A. Smith, 'Masculinity in Transition: Peasant Migrants to Late-Imperial St Petersburg', in B.E. Clements, R. Friedman and D. Healey (eds), *Russian Masculinities in History and Culture* (Houndmills, 2002), pp. 94–112. Placing an ad cost 30 kopecks per line on the front page and 20 kopecks on the back page, at a time when the daily wage for a young worker at a Moscow factory was likely to be only a few dozen kopecks.

55. As might be expected, religious and ethnic diversity was at its greatest in the Odessa matrimonial press. Variations in social status, however, were less extreme in the provincial publications.

56. I spotted only one ad in the whole run of *BG* that required 'persons of Jewish origin not to trouble themselves.' Perhaps unsurprisingly, this came at a moment when the First World War was already several months under way: see *BG* 51 (1914): 1.

57. M. Rogovich, 'O svobodnykh soiuzakh', *Zhenskii vestnik*, 2 (1910): 33–4.

58. This ad, however, came top of the popularity stakes that the paper ran in the early phase of its existence. By the following week it was reported to have elicited forty-two replies, which comfortably made it the champion.

59. Abu-Lughod and Amin make a similar point with respect to Egypt: in their sample of 100 ads, 60 per cent came from men, which is by no means as large a majority as might have been expected. See 'Egyptian Marriage Advertisements', 129.

60. See for example Cocks, 'Peril in the Personals'.

61. J. Harris, *Private Lives, Public Spirit: Britain 1870–1914* (London, 1993), p. 23. An even more fundamental refashioning of linguistic habits was England's decisive shift – greater than anywhere else in Europe – towards standard pronunciation in the second half of the nineteenth century.

62. Such was the prominence of this term that I have chosen not to translate it where it has occurred in quotations.

63. The argument about usage is borrowed from A.B. Liarskii, 'Chastnaia i obshchestvennaia zhizn' peterburgskoi intelligentsii (1907–1914 gg.)', candidate's dissertation, Sankt-Peterburgskii Gosudarstvennyi Universitet Ekonomiki i Finansov, St Petersburg, 1999. To my knowledge, this work is the most sustained and focused sociocultural history of the late tsarist intelligentsia.

64. S. Kassow, J. West and E. Clowes, 'Introduction: The Problem of the Middle in Late Imperial Russian Society', in Clowes, Kassow and West (eds), *Between Tsar and People: Educated Society and the Quest for Public Identity in Late Imperial Russia* (Princeton, 1991), p. 4.

'A MERCIFUL, HEAVEN-SENT RELEASE'?

THE CLERK AND THE FIRST WORLD WAR IN BRITISH LITERARY CULTURE

Jonathan Wild

Department of English Literature, University of Edinburgh

ABSTRACT This article traces the profound social repercussions that resulted from the mass enlistment of British office workers into the armed forces during the First World War. Drawing heavily upon fictionalized autobiographies of the period, my study examines the various stages of the clerk's experience of the conflict and argues that the confidence gained during warfare by surviving office workers fundamentally shaped a more democratic postwar society. This change is evidenced, I argue, in the profile of the fictional clerk that emerges in British literature after 1918.

Keywords: office clerk(s), World War One, popular literature and history, temporary gentlemen

The cultural stereotype of the British office clerk prior to the First World War was securely locked and bolted in place. This image, epitomized by E.M. Forster's portrayal of the feeble body and 'half-baked mind' of Leonard Bast in *Howards End* (1910), had become so conventional before 1914 that any attempts to provide alternative representations were greeted with surprise by critics.[1] When Frank Swinnerton's novel *The Merry Heart* (1909), for example, depicted a healthy, intelligent and articulate clerk, a number of reviewers were inspired to comment on the originality of its characterization and scene: as the *Morning Post* noted, 'we get some interesting and life-like glances into a business life from the unusual point of view (in a novel) of the drudges in it'; and in a similar vein, *Athenaeum* commended the setting of the novel, 'drawn with a freshness and accuracy altogether unusual from lower middle-class English life.'[2] Even with this spirited challenge posed by Swinnerton's antithetical office employees, the dominant literary image of the ineffectual clerk appears unlikely to have undergone any short term reassessment.[3] Only after the outbreak of war when the apparently meek, hollow-chested, and morally fallible clerks formed the vanguard of Kitchener's New Armies, were prewar cultural stereotypes destabilized. Those clerks who enlisted in the first weeks of the war were doing so, in part, to effect this destabilizing process.

In this paper I will investigate the consequences of this exchange of business suits for khaki uniforms by tracing the clerk's experience of war in a variety of print cultural

Address for correspondence: Dr Jonathan Wild, Department of English Literature, University of Edinburgh, David Hume Tower, George Square, Edinburgh, EH8 9JX. 0131 6511 838. E-mail: jwild@ed.ac.uk

sources. While several of these documents represent 'traditional' foundations for socio-historical research (life writing, letters, newspapers), the majority of my sources are taken from creative writing (novels, plays and poems). Using fiction to approach fact is undeniably a problematic enterprise, however, the nature of my investigation to some degree makes this method a necessary one. Any attempt, after all, to analyse the ways in which a cultural image might affect (and be affected by) collective behaviour needs to track the development of this image over time. Further, I would argue that my creative writing sources can shed light on aspects of history arguably untouched by more 'traditional' source material. As Trevor Wilson suggests:

> The historian's task is to know [the past] as completely as is possible. The experiences of poison gas, and lice, and sentry-duty, and the chance encounter with a rodent, are part of the fabric of life lived by a particular body of people during this segment of the past. Where we cannot easily generalise about that segment, the historian has cause to welcome the opportunity to provide particular instances that, although they cannot be incorporated into generalisations, seem to illuminate an area much wider than themselves. Creative writing is a prime source for this general-embodied-in-the-particular . . .[4]

While at times in this paper I break with Wilson's scrupulousness when I seek to draw generalizations from my chosen fictional texts, I remain cognizant of Wilson's subsequent warning that 'creative writers are often partial witnesses'. Taking these caveats into consideration, however, I think that my blend of research materials both demonstrates the changing image of the clerk in print culture while simultaneously allowing us to apprehend something of the wider experiences of the individuals behind these images. These aims, both specific and more general, permit a textured understanding of evidently important aspects of social and cultural history that have, until now, been badly served by scholarship.

*

During the first week of the war, the Prime Minister's son, Herbert Asquith, reminded the *Spectator*'s readers of the clerk's putative position in British society in The Dead Volunteer:

> Here lies a clerk who half his life had spent
> Toiling at ledgers in a city grey,
> Thinking that so his days would drift away
> With no lance broken in life's tournament:
> But ever 'twixt the books and his bright eyes
> The gleaming eagles of the legions came,
> And horsemen charging under phantom skies
> Went thundering past beneath the oriflamme.
>
> And now those waiting dreams are satisfied,
> For in the end he heard the bugle call,
> And to his country then he gave his all
> When in that first high hour of life he died.
> And falling thus, he wants no recompense

Who found his battle in the last resort;
Nor needs he any hearse to bear him hence
Who goes to join the men of Agincourt.[5]

Even if it had reached a clerkly readership, however, Asquith's rallying cry to this audience was largely superfluous. The work of convincing clerks of their institutionalized inferiority, and thus their need to accept the chance for liberation, had already been substantially achieved in the years prior to 1914. The extent to which clerks enthusiastically offered their services for war without undue persuasion can be assessed from the recruitment statistics. During the period from August 1914 to February 1916, when conscription was introduced, over half a million men, or 40.1% of the total prewar labour force, had enlisted from the finance and commerce section alone; this represented the biggest percentage of employees drawn from any of the major employment groups.[6] We can reasonably assume from these figures that by the time of conscription, the vast majority of able-bodied clerical workers under forty years of age had already volunteered their services. The patterns of clerkly recruitment already evident in the South African War, (in which, as Richard Price has noted, 'young clerks were more eager to volunteer than young labourers') were therefore repeated here but on a much larger scale.[7] The preponderance of straw-boatered clerks seen in the photographs of enlistees assembling at recruiting stations in August 1914 offers a visual endorsement of the statistics.

A personal testimony that helps to account for the willingness of clerks to volunteer is provided by J.B. Priestley. In his autobiography, Priestley, a peacetime clerk in a Bradford wool exporter's firm, acknowledged that he joined the army in September 1914 in order to prove his worth:

> There came, out of the unclouded blue of that summer, a challenge that was almost like a conscription of the spirit, little to do really with King and Country and flag-waving and hip-hip-hurrah, a challenge to what we felt was our untested manhood. Other men, who had not lived as easily as we had, had drilled and marched and borne arms - couldn't we? Yes, we too could leave home and soft beds and the girls to soldier for a spell, if there was some excuse for it, something at least to be defended. And here it was.[8]

Priestley's perception of an individual response taking on the characteristics of a collective enterprise goes some way towards explaining the astonishing success of the recruitment drive made by Kitchener at the onset of war. Rather than prompting a moral desire to defend 'gallant little Belgium', which might have solicited a respectable though modest response (Priestley felt sorry for Belgium, but did not feel that 'she was waiting for me to rescue her'),[9] the more personal implications of the call accounted for its extraordinary effectiveness amongst the clerk volunteers. R.C. Sherriff, like Priestley a prewar junior clerk, similarly confirms in his recollections of 'joining up' the redundancy of Asquith's poem as a tool of persuasion. Coming to his London office directly from school at which he had been 'captain of rowing and cricket' Sherriff had become just another City clerk. Not surprisingly perhaps, the youthful Sherriff found his workplace 'a demoralising come-down', and recalled how he had wistfully looked out of his office windows lamenting the loss of 'the river and playing fields'. Under these circumstances we can appreciate why Sherriff considered that the war arrived for him not as an ominous black cloud, but instead as 'a merciful, heaven-sent release'.[10]

In addition to the personal motivation described by Priestley and Sherriff, the rush to volunteer was no doubt underpinned by the sense that this (potentially fleeting) opening for heroism might not occur again. One postwar novel sums up the prevailing mood by suggesting that the conflict provided an 'opportunity, single and unrepeated, for distinction and fame!'[11] Alongside this climate of excitement and urgency, several other reasons more specific to the office environment ensured that clerks were at the forefront of the successful recruitment drive. Of central importance here was the composition and structure of personnel in large urban offices. These working environments provided the perfect stock and breeding farms for the production of young soldiers. The relative youth and unmarried status of much of the workforce, and the ease with which these employees could be replaced by substitute female labour, were undoubtedly key factors here. For the army, however, a more important consideration was the ease with which business offices were able to supply the ideal physical specimens for soldiering. Ironically, in view of the prewar literary stereotyping of their hollow chests, curved spines, and weak hearts, supposedly 'degenerate' clerks proved at medical assessments to be of generally superior health to their working class urban counterparts: Jay Winter comments that 'bank clerks or estate agents', for example, were 'better-fed, healthier, and by and large more able to stand the rigours of army life.'[12] This fitness, honed at city sports clubs and gymnasia, was able to be maintained during the working day in the relatively healthy environment of the business office.[13]

To these fit and healthy clerks, unencumbered by the demands of a reserved occupation, the opportunity to become one of the 100,000 soldiers of Kitchener's New Army was understandably the primary topic of conversation during the war's first days. The departmental structure of the modern office facilitated this intense discussion of current events and proved a crucial element in propelling the clerk from speculation into definite action. The qualities of team spirit which the commercial departments had been keen to inspire (in, for example, their support for team sports and social groups) helped to foster the form of group mentality that would result in clerks joining-up *en masse*. Clerks witnessing their 'heroic' colleagues enlisting would understandably feel considerable pressure to follow their lead. The novelist R.H. Mottram remembered that during the first week of war, at least eight of the clerks in his branch of Barclays Bank in Norwich wore red armbands to show that they had enlisted.[14] This unprecedented phenomenon in the business community appears to have caused much anxiety amongst office managers who could foresee, in the words of one City clerk who walked out to enlist with a dozen of his colleagues, that 'nothing but chaos would follow such a depletion of his staff'.[15] Elsewhere, these concerns were further exacerbated by the formation of Pals' battalions, which were recruited specifically from amongst office workers. The logic behind recruitment of this kind is illustrated in the following passage taken from the *Hull Daily Mail* dated 1 September 1914:

Today has seen the commencement of recruiting for the middle-class, clerks, and professional men, or the 'black-coated battalion'. It must not be thought there is a desire for class distinction, but just as the docker will feel more at home amongst his every day mates, so the wielders of the pen and drawing pencil will be better as friends together.[16]

The success of this marketing, which capitalized on prewar class factionalism, is witnessed in the raising of the first battalion of Hull Commercials in four days, followed by a further two battalions within a month.[17]

Other than those staff who impulsively enlisted in groups, urban offices also lost those clerks who, as members of the territorial forces, were immediately mobilized at the outbreak of war. Phillip Maddison, the central character in Henry Williamson's autobiographical *roman-fleuve*, *A Chronicle of Ancient Sunlight* (1951–1969), finds himself in this position in August 1914. The immense detail and extraordinary recall that Williamson employs in *How Dear is Life* (1954), the volume dealing with Maddison's transition from clerk to soldier, sheds light on this experience. Williamson's wartime novel series indeed epitomizes Trevor Wilson's suggestion of the potential worth to historians of the 'general-embodied-in-the-particular' found in creative writing. The *Chronicle*'s novels illustrate the ways in which Maddison, a meek and unheroic young clerk in the Moon Fire Office (a fictionalized version of Williamson's own clerkship in the Sun Fire Insurance Company) had joined the territorials, in common with thousands of other clerks, purely to take advantage of its significant perquisites. Maddison, once a member, is able to enjoy the facilities of 'a top-hole club, with no subscription',[18] and in addition, the prospect of a fortnight's army camp each year, taken as paid leave, with an extra shilling a day as soldier's pay. As a youth with little interest in world affairs, Maddison remains, until the outbreak of war, relatively unconcerned about the commitment that his territorial membership brings. Williamson's evocation of Maddison's experience conveys a sense of the insularity of the City clerk's world, an impression shared by both fictional and non-fictional accounts of the life of the prewar clerk: 'What happened in the big world outside his private world, Phillip little knew nor cared. He never read the main items of news in the ha'penny paper' (*HDIL* 78). This lack of comprehension regarding the implications of his position is further exposed in Maddison's response to his aunt who enquires about his potential mobilization: 'The Terriers are home defence, you know. We're really more a sort of club than anything else' (*HDIL* 113). When war is declared and the order for General Mobilization of the territorial soldiers is made, Maddison's feelings are curiously mixed: he expresses on the one hand a desire, like Priestley and Sheriff, to break away from City work; and on the other hand, a fear of the 'vast, fathomless darkness', which, for him, is condensed into images of ragged armless soldiers walking 'listlessly, from nowhere to nowhere' (*HDIL* 116–17). For Maddison, despite his reservations, there is no choice about his entry into the conflict. Indeed on the day war breaks out, he and his fellow territorial clerks have already submitted to the inevitability of martial life: 'Almost every one of a hundred thousand faces under straw-hats undulating on the pavements of London Bridge bore a look of new resolution . . . Feeling themselves to be marching, they crossed London Bridge' (*HDIL* 131).

But even for those clerks uncommitted by either a prewar obligation, or a more immediate desire to enlist, it was evidently difficult to resist the call to arms. The pressures placed on clerks to enlist prior to the introduction of conscription in 1916 are illustrated in Herbert Tremaine's (Maude Deuchar's) overlooked pacifist novel *The Feet of the Young Men* (1917). This work focuses on the experiences of a young and ambitious estate agent's clerk, Harry Manwell, for whom the war provides no inspiration and little incentive to trade his comfortable, relaxed office for 'a wild whirling struggle'.[19] Whilst the army barracks, close to his office, offer him a constant reminder of the country's state of war, the marching soldiers exist only in the background of his life: 'they were subdued in his consciousness to frame the vividness of daily life in the Manwells' cottage and in Bliss's office' (21). This isolation is, however, challenged by his employer (Mr Bliss), who after attending a recruiting speech in the Town Hall, returns to inform Manwell that he 'oughtn't to be here' (13). The argument that convinced Mr Bliss to give Manwell notice to quit is repeated by Bliss to justify his actions to his clerk :

> Well, as [the recruiting speaker] said, what's to prevent the women doing their bit, too – taking the places for the men? And the employers ought to be willing, as their bit, to train those women and to have patience if things don't go exactly – well, not exactly on oiled wheels . . . he put it to the employers they oughtn't – just for the sake of the smooth running of their business, and the profits and so on – they oughtn't to keep back any men who might be in training for the front. (18)

Later, Eva (the office typist) reveals to Manwell her suspicions that Bliss's real reasons for taking a female clerk in his place are economic rather than patriotic: '"Cheaper!" Eva said bitterly' (40). Manwell, seeing through Bliss's disingenuous argument, remains determined not to enlist, even after his dismissal from the office. His genuine indifference, tempered with a 'deliberate intellectual detachment' is hardened by a growing sense of externally imposed compulsion to conform. This feeling of detachment allows Manwell to observe objectively his fellow clerks, whom he believes to be mesmerised by the myth growing around the noble 'Tommy': 'what a dare-devil he was, what a brick he was, how the girls all went mad about him' (31). Too wise to believe this propaganda, for him the army is instead 'a great cephalopod' whose 'long sucker-provided arms' are attempting 'to make a clammy clutch at [his] life' (24).

This stand is, however, seen to become progressively more difficult to maintain. Manwell's initial optimism that 'he would be sure to fall into one of those decent ordinary posts left vacant by those normal clerks who had exchanged their respectable shabby greys and brown and blacks for khaki' (27) proves unfounded. His later decision to reduce his sights to enable him to apply for porters' and shopmens' jobs is equally fruitless: at an unsuccessful interview for the post of tramway manager, Manwell is asked the ubiquitous question 'Have you offered your services to your country?' (63). After a year of miserable unemployment, with his savings gone and additional public pressure placed on him following a Zeppelin raid on his town, Manwell finally succumbs to enlistment. With his 'pride in his intelligence' (160) dulled by his recent experience, there is a sense of relief in submission:

> There was a luxurious sort of pleasure in surrender to the brown-green monster which had got a hold of him at last. To struggle any longer would have been too much for the strength of an ordinary man, a clerk who indeed had the Dumb Literary Temperament, but who had no heavy clogging principles nor theories of life . . . To sell himself body and soul . . . seemed to him the only way to get sound boots and warm clothes and to secure a little weekly sum for his mother. (163)

Although Tremaine's novel is a polemical work, the rare glimpse it affords us of eroded resistance on the home front is of considerable interest. Its existence (taken together with Williamson's delineation of Phillip Maddison's emotional turmoil at the onset of war) offers a necessary counterweight to the more familiar clerkly narrative of enthusiastic escape from dull routine. These fictional accounts offer us an indication of the sorts of pressures that were placed on office workers to enlist prior to enforced conscription. While we clearly need to remain sceptical about treating these sources as reliable evidence for social history, they do provide clues as to the reasons why almost the entire population of young and healthy British clerks were transformed – at their own behest – into soldiers in the first half of the war. Tremaine's admittedly emotive image of the doomed Manwell in uniform encapsulates the pathetic shift from business suit into khaki uniform: 'his walk was no longer the quick, light tread of the young business clerk. His feet fell regularly and heavily now – left – right – left – right . . .' (198).

*

The literature – both fictional and non-fictional – that attempts to convey the clerk's initial experience of army life understandably concentrates on the extent to which the war forced together individuals from diverse backgrounds. That this phenomenon should provide such a source of fascination both for those involved in the process, and for those observing from outside, was conditioned by the seemingly strict lines of division that separated prewar urban social groups. When C.F.G. Masterman offered his system of classification for the different strata of society in *The Condition of England* in 1909, he acknowledged the extent to which the tribal nature of the modern city had separated the suburb-dwelling clerks from their inner-city neighbours:

> Every day, swung high upon embankments or buried deep in tubes underground, he ['The Suburban'] hurries through the region where the creature ['The Multitude'] lives. He gazes darkly from his pleasant hill villa upon the huge and smoky area of tumbled tenements which stretches at his feet. He is dimly distrustful of the forces fermenting in this uncouth laboratory. Every hour he anticipates the boiling over of the cauldron. He would never be surprised to find the crowd behind the red flag, surging up his little pleasant pathways, tearing down the railings, trampling the little garden.[20]

While these lines of social division were almost certainly not as strictly demarcated as Masterman suggests, (particularly when we remember that many Suburbans had only recently emerged from among the ranks of the Multitude), the general atmosphere of disharmony and distrust that he describes between these classes did exist in some degree. Some five years after Masterman's account was published, however, the suburban clerk was marching alongside the abyss-dwelling 'creature', united in a common cause.

R.H. Mottram offers a characteristic recollection of these unprecedented events through the experiences of his bank clerk-turned-soldier Stephen Dormer, in the final volume of *The Spanish Farm Trilogy* (1924–6). Drawing on his own experience of volunteering, Mottram, through his fictional clerk, recalls the diverse social mixture represented in the occupations of his training troop; these encompass labourers, clerks (in ascending order of rank from warehouses, railways, insurance offices, banks, and 'one gorgeous individual who signed himself a Civil Servant'), and persons of private means. Mottram imagines this group overlooking prewar enmities, and instead marching forward together, 'the immense disparity of taste and outlook cloaked by shoddy blue uniforms and dummy rifles, equal rations and common fatigues'.[21] Similarly, C.E. Montague's non-fiction work *Disenchantment* (1922), an early text charting the increasingly negative reactions of the troops to the war, begins with the optimism engendered by the egalitarianism of a recruitment inspired by 'one clear aim':

> Here were hundreds of thousands of quite commonplace persons rendered, by comradeship in an enthusiasm, self denying, cheerful, unexacting, sanely exalted, substantially good . . . Little white, prim clerks from Putney – men whose souls were saturated with the consciousness of class – would abdicate freely and wholeheartedly their sense of the wide, unplumbed, estranging seas that ought to roar between themselves and Covent Garden market porters.[22]

Although Montague invokes here the prewar stereotype of the prim Putney clerk, the impression he offers of prejudice eroded under extraordinary circumstances appears authentic. While it would be folly to assume that old partiality was entirely erased by the emergency, we can similarly appreciate that, under these circumstances, opinions long conditioned by reflex were undermined.[23]

It is, however, also apparent that the more lasting repercussions of this softening of class prejudice took time to take effect. Indeed, following the near euphoria of the first days, the effect of intimate association with those whose standards of social behaviour were perceived as debased appears, to some extent, to have confirmed previously imagined prejudices. Williamson's fictional alter ego Phillip Maddison, for example, retains the class snobbery learned at his grammar school throughout his basic training. Convinced of his innate superiority over recruits from the working class, he describes fellow territorials with slight cockney accents, who occupy an adjacent tent, as 'Leytonstone Louts', Leytonstone being 'a district he knew only from the many renewal notices he had made out' and from a fellow clerk's 'remark about it being a ghastly place to live in' (*HDIL* 181). But once in the trenches, during the Battle of Ypres, his fear of imminent death consigns these enduring prejudices to an unenlightened past. Maddison's new perspective is conditioned by the kindness of the working class soldiers and their willingness to 'help the newcomers' (*HDIL* 296). His initial reservations about fighting alongside professional soldiers (who in peacetime he had considered on a par with 'street-walkers') is overcome to a point where he can later reflect that 'the warm and comradely strength, and the security it gave to be among the regulars, was what kept him going' (*HDIL* 309).

Maddison's appreciation of the irrelevance of prewar social boundaries when tested under these extreme conditions also appears to have been a two-way process. Frank Richards, a prewar regular soldier and sometime coal miner, illustrates, in *Old Soldiers Never Die* (1933), how the music-hall image of the clerk was, for the working classes, capable of disruption in battle. He describes how, in March 1917, his battalion had received amongst a new intake a bank clerk, schoolteachers and an architect. Presumably, at first dubious about their potential, Richards was later moved to remark that 'during the time the bank clerk had been with the Battalion he had seen much and endured much and become a pukka old soldier in action'.[24] This testimonial constitutes a high accolade from an old campaigner whose prewar impression of a clerk's fighting ability is easy to envisage. Richards' memoirs, compiled a dozen years after the war's end, further suggest the enduring quality of impressions of worth formulated under extreme conditions.

Evidence of this type of reassessment is also intriguingly revealed in *One Young Man* (1917), a non-fictional text that attempted to address the misguided peacetime image of the 'puny' clerk. Composed of the letters and recollections of Sydney Baxter (a pseudonym for Reginald Davis), the book's pro-clerk objective is implied on its title page: 'The simple and true story of a clerk who enlisted in 1914, who fought on the Western Front for nearly two years, was severely wounded at the Battle of the Somme, and is now on his way back to his desk.' Although, as this outline suggests, *One Young Man* provides a somewhat conventional account of hardships valiantly borne and overcome, its narrative is engineered to remind its readers of their enduring debt to 'unlikely' heroes. In one section, for example, the text's editor, J.E. Hodder Williams, describes the young man's re-encounter with his peacetime employer:

> Sydney Baxter's chief saw him once or twice during these camp days. And he marvelled. The spectacles had gone. The lank, round-shouldered figure had filled and straightened. Suddenly a man had been born. A soldier, too. This fellow of the pen and the ledger, this very type of the British clerk who had never handled a rifle in his life and didn't know the smell of powder from eau de Cologne, who had never experienced anything of hardship or even discomfort; whose outlook in life had hitherto never stretched beyond a higher seat at the office desk . . . How many times have you and I said 'he was the last man I should have thought would have made a soldier.' Well, Sydney Baxter was that last man. And he made a first-class soldier. Let this country never forget it.[25]

This passage is especially interesting because of the ways in which it confirms prewar stereotypes of the clerical worker as a physically inferior specimen and then goes on to suggest the transforming effect of martial life. Where Hodder Williams as editor deviates from the conventional image of the clerk is in suggesting that their City-bred weakness might, given the right circumstances, be addressed and corrected. Earlier cultural impressions of the clerk that implied more indelible patterns of physical degeneration were, Hodder Williams argues, insupportable in the light of wartime evidence to the contrary.

Alongside the wartime demystification of erstwhile entrenched views of 'effete' office workers, the clerks themselves were also able to gain similar insights into previously elevated social groups. Individuals viewed indistinctly before the war as names in society columns, characters in novels, or more closely as respected clients were, for the duration of the war, locked together with their former servants in the democracy of the battlefield. This process had begun at the recruiting grounds, with clerks like Henry Williamson's John Bullock in *The Patriot's Progress* (1930) impressed at the close proximity into which the war had brought these formerly distant beings:[26]

> In front of John Bullock marched a real gentleman – John knew he was that, because he wore a top-hat, like some of the rich directors of the other companies in the building, in whose presence he had always felt subdued and inferior. Now he spoke to the top-hatted gentleman with friendly ease, and even offered him a cigarette. (12)

But after this initial glimpse of the democratic possibilities of war, the public school-educated recruits were largely separated from the ranks to enable them to take up commissions. Thus, in the war's early phase, the class lines dividing the lower middle classes from those above were re-established in the new division between officers and men. This, we assume, would replicate the peacetime norm, with the clerk, trained to offer due deference to an affluent or aristocratic customer, seamlessly transferring that respect to a university-educated officer. Williamson's Phillip Maddison illustrates this resumption of roles in his relationship to the company's superiors:

> The company officers . . . were from that other world, high above him. Their faces were different from those of ordinary people. They looked cleaner, somehow, although not all of them were good-looking. Many of them, he imagined, lived in Park Lane, and, until the war, their hats were faultless Lincoln Bennetts. No doubt they drank champagne with their evening dinners in expensive hotels of the West End. (HDIL 155)

The illusion of the officers as demi-gods was, however, unsustainable in warfare. Following catastrophic casualties amongst Infantry Officers during the first months of the war, the authorities reluctantly acknowledged that replacements, who lacked the social pedigrees traditionally associated with military commissions, would be urgently required. At this stage many clerks applied for and received the promotions that offered them parity of rank with the sons of the aristocracy. That the black-coated workers were to form so significant a proportion of the temporary commissions awarded after the Spring of 1915 is, with hindsight, unsurprising. Their standards of education, typically far beyond those of their working-class counterparts, married to the ambition for social mobility traditionally bred in business offices, made the clerks ideal and willing substitutes.[27] Martin Petter indeed argues with 'some certainty' that the largest single element of wartime officers 'came from what Masterman called 'the suburbans'.[28]

But those numerous clerks who took up commissions did so in the express knowledge that their new status was good for the duration of the war only. This sense of the impermanence of their elevation is reflected in the term 'temporary gentlemen' with which they became indelibly branded.[29] It was a formulation that encapsulated economically the sense of reluctant compromise forced on the establishment by the emergency. A mean-spirited term, it carried with it the hope that rigid class boundaries would again be established after the war, at which time the gentlemanly licences would be revoked. But both the temporary officers and their detractors must have realized, as the war dragged on, that there would be considerable difficulties in effecting this later reversal, at least to the extent that the reversal would mean a return to the sort of prewar subservience towards a social 'superior' that Williamson had illustrated in his characterization of Phillip Maddison. The liberating effect of living (and dying) with those of a higher peacetime social rank, whilst subject to the relative equality provided by combat, was calculated to be an irreversible process.

Ernest Raymond's novel *The Old Tree Blossomed* (1928) offers a useful illustration of the effect of a swift elevation in social status on a prewar clerical worker. Raymond, himself a prewar clerk, depicts the career of Stephen Gallimore, who until 1914 had, like his father, worked in the office of a London department store. Gallimore, at thirty, after thirteen years' clerical experience, has resigned himself to his existence as a three-pounds-a-week clerk living (with his waitress wife) in two rooms in the suburbs. But with the coming of war Stephen sees the chance to transform his prospects. In an echo of Priestley's non-fictional account of his motivation for volunteering, Stephen is described as unconscious 'of any nobility or self-sacrifice in thus going to the wars; such things seemed the opposite of war's gift to him; for he saw only the opportunity' (184). Swiftly taking this opportunity in the form of an early commission, Stephen is able to enjoy the various perquisites of his new status, experiencing, for example, the privileges 'of an Officers' Mess where deferential orderlies sped to his summons; of an officer's first class travelling; of an officer's personal servant; of all the London clubs of which an officer was an honorary member; and of the ladies an officer might be expected to meet' (199). The attraction of these entitlements is placed in particular relief when Gallimore returns home on his first post-commission leave. Here he receives 'dull blows of shame' at his house's 'narrow dingy hall', at his 'lodgers coming in and going out', and at his wife's need to work hard 'in her scullery' (200). The increasing estrangement from his wife is further symbolized in their diverging reading matter; whilst his wife enjoys '*Polly's Paper*, Price 1d' and '*Fanny's Threepenny Fiction*', Stephen 'had been reading the highest literature under an inspiration from one of the Birminghams' officers' (204). Raymond juxtaposes Stephen's two worlds to suggest the growing sense of distance from his former existence that the peacetime clerk encounters. Whilst the narrative of Gallimore's experience is understandably coloured by Raymond's evidently negative feelings towards the suburban clerk's life, his account of Stephen's displacement does offer a reasoned imaginative engagement with the officer's dilemma. The vast gap between life on a clerk's limited salary, and that lived with access to the trappings of affluence that accompanied the officer's uniform, was evidently destined to create social disorientation.

A similar sense of the problems created by a potentially rapid social advancement during wartime is captured in Williamson's account of Phillip Maddison's experiences of promotion. Maddison, having survived the battle of Ypres, in common with most of the remnants of his battalion, applies for and receives a temporary commission. To complete his officer training he is sent to a territorial county regiment, where prewar ideas of soldiering are, as yet, unaffected by wartime conditions. This atmosphere, carefully maintained by a battalion commander used to approving his junior officers for their connections with the county, is an uncomfortable one for Maddison. Lacking the established middle-class connections of his fellow junior officers and marked out as a representative of one of the '"band-box" establishments of the New Armies',[30] the former clerk is keenly aware of his outsider status. Reactions toward Maddison range from the puzzlement of the colonel who, unfamiliar with his new officer's grammar school, attempts to place him socially through other means: 'was there a hint of Kent, or was it Cockney, in some of his vowels?' (*AFUMC* 165); to the overt hostility of his fellow trainees who, having variously described him as a 'young tick', a 'damned outsider', and a 'blasted little Cockney' with 'abominable manners' (*AFUMC* 171,174,187), attempt to force him to resign his commission. These reactions to his presence encourage Maddison to reflect, like Raymond's Gallimore, that his new status has left him in an uncomfortable space between old and new lives: 'he was a sort of mongrel, a half-and-half person' (*AFUMC* 77).[31]

Maddison's unhappy isolation, exacerbated by his ignorance of public school codes of behaviour, contrasts revealingly with his experience amongst the infantry in France. It is only when Maddison is again in combat, during the Battle of Loos, that he is able to witness the relaxing of the snobbish attitudes that had proved such an integral part of his training. In a direct parallel with his experience amongst working-class regulars, Maddison senses an evaporation of class consciousness while in extreme danger. This is evident in the novel when, as a combat-hardened veteran, Maddison again encounters the snobbish officers of the county regiment who have recently arrived from England. In combat, those pre-existing attitudes towards Maddison's inferiority are instantly cast aside in the knowledge that the veteran's familiarity with the battlefield offers a potential lifeline to them as newcomers. Maddison's assistance is indirectly acknowledged by the regiment's commander, who later concedes that it was a pity that Maddison had 'never been to school' (*AFUMC* 386).

If we can consider this shaking-up of old social boundaries a potential dividend of the war, we can equally recognize positive benefits in Williamson's evocation of Maddison's rapidly-growing confidence and maturity. Later, as his relative longevity (coupled with a high casualty rate amongst fellow officers) ensures that Maddison wins further rapid promotion, his transformation from an awkward and timid youth into an authoritative leader is complete. This induces recognition of Maddison's changing perception of himself:

> Strange thoughts of his new self passed in his mind; he was commanding men; *he* was one of those superior beings to whom men looked, as having power over their lives. It was a surprising thought that he, Phillip Maddison, could stand up to real officers like Captain West, M.C.; could speak to staff officers as an equal. How remote seemed his old self, that used to feel small in the presence of such people as Captain Whale, Major Fridkin, and Lieutenant Brendon, who had remarked, with slight contempt, 'As a soldier, Maddison is in that state known as non est.' (*AFUMC* 302)

In his early twenties, Maddison had therefore undergone an education, contingent on his rapid assumption of authority, unavailable to him in peacetime. An army rank may for these volunteers have been, according to a familiar army expression, 'for the duration only', but this sense of impermanence could not extend to personal development. This is particularly evident in Maddison's feelings of equality with those 'superiors' of whom he had once been in awe. Later volumes of the *Chronicle* witness his ease of familiarity with those once-distant individuals who, only months earlier, would undoubtedly have overawed him: by late 1915, for example, Maddison reflects, whilst staying with a fellow officer at his country house, 'what wonderful people he had met, owing to the war!'[32]

That a more widespread feeling of permanent change was developing amongst the surviving temporary officer clerks is also suggested by R.H. Mottram's Stephen Dormer in *The Spanish Farm Trilogy*. In this novel sequence, the former bank clerk's impressions of the army as a form of alternative university anticipate those of Maddison: 'He had become during the three years that had contained for him an education that he could not otherwise have got in thirty, a more instructed person' (735–6). But in contrast to Maddison, whose experiences effect a radical alteration in his character and outlook, Mottram's clerk's new confidence primarily offers instead an affirmation of, and a fresh perspective on, his pre-existing worth. This manifests itself in the sense that, from Mottram's perspective, Dormer does not substantially develop from his connection with the army, as much as the army is immeasurably strengthened from the contribution of Dormer and those like him. The novels of the *Trilogy* in this way offer an unashamed celebration of those undemonstrative qualities possessed by the clerk, qualities that had, prior to 1914, regularly proved a source of mockery in literature. An impression of a changing perception of these qualities is conveyed in Mottram's constant references to Dormer's conservatism and resoluteness: he is described variously as possessing a 'tidy mind' (616), a 'precise and town-bred spirit' (620), 'no superfluous imagination' (729), a 'detached, civilian mind' (607); and of being 'mild and quiet-mannered' (740), and capable of distinguishing 'himself at [routine] by his thoroughness and care' (658). Rather than indicating here that Dormer is a dull and plodding soul, these characteristics, in the context of war, proffer a much-needed solidity and reliability.

Both in battle, and behind the lines (where Dormer becomes a temporary captain attached to Divisional Headquarters dealing with civilian liaison and troop morale) his quiet steadfastness is, in the context of the *Trilogy*, highly prized. Mottram's portrayal of Dormer suggests that he and his ilk represent the epitome of a modern yeoman breed. Dormer is, Mottram's omniscient narrator suggests, typical of an undervalued stock that had emerged from the period of the 'history of the world that mattered'; it was an epoch that had begun only 'after the battle of Waterloo, with Commerce and Banking, Railway and Telegraph, the Education and Ballot Acts' (719). The war, much as it had created carnage on an unparalleled scale, Mottram implies, might also offer the country an opportunity to reassess the generation that Dormer represented. Mottram implies that this reassessment should take into account not only that steadiness of temperament that kept afloat the British army in France, but also the new yeoman stock's refusal to countenance those mutinous thoughts that had surfaced during the conflict. These feelings are concentrated in the following reflections on Dormer, which typify the novel's prevailing philosophy:

> He was no revolutionary. No one was further than he from being one. He only hated Waste. He had been brought up and trained to business, in an atmosphere of methodical neatness, of carefully foreseen and forestalled risks. Rather than have recourse to revolution he would go on fighting the Boche. It was so much more real. (716–17)

Dormer's conservative thoughts, evoked here after he is a witness to the Etaples mutiny, suggest the reasons why the potential for an escalation of unrest among the British Army failed to materialize.

Rather than anticipating the rejection of his former life on return from the war, Mottram's Dormer instead looks forward to its resumption with increased relish. Prewar England, represented for him by 'real proper tea' and 'tea-cakes', 'the Choral Society', 'the local theatre', and 'Vestry or Trust meetings', offered pleasures that the war had thrown into relief.[33] These suburban treats and employments, so often the targets of satirists, made for Dormer 'a fitting termination to a day which he had always felt to be well filled at a good, safe, and continuous job, that would go on until he reached a certain age, when it culminated in a pension, a job that was worth doing, that he could do, and that the public appreciated' (664). Dormer's honourable participation in the war seemed to offer Mottram a licence now to record these pleasures without qualification.[34] Mottram's postwar confidence in presenting his clerk without comic or tragic adornment, therefore, represents a breakthrough in the literary representation of members of his class.[35] Quite apart from Swinnerton's youthful ambitious clerks, Dormer represented a sort of Everyman figure whose conservative inclinations and reliability had (until now) rarely found a literary stage uncoloured by comedy.

*

Even for Mottram himself, however, the peace finally achieved in November 1918 brought with it a sense of anti-climax. The new-found feelings of worth discovered in uniform (and later imaginatively reworked in his characterization of Dormer) were not immediately transferable into civilian life. Indeed, when Mottram himself returned to his branch of Barclays Bank his impression was of being welcomed back from a brief holiday rather than five years of sacrifice:

> Everyone was very nice, but I had just sense enough not to talk about my experiences, or expect any exceptional treatment and to behave as if August 1914 had been the month before, for I did dimly grasp that those of us who had been out in Flanders or farther were not nearly so sick and tired of it all as those who had been kept at home.[36]

Whilst Mottram's temperament allowed him resignedly to resume his old occupation, other clerks, such as Williamson, found that the civilian blindness to their wartime transformation made thoughts of a return to the office stool impossible. The need to submit to demobbing might have been prepared for by temporary officers who had looked forward to the resumption of their civilian lives, but the process of being 'de-officered', as Mottram termed it, was another matter. This implicit procedure appeared to demand that the wartime commission holder should hand in his experience, education and hard won self-esteem, along with his pistol.

Martin Petter's excellent article, '"Temporary Gentlemen" in the Aftermath of the Great War: Rank, Status and the Ex-Officer Problem', identifies various individuals who attempted to police the 'deofficering' process. Amongst the most insistent of these controlling voices was that of H.F. Maltby, whose successful play *A Temporary Gentleman*, staged in 1919, was written in response to what he perceived as the problem of postwar resettlement. He outlined this motivation in his autobiography *Ring up the Curtain*:

> I had often wondered where some of our officers and V.A.D. girls came from; they were
> so obviously lower-middle class and suburban and gave themselves such airs and graces.
> I wondered what would happen to them when the war was over, I could see a terrible
> de-bunking before them.[37]

Maltby's play, which was (according to him) the product of altruism, depicted Walter Hope, a former junior warehouse clerk who had gained a wartime commission in the Royal Army Service Corps. On his return to civilian life he had, in Maltby's formulation, 'ideas above his station' which 'unfitted him for any useful livelihood'. This led to Hope becoming 'out of work because he [was] too swollen-headed to go back to his old job'.[38] Maltby's conclusion sees the clerk's untenable position eventually revealed to him, and witnesses his subsequent return to a more 'realistic' outlook that allows him to become a commercial traveller. The play also concurrently records his move from courting his former employer's daughter to a more 'reasonable' engagement to a housemaid. The plot's parabola and evident success (it became a film in 1920) indicates the resumption of a significant strain of prewar thinking that looked forward to a return to the status quo; Petter's research uncovered the breadth of this thinking, revealing for example the reaction to the play of the *Manchester Guardian's* critic, who had considered its conclusion, an 'admirably worked-out solution to [Hope's] difficulties . . . that he shall in a word 'buckle to' . . . and do his best in some employment open to him in his prewar status as clerk.'[39]

Elsewhere, those who had participated in the war tended to be more sympathetic to their fellow veterans, appreciating the considerable problems of resettlement which war service had brought about. Such individuals tellingly included temporary officers such as Richard Aldington, a prewar university student and poet who considered that Maltby's play dangerously oversimplified the problems of the clerk returning to a defamiliarized environment. Aldington here discusses his feelings after attending *A Temporary Gentleman*:

> I beheld a demobilised officer so conceited about having held His Majesty's
> Commission that he refused to know his old friends and considered ordinary jobs
> beneath him . . . The travesty was bitterly unjust. Already, ex-officers were tramping
> the streets looking for any job, and within months thousands of them were sleeping in
> Hyde Park, absolutely destitute.[40]

The support of Aldington – who later wrote a short story 'The Case of Lieutenant Hall', centring on the suicide of a demobbed officer who had seen Maltby's play – and others in exposing the injustice of the 'de-officering' process gained ground in the years following the war.[41] As more of those who had survived began to write of their experiences, the full naïveté and injustice of Maltby's play became exposed.

It is perhaps reductive to argue that the generation that had fought together as temporary officers during the war formed a loose brotherhood united by survival rather than class. But even the most sceptical of critics must recognize some degree of truth in this admittedly grand assumption. Alan Thomas's novel *The Lonely Years* (1930) certainly suggests the sense of a new egalitarianism that looked to counter the patronizing depiction of the returning officer in Maltby's *A Temporary Gentleman*. Thomas's central character John Penrose differs from Walter Hope in that his prewar background is more typical of the traditional officer class, but following his demobilization as a temporary Captain, Penrose's financial circumstances leave him with little choice but to rearrange his peacetime life. Unlike Hope, however, who is too self-important to accept lesser work, Penrose pragmatically accepts a post at the Bell Insurance Company in Bishopsgate. Penrose's stoicism in accepting a 'fifty bob a week' clerk's post after having served as a wartime Company Commander is sensitively handled by Thomas. One senses, in the ex-officer's reflection 'I'm not complaining . . . I'm lucky to have a job at all these days', a closer understanding of the post-war scene than that suggested by Maltby's bumptious Hope.[42] Thomas counterbalances Penrose's acceptance of his lot with the delineation of events within the office that illustrate the arguably inequitable nature of the character's situation. Penrose is, for example, at twenty-six, and after developing leadership skills, expected to remain patiently in line for promotion behind those too young to fight. Told by his patronizing boss not to run before he can walk (226) and that he should be patiently 'absorbing the routine of the office' (227), Penrose is moved to silently recall: 'I was running – running over the top – while you were sitting in that chair!' (226). When Penrose does eventually speak to his manager about his frustrations, his impatience is criticized and his war experience dismissed as an irrelevance:

> The work's the same. It's you fellers that are different. You don't seem to be able to settle down. You've got no patience . . . I know exactly how you feel. I know what you've been through . . . But you've got to remember that you're not the only one. There are hundreds – thousands, in fact – like you. And what you've got to do now, is to try and forget the war.
> What we've got to do! [thought John] *We! Forget!* (226–7)

Thomas suggests that Penrose's inability to achieve this sort of tactical amnesia is not indicative of the innate superiority of an individual forced down the social scale by family reversals, it is more because his war experiences have left him, and others, as 'fragments of the old order, incapable of fitting into the new!' (250). It is ultimately and ironically the 'positive handicap' (228) of his army service that ensures he leaves the office for an uncertain future.

The pessimism evident in this fictional account of civilian indifference to hard-won potential was, to some extent, tempered by its very articulation. Aldington, Thomas and others, in issuing their support to those returning to office work, ensured that the process of mental 'deofficering' might be exposed and checked. And in addition to those new voices emerging from the war, and thus keenly aware of injustice to their fellows, there were other less likely advocates. Amongst these was John Galsworthy, whose patrician characterization of the clerk Falder in his play *Justice* (1910) had epitomized the prewar liberal humanist perspective on this group.[43] Now, in his *Forsyte Saga* novel *The White Monkey* (1924), Galsworthy was prepared, in the character of Butterfield, to suggest a small but significant change in attitude towards those of the clerk class. Initially Butterfield does appear to duplicate the ineffectuality of Falder, being described as 'commonplace', 'modest looking', and as one 'who made [his] living out of self-suppression and respectability'.[44] But later Michael Mont, the publisher and poet, is moved to see in Butterfield something more than what Jolyon Forsyte had described as 'a pale martyr with his shirt on fire' (192). Revealingly, this occurs after Mont has established his feelings of fraternity with Butterfield following a commonplace observation: 'From your moustache, you were in the war, I suppose, like me?' After this establishment of connection, Mont can, 'as between fellow-sufferers' (201), accept that a sense of perfect trust will exist between him and his future employee. This trust encourages Mont both to employ Butterfield, and to offer his example to his father-in-law, Soames Forsyte, as proof that the war has radically reformed society. Butterfield, who in modern terms would be considered a 'whistle-blower' for his decision to inform against Elderson (a corrupt former employer), has in Mont's view, acquired the steeliness required for this act through the experience he had gained during the war. While Mont admits to Soames Forsyte that the war 'took the lynch-pins out of the cart', he also enthusiastically reflects that 'it did give you an idea of the grit there is about, when it comes to being up against it . . . Look at young Butterfield, the other day . . . going over the top, to Elderson!' (276–7).

A further indication of Galsworthy's reassessment of the potential of this social group is observed in *Reveille,* a magazine for disabled soldiers and sailors, which he edited from August 1918. Here, in an article entitled 'The Ex-Officer Problem', published in February 1919 (and therefore prior to the staging of Maltby's play), H.B.C. Pollard had argued:

> Everyone recognizes that the warehouse clerk who has shown himself fit to be a colonel should not have to go back to his old job, because it is such obvious waste of a man of higher capacity . . . The nation must realise what magnificent material it has available in the non-regular officers of the Army, the Air Force, and the Navy, and it must wake up to the absolute necessity of making the best possible use of them when they revert to civil employment . . . The officer of to-day and the ex-officer of to-morrow are one and the same thing . . .[45]

Whilst the full implementation of Pollard's (and presumably his editor's) wishes were, due to the postwar economy, never likely to be fully realized, a reward of a less tangible kind was, in due course, paid. It was paid in the sense that attitudes clearly changed towards the clerk class over the 1920s and 1930s, resulting in some part from the recognition of this group's contribution to the war effort. That this was indeed the case is witnessed in the extent to which the sort of stereotype represented by Walter Hope – and by extension Leonard Bast – had largely disappeared by the time that Alan Thomas's John Penrose had arrived in 1930.

*

The gap between the appearance of Hope in 1919 and Penrose in 1930 is not marked by the emergence of any single clerk character in English literature who might be considered to herald the change in attitudes. Literary recognition of this change was a gradual process marked more by the absence of the old than by the coming of the new.[46] Whilst established writers such as Frank Swinnerton and W. Pett Ridge continued to publish novels and short stories which were wholly sympathetic to the clerk's cause, there was little sense of domestic literature producing anything as fresh as, say, Sinclair Lewis's *Babbitt* (1922) or Elmer Rice's *The Adding Machine* (1923) in America. But certain significant signs emerged to suggest the male clerk's new standing in print culture. Of these, the following two diverging examples offer glimpses of the postwar reformation of this cultural image. Firstly, one might cite as an index the postwar willingness of the satirical magazine *Punch* to include cartoons which focused on office life. Prior to 1914, clerks other than Mr. Pooter had been a rare sight in the magazine's pages, but following the war, as if in response to a more general recognition of their new status, office workers were ever-present: in the edition for 14 November 1923, for example, there are three separate cartoons featuring office workers.[47] Furthermore, these cartoon clerks are not mere Pooters, designed to amuse a 'superior' reader; they instead tend to suggest a parity of social position with the readership. As a second example we might look towards the clerk's changing literary profile in the work of new modernist writers emerging after the war. An inclusive vision of modern society is, for example, offered in Richard Aldington's modernist poem *A Fool i' the Forest* (1924). The poem offers a spiritual autobiography of three symbolic characters who are also a single individual. Of these, according to Aldington's prefatory note, '"I" is intended to be typical of a man of our own time':

> Every morning now at half-past seven
> Ethel thumps me in the back;
> Up I leap, a loyal English husband,
> Whistle in the bath-room, gulp my bacon...
> Buy the morning papers as I hasten to the Tube
> And read of all the wonders of the age.
> At the office I am diligent and punctual,
> Courteous, well-bred, and much respected;[48]

As in T.S. Eliot's *The Waste Land* (1922), to which work Aldington's poem was indebted, suburban man is imagined here as the figure who epitomized the norm of British society in the postwar era.

The contrasting literary signs of democracy evident in *Punch* and Aldington's modernist poem say very little on their own, but taken together they suggest the changing postwar conception of the clerk class. These contrasting print cultural examples demonstrate the ways in which the rigid prewar social boundaries that had helped to mould the enduring image of the clerk were shaken by the imperatives of extended conflict. Whilst no one would argue that the war brought an end to the divisions of society indicated by Masterman, most would agree that the war had disrupted the strict nature of the dividing lines. If the relative egalitarianism of the trenches was not immediately transported back into civilian life after November 1918, more lasting impressions did remain.[49] Clerk-soldiers returning from the war did so with a greater confidence of their worth as individuals, and of the value of their ideas. This new assurance was translated into the literature of the 1930s, in which a generation of prewar clerks emerged as playwrights and novelists: amongst these were J.B. Priestley, R.H. Mottram, Cecil Roberts, Gerald Bullett, Henry Williamson and R.C. Sherriff. Whilst it would be misleading to rope these individuals together into a literary movement, they do collectively lend postwar print culture a distinctive quality largely lacking before 1914. Like the editor of *One Young Man,* these writers resolved in their work to 'let this country never forget' the sacrifices made by their generation of unlikely warriors.

NOTES

1. E.M. Forster, *Howards End* (Harmondsworth, 1989), p. 62.

2. These reviews were printed by way of an advertisement for *The Merry Heart* at the end of the first edition of Swinnerton's subsequent novel *The Young Idea* (1910).

3. Further abundant evidence of the negative typing of clerks can be found in the influential work of George Gissing. The following examples offer only a brief selection of Gissing's characterizations of clerks in his novels and stories: in *The Odd Women* (1893), for example, Mr. Newdick is identified as 'musty and nervous' and 'trembling and bloodless' (George Gissing, *The Odd Women* (London, 1980), p. 121); Thomas Bird in 'The Salt of the Earth' (1894) possesses the gait 'of a man who takes no exercise beyond the daily walk to and from his desk' (George Gissing, *The House of Cobwebs* (London, 1926 (1906)), p. 266); the man who 'seemed to be some species of clerk' in 'The Tout of Yarmouth Bridge' (1895) presents a 'bloodless face and a tired, anxious expression' (George Gissing, *Human Odds and Ends* (London, 1911 (1898)), p. 212); while Robert Winder in 'A Well Meaning Man' (1895) has a 'pallid . . . countenance, [and an] air of nervous conscientiousness' (*Human Odds and Ends*, p. 219).

4. Trevor Wilson, *The Myriad Faces of War: Britian and the Great War, 1914–1918* (Cambridge, 1988), p. 676.

5. 'Xanthus' (Herbert Asquith), 'The Dead Volunteer', *The Spectator*, 8 Aug 1914, p. 202. We might usefully compare this with Rudyard Kipling's poem 'Ex-Clerk', taken from the 'Epitaphs of the War' series published in 1919:

    Pity not! The Army gave
    Freedom to a timid slave:
    In which Freedom did he find
    Strength of body, will and mind:
    By which strength he came to prove
    Mirth, companionship, and love:
    For which Love to Death he went:
    In which Death he lies content.

(Rudyard Kipling, *Rudyard Kipling's Verse: Inclusive Edition 1885-1918: Volume II* (London, 1919), p. 190.

6. These figures contrast with those from the industrial, agricultural, and transport sectors, from which an average of just 26.35 per cent of the prewar total workforce enlisted. Figures taken from J.M. Winter, *The Great War and the British People* (London, 1985), p. 34.

7. Price's research confirms that greater numbers of clerks than labourers aged between 17 and 25 volunteered for the Imperial Yeomanry in 1900 and 1901. Richard Price, *An Imperial War and the British Working Class: Working-Class Attitudes and Reactions to the Boer War 1899–1902* (London, 1972), pp. 228, 241. See also, Richard Price, 'Society, Status and Jingoism: The Social Roots of Lower Middle Class Patriotism, 1870–1900', in Crossick (ed.), *The Lower Middle Class in Britain* (London, 1978 (1977)), pp. 89–112.

8. J.B. Priestley, *Margin Released* (London, 1963 (1962)), p. 79.

9. J.B. Priestley, *Margin Released*, p. 78.

10. R.C. Sherriff, *No Leading Lady: An Autobiography* (London, 1968), p. 317.

11. Ernest Raymond, *The Old Tree Blossomed*: *A Realistic Romance* (London, 1930), p. 184. All subsequent page references are to this edition.

12. Winter, *The Great War,* p. 49.

13. The relatively healthy working conditions in British offices contrasted with those existing in industry which, according to Winter, had contributed to the 'appallingly low standards of health in many urban working-class districts'. Winter, *The Great War,* p. 49.

14. R.H. Mottram, *Bowler Hat: A Last Glance at the Old Country Banking* (London, 1940), p. 200.

15. Quoted in Peter Simkins, *Kitchener's Army: The Raising of the New Armies, 1914–1916* (Manchester, 1988), p. 170.

16. Simkins, *Kitchener's Army*, p. 88.

17. Given the large component of clerks among the troops who joined up in 1914 it is perhaps unsurprising that contemporary critics were sceptical about the likely effectiveness of the New Armies in facing up to professional Prussian soldiers. One wartime account of a clerk's contribution to the war effort reminds these sceptics of their misplaced reservations: 'Those were very dark days in England . . . We were arrayed in battle against men who had been trained through all the years of their manhood . . . And we had to meet them with – clerks!' . . . [But] in equal fight they thrashed them. Think of it in the light of history. The greatest and most wonderfully equipped and trained army the world has ever know beaten in fair fight by an army of clerks . . .' J.E. Hodder Williams (ed.), *One Young Man* (London, 1917), pp. 39, 40.

18. Henry Williamson, *How Dear is Life* (Stroud, 1995 (1954)), p. 48. All subsequent page references are to this edition.

19. Herbert Tremaine (Maude Deuchar), *The Feet of the Young Men: A Domestic War Novel* (London, 1917), p. 25. All subsequent page references are to this edition. C.W. Daniel was a pacifist publisher who, as Imogen Gassert notes, 'was very publicly prosecuted and almost closed down for publishing the novel *Despised and Rejected* by Rose Allatini (as "A.T. Fitzroy").' Imogen Gassert, 'In a Foreign Field: What Soldiers in the Trenches Liked to Read', *Times Literary Supplement*, 10 May 2002, p. 17.

20. C.F.G. Masterman, *The Condition of England* (London, 1960 (1909)), p. 59.

21. R. H. Mottram, *The Spanish Farm Trilogy 1914–1918* (London, 1929 (1927)), p. 775. All subsequent page references are to this edition. The individual volumes of the trilogy were published as follows: *The Spanish Farm* in 1924, *Sixty-Four, Ninety-Four!* in 1925 and *The Crime at Vanderlynden's* in 1926.

22. C.E. Montague, *Disenchantment* (London, 1922), pp. 7–8.

23. Several autobiographical accounts point towards the initial embarrassment that might be caused by these new relationships. A.H. Davis, a clerk at Lloyds Bank, recalled marching through local streets following his enlistment, with 'one particularly rough chap [who] picked me out as his pal on progress to R.E. Headquarters . . . [On the way] I seemed to meet all my more exclusive friends, and consequently did not feel particularly proud of my position.' A.H. Davis, *Extracts from the Diaries of a Tommy* (London, 1932), pp. 12–13. Similarly Pooteresque was Private Charles Jones, a prewar solicitor's clerk, who wrote to his wife, describing his experiences three days after arriving at his depot: 'The language used by the majority of recruits, consisting mainly of London roughs and country yokels of the worst description, I cannot repeat here but Damns and Bloodys etc etc were introduced into every sentence . . . We had to sleep packed like sardines and with one of the noisiest and obscene collections of human beings it has ever been my misfortune to meet, and the smell of them packed into a small building after a hot day was truly sickening.' Simkins, *Kitchener's Army*, p. 195.

24. Frank Richards, *Old Soldiers Never Die* (London, 1964 (1933)), p. 285.

25. J.E. Hodder Williams (ed.), *One Young Man*, pp. 38–40.

26. R.H. Mottram remembered at his enlistment that next to him 'stood one for whom a large car called to take him home from drill and who gave sumptuous dinners after which officers were invited to take wine with him.' R. H. Mottram, *Three Personal Records of the War* (London, 1929), p. 22.

27. Donald Hankey commented in his popular war essays, collected together in *A Student in Arms* (1916), that 'the youngster who wants promotion has probably been a clerk and lived in a suburb. He is better educated and has a smarter appearance than the general run of the men.' Donald Hankey, *A Student in Arms* (London, 1917 (1916)), pp. 46–7.

28. Martin Petter, '"Temporary Gentlemen" in the Aftermath of the Great War: Rank, Status and the Ex-Officer Problem', *The Historical Journal, 37* (1994), p. 139.

29. The indeterminate status of the temporary officers of the New Armies is identified in the following passage from Henry Williamson's *The Golden Virgin*:

    What did Georgina Lady Dudley think of them? They were the half-and-half people, so very polite, poor dears, so formal, trying hard to appear above themselves; but all was forgiven them for being what they were. Had they not come out of their unknown places and answered the call, from their obscure streets and small houses, to replace, with their plain names in the casualty lists, those of the splendid young men who had fallen in 1914 and 1915.

    Henry Williamson, *The Golden Virgin* (London, 1966 (1957)), p. 340.

30. Henry Williamson, *A Fox Under my Cloak* (Stroud (1955)), p. 164. All subsequent page references are to this edition.

31. Alfred Burrage, writing under the pseudonym 'Ex-Private X', confirms the temporary gentleman's indeterminate status as seen from the ranks. Whilst Burrage's memoir commended the lower middle-class officer's fighting ability, he was less accepting of them on the home front. Describing the scene at a West End restaurant he comments that: 'The place was full of officers and their lady-loves, and judging by the manners and accents of the former they were nearly all "Smiffs", late of Little Buggington Grammar School, who had been "clurks" in civilian life, and were now throwing their weight about on seven and sixpence a day and half salary.' Ex-Private X [A. M. Burrage], *War is War* (London, 1930), p. 217.

32. Williamson, *The Golden Virgin*, p. 73.

33. Sydney Baxter ('One Young Man'), writing a letter to his mother on the eve of the Battle of the Somme, similarly relished the prospect of a return to his 'Church secretaryship' and his 'work in the City'. J.E. Hodder Williams (ed.), *One Young Man*, p. 160.

34. Prior to 1914, characters who stood up for, or merely represented suburban life, appeared to require an apology for their existence: examples might include Shan F. Bullock's Robert Thorne (in *Robert Thorne: The Story of a London Clerk* (1907)) who wished that 'someone more capable' had taken his story in hand; or Keble Howard's 'Note of Warning', prefacing *The Smiths of Surbiton* (1906), that 'if you happen to be a Superior Person, you will not like this story.'

35. As Alison Light has argued in relation to the literature of the postwar period, 'what had formerly been held as the virtues of the private sphere of middle-class life take on a new public and national significance.' Alison Light, *Forever England: Femininity, Literature and Conservatism Between the Wars* (London, 1991), p. 8.

36. R.H. Mottram, *Bowler Hat*, pp. 198–9.

37. H.F. Maltby, *Ring up the Curtain* (London, 1950), p. 146.

38. Maltby, *Ring up the Curtain*, p. 149.

39. Petter, 'Temporary Gentleman', p. 133.

40. Richard Aldington, *Life for Life's Sake* (London, 1968 (1941)), p. 188.

41. 'The Case of Lieutenant Hall' in Richard Aldington's *Roads to Glory* (London, 1992 (1931)).

42. Alan Thomas, *The Lonely Years* (London, 1930) p. 220. All subsequent page references are to this edition.

43. Sympathetic though *Justice* is to Falder's plight, Galsworthy leaves us with no illusions about the difference between the feeble clerk and those of more stalwart qualities. Falder admits his own congenital lack of stamina when he is imprisoned for stealing money from his office: 'I was always nervous. Everything seems to get such a size . . . I feel I'll never get out as long as I live' – John Galsworthy, *Justice* (London, 1977 (1910)), p. 56.

44. John Galsworthy, *A Modern Comedy* (including *The White Monkey*) (London, 1948 (1929)), pp. 122 and 192. All subsequent page references are to this edition.

45. *Reveille: Devoted to the Disabled Sailor and Soldier,* 3, Feb 1919, p. 425.

46. This change in literary attitudes can be usefully located in the wider debate on the erosion of deferential behaviour among 'servile' and black-coated workers in the postwar period. Bernard Waites, while acknowledging the existence of this phenomenon, adds the following caveat with which I concur: 'generalised reference . . . to an erosion of deferential or servile behaviour is difficult to substantiate in terms of reliably recorded social habits and their changing patters.' Bernard Waites, *A Class Society at War: England 1914–1918* (Leamington Spa, 1987), p. 241.

47. *Punch*, 14 Nov 1923. These included cartoons by H.M. Brock (p. 479), J.H. Thorpe (p. 475) and D.L. Ghilchik (p. 466).

48. Richard Aldington, *A Fool i' the Forest: A Phantasmagoria* (London, 1925), p. 60.

49. Waites notes that the 'new temper of the clerks who returned from the forces' was recognizable in the ways in which, for example, railway clerks and lower-grade civil servants evinced 'a political radicalism which had no precedent in the prewar world.' Waites, *Class Society*, pp. 250 and 257.

THE LIMITS OF CULTURE?

SOCIETY, EVOLUTIONARY PSYCHOLOGY AND THE HISTORY OF VIOLENCE

J. Carter Wood

The Open University, Milton Keynes

ABSTRACT Recent debates about the meaning and role of cultural history have focused on the relationship between 'culture' and 'society'. Some have taken this opportunity to position cultural history as a site of resistance to 'biological' explanations of human behaviour. In contrast, this article argues that 'biological' methodologies – particularly the perspectives of evolutionary psychology – can usefully contribute to the historical understanding of culture and social development. To this end, it outlines the fundamentals of Darwinist psychology, suggests options for interdisciplinary cooperation and uses the topic of interpersonal violence to explore the potential for uniting cultural, social and evolutionary psychological methodologies.

Keywords: culture, violence, biology, evolution, psychology

Cultural historians' enduring conversation about the state of their field, especially its relationship to social history and the social sciences more generally, received new impetus from Peter Mandler's survey of the 'problems' facing cultural history.[1] At about the same time, some social historians were reconsidering methodologies derived from a 'cultural turn' which appeared to be slowing.[2] Both discussions focused particularly on the boundaries between 'culture' and 'society', and Mandler's farthest-reaching 'modest proposal' for addressing cultural history's shortcomings calls for a methodologically more rigorous 'theory of meaning' rooted in sociological theory. A similar goal leads Paula S. Fass to conclude, 'Now, more than ever, cultural history needs exposure to the methods, ways of thinking and questions that social history can provide.'[3] The search for new theoretical inspiration and innovative approaches is to be welcomed and (re)anchoring cultural history in sociological methodology and (re)building bridges with the social sciences is one way forward. Yet, while the time may be ripe for a new theoretical synthesis, cultural historians should be prepared to cast their conceptual nets more widely.

Nonetheless, despite continuing debates about the relationship between society and culture or ongoing battles around literary and linguistic theories, there is one menace on which many cultural historians seem to agree: biology. Although the literal

Address for correspondence: Dr John Carter Wood, Research Fellow, Department of History, International Centre for Comparative Criminological Research, The Open University, Walton Hall, Milton Keynes, MK7 6AA, UK. E-mail: jcarterwood@yahoo.com

meaning of 'biological' might seem innocuous (anything related to, caused by or affecting living organisms), analyses of human life in terms of genetics or evolutionary theory are often seen as reductive, deterministic and threatening (or, alternatively, irrelevant) to historical studies. The 'othering' of biology was built into some recent debates from the start, with Mandler, for instance, suggesting a cultural history reinforced by social science could act as a bulwark against 'biology envy' and the 'vast claims made by socio-biology and evolutionary psychology to have unlocked the secrets of human behaviour'.[4] In a response, Carla Hesse, although otherwise critical of Mandler's views, agrees on cultural history's position *vis-à-vis* the natural sciences. For her, the 'fundamental aim' of psycholinguistics, socio-biology and evolutionary psychology is to 'discover immutable laws of human behaviour'; their interests are 'essentially at cross purposes with what historians want to know about "meaning", "identity", "needs", "desires", "discourse" and "narrative"', and their levels of analysis are 'deeply incommensurable with those of the historian'.[5] Even from a point of view that is ostensibly more informed by Darwinian thinking, evolutionary psychologists have been accused of presenting arguments which are either 'dangerous' or 'innocuous'.[6] More often than provoking overt hostility, biology is simply ignored: a recent, wide-ranging and theoretical introduction to cultural history, despite its other merits, avoids a single reference to evolutionary, cognitive or neuropsychological perspectives on culture.[7]

Thus, cultural historians are being urged to turn to sociology without considering approaches that critique (or usefully supplement) sociological thinking on society and culture. Constructive discussions of the relationship between culture, society and biology have – with a few exceptions – largely taken place outside of the field of history. I suggest that rather than raising disciplinary drawbridges, however, cultural historians should be contributing to emerging interdisciplinary understandings of the interactions between psychology and society. The incorporation of 'biology' may mean recognizing limits to 'culture' as an independent explanatory principle, but it also presents an opportunity for scholars of culture to increase the depth and relevance of their work and to participate in a broader rethinking of the human condition. What follows is an argument for reconsidering and, when possible, making use of natural science approaches to key topics in cultural and social history. First, I will summarize evolutionary psychology and some of its perspectives on culture. Second, a few typical objections to Darwinist views of culture will be addressed as part of describing a possible *modus vivendi* between culturalist and naturalist theories. Finally, I shall use the topic of violence to suggest the opportunities for connecting cultural history, sociology and psychology.

EVOLUTIONARY PSYCHOLOGY: A METHOD OF ANALYSIS

There have been a variety of efforts to unite 'evolution' and human social development, which, while sometimes overlapping, can be distinguished. One sees culture 'evolving' in ways analogous to biological change: pieces of cultural information – such as 'cognitive units', 'memes' or 'mentemes' – are replicated and subjected to selection pressures, which cause cultural phenomena to arise, thrive or go extinct.[8] While cultural and genetic change are both seen as processes of replication and selection, they remain separate realms. A second approach argues for a form of 'coevolution': genes act as a 'leash' (or 'elastic') upon cultural development, which, in turn, influences long-term patterns in genetic inheritance.[9] Both 'cultural evolution' and 'gene-culture coevolution' are intriguing and potentially useful theories. However, I will mainly focus on a third methodology, evolutionary psychology, which I think offers the most to cultural historians. Interest in what evolutionary psychologists have to say about culture has hitherto been mainly confined to anthropologists, psychologists and sociologists, but, while history and evolutionary psychology differ, they nevertheless share a concern with explaining how individuals understand their societies and interact with one another. Some evolutionary psychological arguments have even borrowed directly from history, using, for example, historical data on mate choice, homicide or demography.[10] This suggests that an interdisciplinary exchange in the opposite direction is not only possible, but also necessary.

Furthermore, it is not difficult to imagine how a better understanding of human psychology might be relevant to the study of culture and *vice versa*. As Mark Flinn asserts, 'a historical theory of culture without psychology is as incomplete as is a psychological theory of culture without history.'[11] This notion should not be alien to cultural historians, some of whom have long been able to incorporate a different theory of psychology: that of Freud.[12] 'Psychohistory' has always had a mixed reception. The scepticism and hostility directed toward evolutionary psychology, however, seems to point to a far more fundamental rejection of its intellectual and scientific validity. This may partly result from confusion about its true nature, but it would be too easy to simply reduce a genuine interdisciplinary conflict to a misunderstanding, thereby overlooking basic differences in assumptions and methods. Many humanities scholars would likely deny, for example, that there is a meaningful 'human nature', a concept central to evolutionary psychology. Clearing out the thickets of debate, politics and misapprehension that have grown around that concept is beyond the scope of this article.[13] I am, in any case, less interested in advocating a specific model of evolved psychology (although I will make some suggestions in that direction) than in encouraging a more general openness toward evolutionary perspectives and exploring how they may be of use in historical studies. This requires a brief summary of those elements of evolutionary psychology that I think are most relevant to cultural and social historians.

Leda Cosmides and John Tooby describe evolutionary psychology as an 'approach' to dealing with questions about the human psyche and as a 'way of thinking' about psychology rather than a specific field unto itself.[14] While distinct from cognitive psychology or neuroscience, its relationship to them has often been complementary, serving above all to explain *why* and *how* specific aspects of the human mentality might have developed. Evolutionary psychology need not be connected to the aforementioned theories of cultural evolution or gene-culture coevolution, as it neither posits a selective mechanism for cultural 'units' nor (necessarily) concentrates upon the specific degree to which particular behaviours are influenced by genes or learning.

Asserting the 'fundamental unity' of human psychology, evolutionary psychologists are primarily interested in shared aspects of the psyche that underpin all cultures; their subject matter is 'the evolved architecture of the human mind, or the set of evolved mental mechanisms that comprise the human mind'.[15] (The main exception to the notion of a unified psyche relates to sex differences in some aspects of psychology and social interaction, such as those shaping violence.)[16] Psychology is thus seen as a biological phenomenon subject to evolutionary development. Rather than a 'blank slate' or all-purpose thinking machine, the brain is theorized as a collection of modular 'regulatory circuits' that 'organize the way we interpret our experiences, inject certain recurrent concepts and motivations into our mental life, and provide universal frames of meaning that allow us to understand the actions and intentions of others'.[17] The emphasis is on determining how specific mechanisms manage mental processes and the beliefs and actions which result. Some mechanisms operate unconsciously, but by studying behaviour patterns, brain structures and the selection pressures of the evolutionary past, the outline of an innate psychological structure can emerge.

The behaviour caused by the evolved psyche may not always be 'adaptive' (that is, improving 'inclusive fitness', the reproductive success of oneself and one's kin) in modern contexts. Taking into account the slow process of evolution and the long-term existence of our species as hunter-gatherers, Tooby and Cosmides argue that 'the complex architecture of the human psyche can be expected to have assumed approximately modern form during the Pleistocene, in the process of adapting to Pleistocene conditions, and to have undergone only minor modifications since then.'[18] But while modern human lifestyles may not be directly determined by their contemporary contribution to evolutionary fitness, psychological mechanisms formed during ancestral periods continue to 'govern' certain aspects of human behaviour and culture. Thus, 'although specific modern behaviour may or may not be *adaptively patterned*, both modern and past behaviour is *evolutionarily patterned* and can only be understood by being placed in an evolutionary framework.'[19] Others have argued that many modern behaviours are in fact adaptive, which has led to a lively debate; however, regardless of the specific position taken on the issue of adaptiveness, evolutionary psychology primarily 'addresses not what the mind can do, but what it was designed to do', and as a result 'selection thinking' (which considers the evolutionary sources and functions of behaviour) can provide insight into a wide range of human social activity.[20] This approach has led to theories about patterns in (and the reasons for) abilities, concepts and behaviours of historical interest, such as generosity, attraction, sexuality, morality, violence and aesthetics. In short, it presents an argument for how culture is created, which is – or at least should be – a central concern of cultural historians.

CULTURE AND BIOLOGY: NEVER THE TWAIN SHALL MEET?

Evolutionary psychology is often accused of 'determinism', of seeing people only as directly 'programmed' by genetic instructions.[21] Typically, this encoding is seen as irresistible and malevolent, supporting a pessimistic view of people as inherently rapacious, irredeemably self-interested and perpetually violent. However, evolutionary psychologists have repeatedly denied that there are fixed laws of behaviour and have emphasized the possibility of social improvement. Although admitting how easily misunderstandings arise when speaking of 'a gene for' certain kinds of behaviour, Richard Dawkins has argued at length that 'genetic determinism' is a myth.[22] While critiquing social science's rejection of human nature, Steven Pinker devotes extensive discussion to 'bridging' biology and culture.[23] Martin Daly and Margo Wilson place evolutionary psychology at the centre of their studies of violence; however, they reject biological determinism, address the issue of cultural variability in homicide and draw attention to factors which might reduce violence.[24] Randy Thornhill and Craig Palmer open their study of rape with a lengthy consideration of the interrelationship between culture and biology, arguing that 'every aspect of every living thing is, by definition, biological, and everything biological is a result of interaction between genes and environmental factors'; therefore, 'no behaviour is inevitable'.[25] Cosmides and Tooby express the view of many evolutionary psychologists as follows:

> *Every aspect of an organism's phenotype is the joint product of its genes and its environment.* To ask which is more important is like asking, Which is more important in determining the area of a rectangle, the length or the width? Which is more important in causing a car to run, the engine or the gasoline? Genes allow the environment to influence the development of phenotypes.[26]

There are indeed some who, working from an evolutionary perspective, dismiss any significant role for culture but, as the above comments suggest, this view is far from dominant.[27] Framing the issue as a choice between biology *or* culture, between nature *or* nurture, is pointless, and culture – like other 'environmental' factors – is taken seriously in many current evolutionary perspectives on society and psychology. However, determining what 'culture' is, explaining how it is formed and exploring its role in human life remain important tasks, framing an intellectual effort to which biological perspectives can fruitfully contribute.

Defining 'culture', however, is no easy task. While the 'common ground' of cultural history can be described 'as a concern with the symbolic and its interpretation', this shared interest conceals several different and sometimes mutually antagonistic approaches: some emphasize 'the importance of beliefs and assumptions and their causal role in group behaviour', others are 'more interested in the history of representations than in structures or processes' and a few seem to have abandoned an interest in materiality and causality altogether.[28] Trying to establish a single definition of 'culture' upon which all historians would agree is likely futile. Similarly, there is no single 'Darwinist' theory of culture. Nonetheless, there are common features in outlook and conceptualization among most evolutionary psychologists. For instance, they critique a view of culture – whether derived from the social sciences or postmodern theory – as an omnipotent, disembodied force, independent of individual psychology, environmental conditions and material structures. Instead, culture is given a definite location: 'It is generated in rich and intricate ways by information-processing mechanisms situated in human minds. These mechanisms are, in turn, the elaborately sculpted product of the evolutionary process.'[29] From this perspective, 'culture' derives from the interaction between innate psychological tendencies and dynamic relationships among individuals; thus, 'group level cultural and social phenomena, while they have some emergent properties, are the consequence of the operation of evolved psychological (and morphological) mechanisms functioning in individuals who evolved to live in groups.'[30]

Cultural information, by definition, is learned, but 'learning' is itself governed by mental mechanisms that process socially imparted information. These mechanisms – 'Darwinian algorithms', 'learning biases' or 'constraints on learning' – provide psychological 'aptitudes' for or 'restrictions' on culture.[31] Language, perhaps the most fundamental of a culture's learned aspects, is, in this view, guided by its own set of evolved psychological mechanisms.[32] From a 'coevolutionary' viewpoint, Edward O. Wilson describes the inherited regularities which result from evolved mental structures as 'epigenetic rules',

> . . . neurobiological traits that cause us to see the world in a particular way and to learn certain behaviours in preference to other behaviours. The genetically inherited traits are not memes, not units of culture, but rather the propensity to invent and transmit certain kinds of these elements of memory in preference to others.[33]

This approach questions the notion of culture as an independent, self-creating phenomenon, emphasizing the origins of particular cultural forms and seeking to explain patterns in the ways they change. By pointing to the inherited legacy of mental mechanisms that form universal aspects of the human psyche, evolutionary psychology also inevitably focuses on the commonalities that result.

It may seem, though, that the great historical and cultural diversity of social arrangements, belief systems and behavioural patterns undeniably refutes the existence of a common, evolved mentality. The relationships between the generality and particularity of cultural forms and the issues of global diversity and historical change have thus been key interests of evolutionary psychology. The mere existence of cultural variety, of course, explains neither how it came to be nor the parameters within which it has developed. It may be helpful in this context to differentiate among types of culture, as Tooby and Cosmides have done. First, they propose that there is a 'metaculture', the most direct expression of the human psyche's interaction with 'the recurrent structure of the social or non-social world': the kinds of persistent, long-term problems faced by *Homo sapiens* and its predecessors which would generate the most universal elements species-typical behaviour.[34] Second, different forms of 'evoked' cultures emerge from particular interactions with local environments. Third, there is 'reconstructed' or 'adopted' culture, meaning 'representations or regulatory elements that reappear in chains from individual to individual – "culture" in the classic sense'.[35] Here, observers and listeners have an active role in making sense of the culture that they are taught or observe (hence the emphasis on culture being reconstructed or adopted rather than merely 'transmitted'). Evolved psychological mechanisms enable and guide an individual's assembly of a 'private culture' – an 'individually tailored adaptive system' – out of a variety of sources, including the behaviour and attitudes of the surrounding social group; these are the building blocks of group cultures.[36] (One theory of cultural evolution proposes an 'epidemiology of representations' for examining the ways the elements of private cultures, such as ideas, technologies or ways of doing things, spread.)[37] What often appears to be a uniform 'culture' is actually a roiling pattern of constant cultural transmission and reinterpretation among individuals. The more successful particular ideas or behaviours are, the more likely they will be identified as 'culture'; nonetheless, 'there is no natural dividing point' between that which is or is not culture 'along a continuum of something shared between two individuals to something shared through inferential reconstruction by the entire human species'.[38]

Two further points are important. First, the strength of evolved predispositions is variable, deeply affecting some aspects of behaviour while playing little or no role in others. (Debating whether a single 'evolved psychology' affects something called 'culture' misses the point: neither is a monolithic structure.) Second, evolutionary psychology tends toward a functional view of culture as a 'tool for living'.[39] Thus, social life, competing psychological mechanisms and environmental differences are important factors in creating cultural variation. Such a view sees pre-existing culture – in the sense of the accumulated attitudes and practices of a particular group – as an important part of the environment, providing raw material for private cultures, establishing a framework for social interaction, cementing social arrangements, shaping forms of cultural common sense and generating a social 'inertia' which resists (or guides) change. Another aspect of the environment includes, of course, other people, each with his or her own psychological apparatus and interests. The resulting dynamics of these encounters are among the sources of cultural diversity. From this point of view, mental universality and cultural difference are hardly contradictory.[40]

The existence of a universally similar psyche, which provides certain innate interests and tendencies and actively interacts with the surrounding environment, means that cultural dynamics are connected (though not reducible) to individual psychology, and, from the perspective of evolutionary psychology, a set of assumptions emerges: 'social groups will be arenas of conflict and cooperation'; 'the shared features of culture are the outcome of negotiating individuals'; 'where interests conflict, there is no "best solution" or adaptive culture for all'; and power is 'a constant feature of almost every interaction between individuals'.[41] Such a perspective allows – indeed predicts – a pluralistic structuring of cultures:

> Different social contexts will manifest different arrays of individuals, and so different social contexts will tend to have different local or situation-specific 'cultures' (the home or family will have its culture, the unsupervised children of a family will have their characteristic culture, the peer group will have its culture, the male band its culture, the female group its culture, particular friendship groups will have their cultures, etc.).[42]

By this point, we are far from the mistaken view that evolutionary psychology must be deterministic (by ignoring the influence of historical and environmental contingency) or reductive (by viewing culture as simply the product of genes). To the contrary, it sees both culture and interpersonal interaction as fundamental environmental influences shaping individual and social life, and it has a subtle, differentiated view of culture and human relationships. It follows that evidence of cultural diversity, variability and change does not in itself dismiss evolutionary explanations of human mental development, culture or behaviour.

So, evolutionary psychology convincingly argues that the human psyche has been strongly affected by evolution; nonetheless, applying 'selection thinking' to history is not simple. It will, clearly, be more relevant to some aspects of (and questions about) culture and society than others. Moreover, historians often approach their subjects with different aims and at different levels of analysis than evolutionary psychologists. Whereas the latter seek to describe a mental architecture shared across societies and historical time spans, historians (especially cultural historians) tend to emphasize the primacy of cultural specificity. While historians most often focus on 'proximate' causes – the (largely conscious) motivations which move people to act in particular social and historical situations – evolutionary psychologists emphasize 'ultimate' causes of behaviour – the underlying reasons *why* particular kinds of proximate causes have come to exist at all.[43] Although the 'deterministic' tendencies of evolutionary psychology have been overstated, such broad explanations of behaviour remain anathema to many historians. Evolutionary psychologists' efforts to explain behaviour across cultures (or at least to identify recurrent regularities in culture and behaviour) appear to conflict with cultural history, which, hostile to metanarratives, has often celebrated micro-histories and emphasized difference, marginality and particularity. It is probably this divide more than any other that has stoked cultural historians' hostility toward evolutionary methodologies, but whether this puts evolutionary psychology fundamentally at cross-purposes with cultural history depends on one's view of the latter's goals. As has been astutely noted, the historical focus on cultural margins and fragmentation may mean that 'questions concerning the experience of most people have dropped from sight'.[44] Armed with a perspective celebrating the independent power of culture and assuming the predominance of cultural particularity, many cultural historians are reluctant to generalize about human behaviour. Nevertheless, if only to supplement a focus on diversity and change with an appreciation for commonality, continuity and humanity's 'natural competencies', evolutionary psychology could have a constructive influence on cultural history.[45]

VIOLENCE: PSYCHOLOGY, SOCIETY AND CULTURE

Having generally addressed the potential for dialogue and methodological exchange between cultural history and evolutionary psychology, I would like to consider a specific phenomenon about which both disciplines have had a great deal to say: interpersonal violence. Evolutionary psychologists' interest in this topic is perhaps unsurprising, as violence is present in all societies (though at varying rates and with diverse meanings) and has likely accompanied human evolutionary development, influencing survival and access to resources. Thus, it seems initially plausible that some forms of violent behaviour – or, more specifically, the psychological mechanisms which guide them – may have been 'adaptive' (or at least side effects of other adaptations). For their part, historians have always been interested in violence, even if until recently this has largely meant war, empire and conquest; the detailed study of small-scale or individual interpersonal violence has flourished only within the last few decades.[46] Building on earlier quantitative work, historians of violence have increasingly adopted cultural approaches to violence, making it an apt topic for examining the specific opportunities for interdisciplinary exchange between cultural history and evolutionary psychology.

Discussing the evolutionary psychology of interpersonal aggression means considering the work of Martin Daly and Margo Wilson. Their studies of violence are based upon common evolutionary assumptions such as, for instance, the assumption that individuals have 'intricately structured information-processing abilities and self-interests' that cause them to tend toward certain ways of dealing with the social reality they face.[47] Most kinds of violence are seen to grow out of conflicts over particular kinds of resources, which may be material (such as wealth or family property) or non-material (such as honour or status). Every interpersonal relationship involves specific types of conflicts; thus, there is no single evolutionary explanation of 'violence', which is a blanket term covering an extremely wide range of behaviours, each with different causes, forms and consequences. Evolutionary perspectives highlight the need for a differentiated theorization of violence, stressing the discrete psychological mechanisms and social relationships that cause physical aggression: violence between young male acquaintances results from interpersonal tensions distinct from those which contribute to the abuse of children by step-parents.[48] Although the 'cultures' of each kind of violence do differ, culture – at least insofar as it affects behaviour – is less a power unto itself than a combination of evolved psychological mechanisms and social circumstances. This suggests that most violence is not 'pathological' or the consequence of a mental failure, as people posses 'complex psychophysiological machinery that is clearly designed *for* the production and regulation of violence'.[49] Far from denying cross-cultural and historical variation in violence, Daly and Wilson see it as resulting from a mental calculus dependent upon interaction with environmental factors or specific social contexts. Nonetheless, they emphasize the underlying regularities of cultural variation, criticize overemphasis on alleged cultural particularities as 'causes' of violence, question the analytical utility of 'subcultures' of violence and critique theories that treat individuals as passive recipients of cultural messages about violence.

What do these perspectives offer the historian? There are several points of mutual interest, and this is not least because the historiography of violence remains guided by social-historical emphases on analysing violence not only as 'culture' (in the form of representations, narratives and discourses) but also as behaviour. This may have to do with the subject: real violence and the symbolic and imagined cultures which surround it are distinct, but they resist separate analysis. Most obviously, narratives of violence not only help to define and express people's attitudes, they also shape the use of (physical) violence. Shani D'Cruze has succinctly described the relationship among discursive structures, individuals and real experience, noting that 'discourse does not float free of social interaction nor does it hypnotize social actors into conformism any more than "social control" terrorises them into acquiescence. Rather, individuals make situated and tactical identifications with these kinds of literatures.'[50] The narrativization of experience can itself be understood as an evolved human capacity, and in my view evolutionary psychology's insights are useful in explaining the 'tactical' (and other) relationships between people and discourse with regard to a range of phenomena, violence among them. Narratives of violence are highly flexible, but they are not limitlessly so, and there are cross-cultural similarities in the ways that violence is understood, employed and experienced. Our understanding of specific historical narratives of violence would clearly benefit from attention to the means by which they were distributed, the purposes to which they were put and the interests (psychological, social and material) they served. 'Cultures of violence' are not simply arbitrarily accumulated traditions, but are also shaped by particular kinds of social contexts, such as those in which personal security is insufficiently protected.

Consider male violence. Throughout history and across cultures, men have committed an overwhelming proportion of violent acts, and that predominance is even more striking with regard to intrasex violence: men kill other men far more often than women kill other women.[51] The universality of such patterns questions how far 'culture', on its own, can provide a complete understanding of violence. Obviously, those who participate in or witness a violent incident at a particular time and in a certain place perceive it largely in terms of their local cultural understandings of violence, and the specific reasons for and forms of male fighting have varied across place and time. Simply to stay within the framework of Western culture, the diversity of cultures of violence seems self evident when comparing, for example, early-modern Amsterdam, nineteenth-century Greece and late twentieth-century Philadelphia.[52] The cultural notions which have shaped male violence, such as 'gentlemanliness' or 'machismo', have also been subject to change. At the same time, it is difficult to overlook what may be the 'inherent rules' of male fighting and the extent to which diverse cultural conventions may be 'labellings of natural tendencies'.[53] Explaining the cross-cultural recurrence of the connection between men and violence cannot be done simply by reference to culture. Taking a broader view, evolutionary psychologists argue that the patterns of male violence are ultimately rooted in selective processes (across vast stretches of prehistorical time) related to competition for social resources; the result is a male psyche that contributes to intrasex conflict (regardless of its adaptiveness in modern settings). Nonetheless, male-on-male violence is one of the most variable types of physical aggression, suggesting that any psychological mechanisms involved are sensitive to social stimuli such as inequality, threats to personal security, the perceived 'legitimacy' of violence, and the social costs of (or potential punishment for) using violence.[54] Some aspects of violence – fighting styles or preferences for particular weapons – may be culturally arbitrary but nevertheless significantly affect the extent, patterns and lethality of violence. There is, though, no inherent contradiction between the variability of male violence and the claim that it is shaped by universal, evolved predispositions: innate aspects of the psyche create a framework within which variability occurs, generating a wide (though not limitless) variety of proximate causes of violence.

The examination of cultural and social phenomena from a variety of mutually consistent theoretical and causal levels can be a rewarding approach, as a study of the 'culture of honour' in southern America by Richard E. Nisbett and Dov Cohen demonstrates.[55] Crime statistics and attitude surveys point to a distinctive southern culture of violence, early manifestations of which social historians have already examined.[56] Nisbett and Cohen are interested in explaining what has caused southerners to see violence used to defend honour, maintain social order or protect oneself as more legitimate than other Americans. Their compelling analysis is based not only on economic and social factors such as patterns in farming, immigration and settlement but also on individual psychology. Moreover, they rely on evolutionary psychology – particularly those insights into male violence provided by Daly and Wilson: the southern culture of honour is thus seen as one example of a global phenomenon, a product of a particular interaction between innate male psychology and variable economic social relations. The result is multilayered study of violence, an example of how biological and social approaches can generate insights about culture.

In a more directly historical context, Jeffrey Adler has sought to evaluate the utility of evolutionary psychological theories by applying them to patterns in violence in late nineteenth- and early twentieth-century Chicago. In particular, he considers the extent to which such theories can be verified by historical evidence, focusing on the notion of an evolved psyche that compels men (especially young men) to be obsessed with social comparisons, prepared to take extreme risks and devoted to achieving and maintaining status. As this argument goes, men become especially reliant upon a reputation for toughness and the ability to use (or threaten) violence in the absence of other social or economic opportunities. Adler finds this view confirmed by the 'strutting, preening, swaggering, and hypermasculinity' of Chicago's bachelor subculture, and the typical male-on-male homicide in the 1870s arose out of a drunken bar brawl of the type ingrained in the local plebeian lifestyle.[57] Although Chicago experienced dramatic demographic and economic changes between 1875 and 1920, evidence of striking continuities in patterns of violence 'supports the evolutionary psychology perspective': the proportion of all homicides which were committed by men remained constant (hovering around 93 per cent), as did the fact that nearly four out of five homicides involved both a male perpetrator and victim.[58] Yet there were also significant changes, as the homicide rate among young men tripled and the archetypal intermale Chicago homicide was no longer associated with a drunken brawl but rather with a robbery; this meant that 'homicide in Chicago became increasingly impersonal, instrumental, and calculated.'[59] Can evolutionary psychology account for these changes? It seems that, at least in part, it can, as Adler concludes after testing its predictions regarding the influence of inequality, social mobility and risk on patterns in aggression. Moreover, the apparently instrumental cold-bloodedness of early twentieth-century robbery-homicides also involved elements of the same kinds of competitive, status-obsessed machismo apparent in late nineteenth-century brawling.

Nonetheless, Adler remains ambivalent about the utility of evolutionary psychological perspectives on violence. Sometimes he seems to suggest that only continuity in macho, impulsive violence would fit a Darwinian perspective; at other times, though, he highlights evolutionary psychology's emphasis on the potential for change. He concludes that 'the evolutionary psychological model is almost as difficult to disprove as it is to prove' since it would support evidence of both continuity and change.[60] However, evolutionary psychology does not simply predict continuity *or* change in male violence. Instead it posits *reasons for* particular forms of long-term continuity or cross-cultural similarity while at the same time specifying social factors that are likely to encourage certain kinds of change or difference. Thus, its provability does not depend on the mere presence or absence of continuity or change. Had Adler's data pointed in the opposite direction (had, for example, the ratio of male-on-male homicides dramatically declined in the face of increasing social competition among low-skilled men, had decreasing economic opportunities been correlated with reductions in violence, or had increasing risks associated with robbery lowered robbers' willingness to use force) specific evolutionary arguments might have been questioned; however, they were not. While not conclusive proof of the validity of evolutionary psychology (which is not going to be decided by a single case study), Adler's fascinating analysis points to the potential for a useful dialogue between evolutionary psychology and history.

It also, however, emphasizes that evolutionary psychology may be most valuable for historians when integrated with other theoretical approaches. For example, the decline in barroom altercations was partly a result of a successful crackdown by police and employers on saloon culture, changes in patterns of recreation and socio-economic factors which encouraged greater self-control. Such topics have been widely addressed by historians of violence influenced by Norbert Elias, whose sociological theories have played an increasing – although controversial – role in the cultural and social historiography of violence.[61] Interest in his theory of the 'civilizing process' has become more intense with the growing historical consensus that overall rates of interpersonal violence in Europe declined significantly between the late medieval period and the middle of the twentieth century.[62] Increasing abhorrence of physical pain, broadening definitions of 'violence', growing sensitivity to the suffering of others, stricter laws against public fighting and domestic abuse, the growth of state policing and changes in social relationships have become central issues in explaining what happened to violence over several centuries. Investigating these topics requires attention not only to social, cultural and institutional changes but also to individual psychology. Elias's theories were not designed to be incorporated with Darwinian psychology, and their psychological assumptions are partly Freudian. Nonetheless, Elias's view of culture and many of the social and psychological processes on which he focused correspond with those emphasized by proponents of evolutionary psychology. Despite its different view of underlying human psychology (which, in my view, is capable of revision), the theory of the civilizing process may provide a solid foundation for a cultural and social history of violence which can incorporate evolutionary perspectives.

Elias strongly emphasized the importance of individual psychology as a cultural force, seeing it as inseparable from both social development and biology. Opposed to a view of 'society' as a unified, disembodied abstraction, he conceived it as a dynamic, historically specific network of individuals (a 'figuration'). From this perspective, as Pieter Spierenburg has argued, 'the traditional opposition of "individual vs. society" is a false opposition. Society consists of individuals; it is the name we give to the network (or figuration) of all social relationships. Hence, society cannot "do" things (like making rules; people make rules)'.[63] This view has parallels in evolutionary psychology's emphasis on 'arrays of individuals' in generating culture.[64] A further point of contact involves human nature. In Elias's view, each individual is driven by an innate set of 'affects' (emotions, urges) which interact with psychological self-control mechanisms. The specific balance among these mental elements also depends upon the individual's socialization as well as conditions in the current social environment. The psyche is shaped by society, with self-control being developed through education and forms of social pressure, but 'society' itself emerges from dynamic interactions among individuals with built-in psychological instincts. Across the historical period that Elias examined, social developments – in general – led to more self-control, with individual behaviour being regulated 'in an increasingly differentiated, more even and more stable manner'; the balance between different psychological elements – between, in Elias's terms, 'drives' and 'controlling agencies' – is affected by the social environment, particularly relations with others.[65] (As Nisbett and Cohen find, the 'psyche' may indeed be moulded by social development: when provoked, the southern men in their study had stronger hormonal responses related to aggression than did northerners.)[66] Nonetheless, the extent to which psychology can be affected by social reality (and culture) varies depending on which aspect of life is being considered. As Elias argued, not all needs 'are replaceable or malleable to the same extent':

> And this raises the question of the limit of the transformability of the human personality. Without doubt, it is bound to certain regularities that may be called 'natural'. The historical process modifies it within these limits. The degree to which human life and behaviour can be moulded by historical processes remains to be determined in detail. At any rate, all this shows once again how natural and historical processes interact almost inseparably.[67]

Such a view is compatible with evolutionary psychological theory, which recognizes that some domains of human behaviour may be more susceptible to social change than others: there is a difference between 'open' and 'closed' behavioural programmes.[68]

Furthermore, in line with evolutionary psychology Elias sees 'power' neither as a disembodied force nor as the possession only of particular social groups but rather as a feature of all human relationships.[69] The nature of power (and its imbalances) depends on a variety of circumstances; however, even 'subordinate' individuals and groups are not entirely powerless. Likewise, the human psyche is seen as having built-in mechanisms for the use – and control – of violence: violence, in most cases, is not a symptom of individual psychological pathology. 'Culture' is an important element of change, but its patterns are dependent upon the shape of social relationships among individuals. From a perspective influenced by Elias, the 'higher levels of aggression which are characteristic of relationships within lower working-class communities' can only be explained with reference to the particular nature of the social figuration; the relative lack of 'civilizing' pressures from above, the lower degree of state protection and the lack of access to (material and immaterial) resources encourage 'their willingness and – at least in some contexts and on the part of some males – also their desire to engage in acts of physical aggression'.[70] The result may indeed be a distinctive 'culture' of violence; however, to what extent is culture an independent causal factor when compared with the weight of social forces which (assuming a psyche with particular mechanisms designed to seek out security or status) generate a particular dynamic of violence? As Daly and Wilson have noted:

> . . . if we think we can explain why poor young men behave violently in terms of the 'transmission' of 'values' within a 'subculture', then we are unlikely to seek more utilitarian explanations. In fact, poor young men with dismal prospects for the future have *good reason* to escalate their tactics of social competition and become violent.[71]

Elias's emphasis on social dynamics such as growing interdependence and increasing state monopolization of violence (making individual self-defence and personal vengeance less necessary) is applicable to cultural change, and these phenomena have also been central to evolutionary psychological commentary on reducing violence.[72]

Without doubt, 'culture' was important to historical shifts in violence, representing a means through which social expectations were inculcated, self-control was regulated, rights to use violence were negotiated, sympathies were encouraged and state and social power was expressed. In many societies, reductions in violence have been dependent upon historical changes that have made the personal use of physical force both less necessary and more damaging to one's status – trends involving interactions among society, culture and individual psychology. As I hope to have shown, evolutionary psychology has at least the potential to be integrated with one of the prominent theoretical models applied to the cultural and social history of interpersonal aggression, providing a useful framework for explaining cross-cultural similarities and cultural variations and helping to analyse the dynamics of continuity and change. However, the role of evolutionary psychology needs to be evaluated subtly. There is, for example, no reason to assume that changes in human aggression will always follow a strictly 'adaptive' script, and, as Peter J. Richerson and Robert Boyd have suggested, cultural institutions such as religions may be 'semi-independent' forces in shaping behaviour.[73] Of course, Darwinist principles may be less applicable to some aspects of cultural history than others, and human behaviour remains far from a 'theory of everything'. However, those principles can provoke new lines of questioning such as those related to the connections between social phenomena and the human life cycle. There are, for instance, cross-culturally valid, age-related patterns in violence (both as perpetrator and as victim), and evolutionary psychology presents a framework for explaining these little-explored trends.[74]

CONCLUSION

Were I, following Mandler, to make my own 'modest proposal', it would be that in developing a 'theory of meaning' cultural historians should be guided not only by sociology but also by 'biological' viewpoints on thought and behaviour. Culture has an identifiable location within the minds of individuals and these minds have been subject to evolutionary pressures likely to influence the ways that culture is formed, experienced and altered. Using cultural history to undermine any variety of 'universalising hubris' – to the extent that it is real – may be a worthwhile goal; however, evolutionary perspectives may usefully confront the particularizing hubris of some forms of cultural studies. Evolutionary psychology has provided insightful analyses of as fundamentally 'cultural' a phenomenon as literature, so what sensible reason is there to reject out of hand its applicability to understanding other areas of cultural and social life?[75] Concerns about disciplinary sovereignty are misplaced: historians have long been able to make use of economic methods without becoming economists, have adopted anthropological perspectives without turning into anthropologists and, despite the massive influx of theoretical influences from literature and linguistics, have remained distinct from those fields too.

I have used the example of interpersonal violence to suggest that it is often necessary to go beyond 'culture' to explain the cultural history of a particular phenomenon. Anchoring culture in 'society' remains important, and most historians need no reminder to do so. In some ways, however, the new 'social turn' remains a half-measure, ignoring a considerable body of natural science commentary on the location, purpose and dynamics of culture. Rather than being incommensurable with the interests of historians, evolutionary psychology addresses issues of great relevance for history, including the origin of 'historical consciousness' itself.[76] Those areas of history that have overlapped most with the central concerns and topics of evolutionary psychology, such as childhood, family, sex, nutrition, physical health and violence and aggression, would have the most to gain. If we are interested in 'identity', 'desire' and 'meaning', we need to understand the mental processes through which they are formed. To have a full understanding of 'power', we need to understand why people are interested in having it and whether there are enduring or global patterns in the ways they pursue it. In many cases (though probably not all), evolutionary psychology is a promising source from which to borrow theoretical and methodological perspectives. As Mandler rightly argues, we should be 'ranging more widely among the possible intellectual frameworks and choosing those appropriate to our problematic and our evidence, rather than deferring automatically to those that other people have used (often for different reasons and with different motives)'.[77] However, neither should we automatically shun those intellectual frameworks which other historians have avoided (for a variety of reasons and motives). As David Gary Shaw has pointed out, 'the gap between science and history is less than historians instinctively believe'; given the 'paradigm shift' in which science has 'gone historical', there is an opportunity to work toward 'a unification of knowledge, in which evolutionary science and history border on each other'.[78] Whether historians are willing to pursue such a goal is another question. Eric Hobsbawm has observed that 'for the first time, we have an adequate framework for a genuinely global history, and one restored to its proper central place, neither within the humanities nor the natural and mathematical sciences, nor separated from them, but essential to both.'[79] I agree. Once evolutionary biology is seen not as a machine for generating universal, reductionist and deterministic laws but rather as a subtle framework for analysing the legacy of an evolutionary past with which individuals, societies and cultures continue to contend, the perceived chasm between the humanities and natural sciences – by no means new – starts to seem less daunting.

NOTES

1. Peter Mandler, 'The Problem with Cultural History', *Cultural and Social History*, 1 (2004): 94–117; Carla Hesse, 'The New Empiricism', *Cultural and Social History*, 1 (2004): 201–7; Colin Jones, 'Peter Mandler's "Problem with Cultural History", or, Is Playtime Over?', *Cultural and Social History*, 1 (2004): 209–15; Carol Watts, 'Thinking about the X Factor, or, What's the Cultural History of Cultural History', *Cultural and Social History*, 1 (2004): 217–24; Peter Mandler, 'Problems in Cultural History: A Reply', *Cultural and Social History*, 1 (2004): 326–32.

2. See a special issue of the *Journal of Social History*, especially Peter N. Stearns, 'Social History Present and Future', *Journal of Social History*, 37 (2003): 9–19 and Paula S. Fass, 'Cultural History/Social History: Some Reflections on a Continuing Dialogue', *Journal of Social History*, 37 (2003): 39–46.

3. Fass, 'Cultural History/Social History', p. 39.

4. Mandler, 'Problem', pp. 116–17.

5. Hesse, 'New Empiricism', p. 207.

6. David Stack, *The First Darwinian Left: Socialism and Darwinism 1859–1914* (Cheltenham, 2003), p. 4.

7. Peter Burke, *What is Cultural History?* (Cambridge, 2004).

8. W.G. Runciman, 'Culture Does Evolve', *History and Theory*, 44, no. 1 (2005) pp. 1-13; Martin Stuart-Fox, 'Evolutionary Theory of History', *History and Theory*, 38, no. 4 (1999) pp. 33-51; Susan Blackmore, *The Meme Machine* (Oxford, 1999).

9. On gene-culture coevolution see C.L. Lumsden and E.O. Wilson, *Genes, Mind and Culture: The Coevolutionary Process* (Cambridge, 1981). The 'leash' image is employed in E.O. Wilson, *On Human Nature* (Cambridge, 1979), p. 167 and 'elastic' in Jerome H. Barkow, 'The Elastic Between Genes and Culture', *Ethology and Sociobiology*, 10 (1989): 111–29.

10. Laura L. Betzig, *Despotism and Differential Reproduction: A Darwinian View of History* (Hawthorne, 1986); Martin Daly and Margo Wilson, *Homicide* (Hawthorne, 1988); Malcolm Smith (ed.), *Human Biology and History* (London, 2002).

11. Mark V. Flinn, 'Culture and the Evolution of Social Learning', *Evolution and Human Behavior*, 18 (1997): 45.

12. With regard to violence see, for example, Peter Gay, *The Cultivation of Hatred. The Bourgeois Experience, Victoria to Freud, vol. 2* (New York, 1993); V.A.C. Gatrell, *The Hanging Tree: Execution and the English People, 1770–1868* (Oxford, 1994).

13. An excellent overview is provided by Ullica Segerstråle, *Defenders of the Truth: The Battle for Science in the Sociobiology Debate and Beyond* (Oxford, 2000).

14. Leda Cosmides and John Tooby, Evolutionary Psychology: A Primer, http://www.psych.ucsb.edu/research/cep/primer.html, accessed 20 June 2006.

15. Dan Sperber, *Explaining Culture: A Naturalistic Approach* (Oxford, 1996), p. 153. Donald E. Brown, 'Human Nature and History', *History and Theory*, 38 (1999), p. 144.

16. Daly and Wilson, *Homicide*, pp. 137–61.

17. Cosmides and Tooby, 'Primer'.

18. John Tooby and Leda Cosmides, 'Evolutionary Psychology and the Generation of Culture, Part I: Theoretical Considerations', *Ethology and Sociobiology*, 10 (1989), p. 34. John Tooby and Leda Cosmides, 'The Past Explains the Present: Emotional Adaptations and the Structure of Ancestral Environments', *Ethology and Sociobiology*, 11 (1990), pp. 375–424.

19. Tooby and Cosmides, 'Generation of Culture', pp. 37–8. Emphasis in original.

20. See Paul W. Sherman and Hudson Kern Reeve, 'Forward and Backward: Alternative Approaches to Studying Human Social Evolution' in Laura Betzig (ed.), *Human Nature: A Critical Reader* (Oxford, 1997), pp. 147–58; Brown, 'Human Nature', p. 139; Daly and Wilson, *Homicide*, p. 7.

21. For example, Peter C. Grosvenor, 'Evolutionary Psychology and the Intellectual Left', *Perspectives in Biology and Medicine*, 45 (2002), pp. 433–48. See also, Segerstråle, *Defenders of the Truth*, pp. 391–6.

22. Richard Dawkins, *The Extended Phenotype: The Long Reach of the Gene* (Oxford, 1999), pp. 9–29.

23. See, for example, Steven Pinker, *The Blank Slate: The Modern Denial of Human Nature* (London, 2002), pp. 30–58.

24. For example, Daly and Wilson, *Homicide*, pp. 8–9, 275–91, 296–7.

25. Randy Thornhill and Craig T. Palmer, *A Natural History of Rape: Biological Bases of Sexual Coercion* (Cambridge, 2000), pp. 20, 153.

26. Cosmides and Tooby, 'Primer'. Emphasis in original.

27. Segerstråle, *Defenders of the Truth*, pp. 141–7.

28. Burke, *Cultural History*, p. 3; Tony Bennett, 'Culture' in Tony Bennett, Lawrence Grossberg and Meaghan Morris (eds), *New Keywords: A Revised Vocabulary of Culture and Society* (Oxford, 2005), pp. 63–9; Stearns, 'Social History', p. 10; Mandler, 'Problem', p. 94; Neville Kirk, 'History, Language, Ideas and Post-Modernism: A Materialist View', *Social History*, 19 (1994): 221–40.

29. Leda Cosmides, John Tooby and Jerome H. Barkow, 'Introduction: Evolutionary Psychology and Conceptual Integration' in Jerome H. Barkow, Leda Cosmides and John Tooby (eds), *The Adapted Mind: Evolutionary Psychology and the Generation of Culture* (Oxford, 1992), p. 3.

30. Tooby and Cosmides, 'Generation of Culture', p. 45.

31. Flinn, 'Social Learning', p. 30.

32. Steven Pinker, *The Language Instinct* (New York, 1995).

33. Edward O. Wilson, *Consilience: The Unity of Knowledge* (New York, 1998), p. 163.

34. John Tooby and Leda Cosmides, 'The Psychological Foundations of Culture' in Jerome H. Barkow, Leda Cosmides and John Tooby (eds), *The Adapted Mind: Evolutionary Psychology and the Generation of Culture* (Oxford, 1992), pp. 117–18.

35. Tooby and Cosmides, 'Psychological Foundations', p. 118.

36. Tooby and Cosmides, 'Generation of Culture', p. 44.

37. Sperber, *Explaining Culture*, pp. 1–2.

38. Tooby and Cosmides, 'Psychological Foundations', p. 120.

39. Pinker, *Blank Slate*, p. 66; Tooby and Cosmides, 'Generation of Culture', p. 32.

40. Tooby and Cosmides, 'Psychological Foundations', p. 45. Jerome H. Barkow, *Darwin, Sex and Status: Biological Approaches to Mind and Culture* (Toronto, 1989), pp. 213–27.

41. Tooby and Cosmides, 'Generation of Culture', p. 45.

42. Tooby and Cosmides, 'Generation of Culture', p. 45.

43. Pinker, *Blank Slate*, p. 54; Thornhill and Palmer, *Natural History*, pp. 3–5; Daly and Wilson, *Homicide*, pp. 6–9.

44. Fass, 'Cultural History/Social History', pp. 42, 45.

45. Cosmides and Tooby, 'Primer'.

46. For a summary in the British context, see J. Carter Wood, 'Criminal Violence in Modern Britain', *History Compass* 4 (2006): 77–90. DOI: 10.1111/j.1478-0542.2005.00200.x.

47. Martin Daly and Margo Wilson, 'Crime and Conflict: Homicide in Evolutionary Psychological Perspective', *Crime and Justice,* 22 (1997): p. 52.

48. Margo Wilson and Martin Daly, 'Competitiveness, Risk Taking, and Violence: The Young Male Syndrome', *Ethology and Sociobiology,* 6 (1985): 59–73; Martin Daly and Margo Wilson, *The Truth About Cinderella: A Darwinian View of Parental Love* (London, 1998).

49. Daly and Wilson, 'Crime and Conflict', p. 57. Emphasis in original.

50. Shani D'Cruze, 'Unguarded Passions: Violence, History and the Everyday' in Shani D'Cruze (ed.), *Everyday Violence in Britain, 1850–1950* (Harlow, 2000), p. 15.

51. '*The difference between the sexes is immense, and it is universal.* There is no known human society in which the level of lethal violence among women even begins to approach that among men.' Daly and Wilson, *Homicide*, p. 146. Emphasis in original.

52. Pieter Spierenburg, 'Knife Fighting and Popular Codes of Honor in Early Modern Amsterdam' in Pieter Spierenburg (ed.), *Men and Violence: Gender, Honor, and Rituals in Modern Europe and America* (Columbus, 1998), pp. 103–27; Thomas W. Gallant, *Experiencing Dominion: Culture, Identity and Power in the British Mediterranean* (Notre Dame, 2002), pp. 117–47; Elijah Anderson, *The Code of the Street: Violence, Decency and the Moral Life of the Inner City* (New York, 1999), p. 34.

53. Robin Fox, 'The Inherent Rules of Violence' in Peter Collett (ed.), *Social Rules and Social Behavior* (Oxford, 1977), p. 133.

54. Daly and Wilson, *Homicide*, pp. 123–61, 284–6.

55. Richard E. Nisbett and Dov Cohen, *Culture of Honor: The Psychology of Violence in the South* (Oxford, 1996).

56. Elliott J. Gorn, '"Gouge and Bite, Pull Hair and Scratch": The Social Significance of Fighting in the Southern Backcountry', *American Historical Review*, 90 (1985): 18–43; Kenneth S. Greenberg, 'The Nose, the Lie and the Duel in the Antebellum South', *American Historical Review*, 95 (1990), pp. 57–74.

57. Jeffrey S. Adler, '"On the Border of Snakeland": Evolutionary Psychology and Plebeian Violence in Industrial Chicago, 1875–1920', *Journal of Social History*, 36 (2003): 542.

58. Adler, 'Snakeland', p. 544.

59. Adler, 'Snakeland', p. 548.

60. Adler, 'Snakeland', p. 553.

61. See Pieter Spierenburg, 'Violence and the Civilizing Process: Does It Work?' *Crime, Histoire et Sociétés / Crime, History and Societies*, 5 (2001), pp. 87–105 and Gerd Schwerhoff, 'Criminalized Violence and the Process of Civilization: A Reappraisal', *Crime, Histoire et Sociétés / Crime, History and Societies*, 6 (2002), pp. 103–26. See also E. A. Johnson and Eric H. Monkkonen (eds), *The Civilization of Crime: Violent Crime in Town and Country since the Middle Ages* (Chicago, 1996) and J. Carter Wood, *Violence and Crime in Nineteenth-century England: The Shadow of Our Refinement* (London, 2004).

62. Manuel Eisner, 'Modernization, Self-Control and Lethal Violence: The Long-term Dynamics of European Homicide Rates in Theoretical Perspective', *British Journal of Criminology*, 41 (2001): 618–38.

63. Pieter Spierenburg, 'Elias and the History of Crime and Criminal Justice: A Brief Evaluation', *IAHCCJ Bulletin*, 20 (1995): 19.

64. Tooby and Cosmides, 'Generation of Culture', p. 45.

65. Norbert Elias, *The Civilizing Process: The History of Manners and State Formation and Civilization* (Oxford, 1994), pp. 445, 487.

66. Nisbett and Cohen, *Culture of Honor*, pp. 41–55.

67. 'The formation of feelings of shame and revulsion and advances in the threshold of delicacy are both at once natural and historical processes. These forms of feeling are manifestations of human nature under specific social conditions, and they react in their turn on the sociohistorical process as one of its elements.' Both quotes from Elias, *Civilizing Process*, p. 131.

68. Tooby and Cosmides, 'Psychological Foundations', p. 46.

69. Pieter Spierenburg, 'Punishment, Power, and History: Foucault and Elias', *Social Science History*, 28 (2004): pp. 607–36.

70. Eric Dunning, Patrick Murphy and Ivan Waddington, 'Violence in the British Civilising Process', University of Leicester Discussion Papers in Sociology, no. S92/2 (1992), pp. 39–40.

71. Daly and Wilson, *Homicide*, p. 287. Emphasis in original.

72. See, for example, Pinker, *Blank Slate*, pp. 320–1, 329–36; Daly and Wilson, *Homicide*, pp. 221–51.

73. Peter J. Richerson and Robert Boyd, 'The Role of Evolved Predispositions in Cultural Evolution', *Ethology and Sociobiology*, 10 (1989): 195–219.

74. Daly and Wilson, *Homicide*, pp. 168–74, 73–93; Thornhill and Palmer, *Natural History*, pp. 70–3, 89–96.

75. Robert Storey, *Mimesis and the Human Animal: On the Biogenetic Foundations of Literary Representation* (Evanston, 1996); H. Porter Abbott, 'The Evolutionary Origins of the Storied Mind: Modelling the Prehistory of Narrative Consciousness and Its Discontents', *Narrative* 8 (2000): 247–56; Jonathan Gottschall and David Sloan Wilson (eds), *The Literary Animal: Evolution and the Nature of Narrative* (Evanston, 2005).

76. Donald E. Brown, *Hierarchy, History, and Human Nature: The Social Origins of Historical Consciousness* (Tucson, 1988).

77. Mandler, 'Problem', p. 96.

78. David Gary Shaw, 'The Return of Science', *History and Theory*, 38 no.4 (1999), p. 4.

79. Eric Hobsbawm, *Interesting Times: A Twentieth-Century Life* (London, 2002), p. 297.

BREAKING MODERNITY'S SPELL – MAGIC AND MODERN HISTORY

Karl Bell
University of East Anglia

Keywords: historiography, magic, modernization, continuity, transformation

Until very recently magic had been consigned to a footnote in modern history. Historiographically fingers of blame can be pointed in various directions, including nineteenth-century folklorists and the sociologist Max Weber. Yet ultimately responsibility for this lies within the academic historical profession, especially with the impact of Keith Thomas's monumental *Religion and the Decline of Magic*. While breaking new ground, this seminal work cast such a shadow over subsequent research that we still naturally articulate our thoughts in relation to it. Thomas's fusion of intellectual, social and cultural history, his innovative use of social anthropology, the wide-ranging exploration of magical healing, witchcraft, astrology, ghosts and fairies, and his multi-causal explanation for the decline of magic seemed, for a generation, to offer the final word on the topic. While it has been subsequently augmented and updated, most consciously in Barry, Hester and Roberts's critical homage, *Witchcraft in Early Modern Europe: Studies in Culture and Belief*, Thomas's comprehensive analysis of the decline of magical mentalities seemingly robbed the subject of a place in modern history.[1]

This view has gradually been challenged in the last decade. This article will briefly explore the range of ways in which historians are undermining Thomas's thesis of decline, pursuing arguments for both the continuation and transformation of magic in the modern period.

Prior to the mid-1990s most studies of witchcraft and magic had been content to conclude with a few anachronistic examples of incidences that spilled beyond the legalistic bounds of the 1736 Witchcraft Act. This provided a clear marker with which to signal the end of (elite) beliefs and, Blecourt notes, student interest.[2] Thereafter magical mentalities were dismissively associated with uneducated rural dwellers. If there was discontent with the view that magic's demise around the late eighteenth century neatly conformed to the arbitrary dates associated with the beginning of the modern period, it remained muted. Historians seem to have taken some time to

Address for correspondence: Karl Bell, School of History, University of East Anglia, Norwich, Norfolk, NR4 7TJ. E-mail: karlrubikon@aol.com

summon the courage to investigate an era that was defined by assumptions that denied or dispelled the need for magic, of elite rationalism, scepticism and encroaching state intervention on the one hand and popular disenchantment and working-class cooperative efforts on the other.

In his 1996 *Instruments of Darkness,* James Sharpe sketched out a range of ways forward. He suggested that nineteenth-century folklorists could provide the written documentation that historians venturing into a new field would instinctively seek. Sensing a trend that others would subsequently cement, Sharpe's ideas focused on the transformation of magical beliefs and witchcraft tropes as much as their continuity. The shift from the malevolent to the comical in references to witchcraft in eighteenth-century theatre, the recategorization of magic and the supernatural in Gothic literature, and the propagation of witch iconography in Victorian children's fiction all suggested magic's transition from a fearful reality to an imaginative form of entertainment. Concurrently, the blurring of natural magic, science and medicine in the early Victorian appeal of mesmerism and, later in the century, the refashioning of the occult in spiritualism allowed for the reality of magic in the period. Cultural and intellectual trends such as Romanticism offered another potential avenue of research. However, Sharpe was reluctant to take the leap himself, stating that 'a book waits to be written (fortunately another book than this one) on the extent, content and functions of . . . nineteenth century beliefs.'[3]

It was Owen Davies who took up the gauntlet thrown down by Sharpe and who almost single-handedly advanced the field. The paucity of research on magic in modern England was revealed when Marijke Gijswijt-Hofstra came to write about it in the *History of Witchcraft and Magic in Europe: The Eighteenth and Nineteenth Centuries.* Her analysis was based almost solely on Davies's PhD thesis, 'The Decline of Popular Belief in Witchcraft and Magic' (1995) and articles stemming from it, noting 'Davies's research into witchcraft in England and Wales is so far the only work that covers the whole of the eighteenth and nineteenth centuries'.[4]

Davies's work crystallized in 1999 with *Witchcraft, Magic and Culture 1736-1951.* His broad geographical survey of England and Wales emphasized continuity rather than decline and, certainly in terms of magic and popular literature, hinted at transformation. Davies's aim was not to use magic and witchcraft as a means of constructing nineteenth century micro-histories of socio-economic or gender relations, as had been done in the early modern period. The strength of his work lay in revealing the multifarious ways in which magic could be studied in the modern period. Unlike Thomas, he focused more consistently on popular beliefs than those of the elite, examining them through various forms of popular literature, folklore and acts of mob justice. The sheer amount of empirical data gathered naturally made one question how historians had missed or blinded themselves to such a large body of evidence. In doing so Davies broke new ground that Thomas's decline thesis had effectively denied. However, even Davies's thesis still operated within the decline paradigm that Thomas had imposed, offering new explanations and pushing the date of witchcraft's decline into the twentieth century.[5] His distinction was to remind us that magical beliefs were not bound together as a unified whole, at least in the mind of their users (contemporary critics tended to lump them together to emphasize the weight of superstition that still enslaved people's minds).[6] Davies clearly shows that while some manifestations declined, others, such as fortune telling, continued and adapted. Considering the scope of topics and the breadth of history covered, it is a remarkably lucid and concise text, undoubtedly destined to become a classic for all subsequent investigation of modern magic.

The question that naturally arises if we challenge the decline thesis is that of where did magic go? The diverse arguments suggested by a recent cluster of books do not amount to a single oppositional thesis, yet they hint at promising ways forward. As detected by Sharpe and Davies, they point not towards a decline, nor unchanged continuation, but towards transformation.

Terry Castle, exploring supernatural beliefs as opposed to specifically magical ones (Thomas felt inclined to include ghosts in his magical world view), demonstrates how the spectral was internalized, how emphasis on romantic sensitivity and individualism led to a developing 'sense of the ghostliness of other people'. Concurrently, new scientific attitudes, the break up of traditional communities and challenges to religious orthodoxy created a more mechanistic view of ghosts as products of the mind. This assault on spirits arose in the seventeenth centuries with the likes of Hobbes, Descartes and Spinoza, and was perpetuated into the nineteenth century by works such as John Ferriar's *An Essay Towards a Theory of Apparitions* (1813) and David Brewster's *Letters on Natural Magic* (1832). Castle's psychoanalytical position finds resonance with these nineteenth-century works that sought to dispel the idea of magic and ghosts as figments of the imagination or a disturbed mind, the difference being that Castle offers this as explaining a transforming mentality while contemporary commentators use it to debunk superstitious beliefs.

Adopting a Freudian approach, Castle notes how ghosts, as products of the unconscious, preserved 'a vestigial magic force and a terrifying, irrational persistence in the life of the mind'.[7] Magic did not decline according to Castle, but relocated itself within 'the new empire of subjectivity'. The rationalizing writers of the early nineteenth century could not banish spirit beliefs or a sense of forces beyond the material world but merely transformed them from metaphysics into psychology with the result that imagination and even thought became demonized. If Castle's intriguing blend of literature, culture and psychology has one weakness, it is to makes us question how much time the average cotton-mill worker or coal miner could spend in such mental self-absorption. Even narrower than a social elite, the subject implied by Castle's thesis largely seems to be a fey dreamer given to reverie, a cultural construction of Gothic romanticism.

In a wholly different vein, Maureen Perkins explores magic in the context of what she calls the 'temporal politics' of the period. She demonstrates how magical prediction was co-opted by factory owners and imperial administrators through time management and planning in the nineteenth century, stating: 'Weber's concept of rationalisation, referring to the rise of a culture of planning, is, in fact, a form of secular prediction'.[8] Magic was embroiled in the conflict over perceptions of time. The middle-class promotion of progress through punctuality and industriousness, aided by eighteenth-century improvements in horology, was undermined by the supposed fatalism promoted by superstition. As a case study Perkins explores the Society for the Suppression of Vice's struggle against astrologers. The defining of both superstition and progress as hegemonic vehicles to ensure the working class subscribed to the era's self-improving agenda, superstition being whatever did not conform to bourgeois work ethics, demonstrates how those possessing power constructed and manipulated these polar opposites in the struggle against popular custom. Despite these efforts, Perkins shows how the popular belief in certain individuals to predict the future remained resilient, resurfacing in nineteenth-century spiritualism and even in today's more tawdry magazine astrology.

Perkins's approach firmly embeds magic within the socio-cultural dialogues and conflicts of the period. Sharing Castle's shift towards psychology, Perkins demonstrates how the popular literary genre of dream-prediction manuals was appropriated at the end of the century by psychoanalysis. Freud changed dreams from a popular method of divining the future to a means of understanding the past. If, Perkins argues, magical prediction was condemned as a political act (in the broad sense of power relations), then we are led to the consideration of 'the construction of scientific certainties as "local knowledges" whose universal claims must each be negotiated.'[9] The study of magic therefore impacts with disproportionate force upon our assumptions about modernity and its epistemological underpinnings. While she never explicitly develops the argument, the politicized nature of Perkins's work suggests that we consider magic mentalities and their varied manifestations in terms of counter-hegemonic stances, an extension, perhaps, of the customary resistance examined by E.P. Thompson and John Rule.[10]

Davies and de Blécourt's most recent work, *Witchcraft Continued* (2004), also suggests a certain amount of readjustment in thinking about witchcraft in Britain and Europe in the nineteenth century. They note that 'far from constituting a monolithic, stable entity, witchcraft was subject to adaptation and alteration'. They argue for a view of fluctuation rather than decline, hinting at the transformation of the witch from someone 'notorious throughout whole villages to being more private personal evil-doers', or even depersonalized to the extent that cunning folk or white witches offered generic counter-magic measures rather than providing the means to identify the individual responsible.[11]

Pamela Thurschwell has shown how magical mentalities were applied in the *fin de siècle* to technologies such as the telegraph and telephone. Contemporary debates about telepathy, the nature of modern technology and their reflection in literary works of the period are used to explore the 'occult reformulations of community and communication'. In this she finds resonance with reconfigured forms of magic noted by Perkins, notably the mid-late nineteenth-century appeal of spirit mediums and the repackaging of the magical in pseudo-scientific guises. Thurschwell describes magical thinking as 'the belief that thoughts and desires can directly transfer themselves to, and transform, the material world, other people, the future', and like technology, telepathy and contact with the dead, magical thinking collapsed distances between minds.[12] Both spirit mediums and telephones allowed previously unimagined communication with disembodied voices. Thurschwell implies that the validity of the latter helped prop up the possibility of the former. Her synthesis of literature, technology, psychical research and the development of psychoanalysis pull us away from popular magic while showing how certain aspects of it were assimilated into 'occult' thinking, the distinction largely implying, in this context, a class divide. In exploring the fusion of these discourses, Thurschwell believes a new sense of the permeability and suggestibility of the individual mind and body was created, a mentality highlighted by her exploration of the hypnotising villain as a staple character in *fin de siècle* horror and fantasy literature. Yet such a view, dressed in the language of psychology and science, in essence harked back to the mentality of those who believed in the intrusive and controlling power of witchcraft. It echoes with the magical 'laws' of contagion and continuing effect sketched out by the likes of Fraser and Mauss.[13]

In terms of transformation in the modern period, interest in the relation between witchcraft and modernity has become a popular area of recent anthropological study. Things have moved on from Evans-Pritchard. Several recent anthropological studies of witchcraft in post-colonial Africa offer ideas to modern historians about the function of magical concepts with regard to urbanization, capitalist development, and the rise of new political and social power structures. Jean and John Comaroff have explored 'occult economies', where witchcraft and other magical phenomena gain ground when access to wealth and opportunities for the poorer sections of society appear unattainable.[14] Peter Geschiere has analysed the flexibility and ambivalence of witchcraft discourses in postcolonial Cameroon. He demonstrates how, in severing itself from its connections with the village and kinship order, witchcraft has been able to become a central aspect of the discourse of modernity. It is used by the middle class and elite to describe power relations with regard to access and control of modern consumer goods, and to forge new identities in opposition to their rural origins. Witchcraft is, he states, 'both a resource for the powerful and also a weapon for the weak against new inequalities.'[15] Geschiere's work has received some criticism, especially that his concept of witchcraft is used so broadly and with such variation as to threaten the basic meaning of the term. However, as with Perkins and Thurschwell, Geschiere offers teasing possibilities as to how magical thinking was or can be applied to the modern period. It has been noted that recent cultural anthropology has been 'obsessed with defining modernity, its pluralities and contradictions, its limitations'.[16] Even if we feel the gap between post-colonial Cameroon and Victorian Britain is too wide, its social, cultural and economic idiosyncrasies too disparate to adapt, perhaps in light of the above research historians should at least join anthropologists in rigorously re-evaluating their concept of modernity.

While these very different works may seem to offer only the thinnest of threads, they do at least suggest that historians have been a little too brusque in arguing for decline. Tentative grounds may yet exist for an alternative to Thomas's thesis based on transformation. Part of my current research attempts to test the validity of this approach. As yet, a transformation thesis pulls in seemingly contradictory directions. On the one hand we have the internalization of magical mentalities hinted at by Castle and the battle for modes of thinking implicit in Perkins. On the other, we find evidence of what might be described as the exposure of magical beliefs, and certainly their tropes, through commercialization and changing forms of entertainment.

These latter developments took a myriad of expressions. Astrology had long been a commercial venture but practitioners' use of handbills and, later, newspaper advertisements to promote their services was given an unprecedented boost by reduced costs following the development of the steam press in the 1810s. London astrologers effectively formed a mutual aid society from the 1820s to the 1850s, mimicking the popular mode of working class organization prior to the rise of large trade unions.[17] In early nineteenth-century English provincial newspapers one finds the promotion of 'magical' folk remedy cures alongside the latest patent medicines with no apparent sense of contradiction. Simultaneously there was the increase from the late eighteenth century in the popularity of public conjurors and the rise of the stage magician, aided by the development of the music hall in the second half of the nineteenth century. Highly popular magic shows by the likes of the 'Wizard of the North' embodied the age with their fusion of commercial entertainment, science and illusion. From the Cock Lane Ghost of 1762, supernatural hoaxes also peddled this blend of the supernatural and the theatrical, thriving in the cultural space between credible belief and thrilling amusement. Technological development aided this, most notably the phantasmagoria displays that arrived in London from Paris in 1801.[18] Popular literature certainly kept images such as witches and magical ideas alive, even if they no longer maintained the immediate fear they had once possessed, their power emptying out into entertaining literary tropes. If, as Stuart Hall has argued, 'everything is destined to be speeded up, dissolved, displaced, transformed, reshaped' by modernity then it seems we must not exclude magic.[19] While the contradictory tension between the ideas of magical survival and transformation are difficult to reconcile within a single framework, even when we accept Davies's position that not all forms of magic changed at the same time in the same way, both have challenging consequences for our perception of modernity. Exploring magic as a survival from an earlier age runs contrary to Weberian theories of progressive rationalism and disenchantment. The obvious extent of that survival also seems to undermine the marginalization implicit in the use of the word. The transformation of magic is less blatantly defiant, subtly entwining itself into some of the very features that have been used to define modernity, such as communication technologies, developing literacy, and the rise of mass entertainment and the consumer.[20] As a result current accounts of re-enchantment, such as New Age manifestations of witchcraft and magical healing, perhaps underestimate the extent to which a sense of magical thinking never went away. This is not to totally refute Ronald Hutton's thesis in *Triumph of the Moon*. Just as he is opposed to the idea of an unbroken link between modern-day pagan witchcraft and its historical predecessors, so the extent of the transformation of magic over the last 200 years renders a singular, untrammelled connection to the past unrealistic.

The recent creation of the Society for the Academic Study of Magic and its *Journal for the Academic Study of Magic* is perhaps indicative of the strength and confidence of current study. Both will certainly be tested as magic continues to push, or, taking the transformation trend, insinuate itself into modernity's domain. Escaping theories of decline, the history of modern magic challenges (largely nineteenth-century) suppositions that many historians have been only too willing to perpetuate – literacy as a force for morality and enlightenment, cities as centres of rationality, an evolutionary doctrine of societal progress from superstition towards reason.[21] In doing so, historians of modern magic, whose work represents a seemingly archaic thread overshadowed by the period's bigger themes of technological, socio-economic and political advance, potentially have a larger impact beyond their research area. Their findings question our construction of the idea of modernity, challenge the ubiquity of some of its components and critically review notions about the way historians think and write about the modern period.[22] Like a counter-witch spell, their diverse research projects are the heated nails that jab at the belly of modernity's self identity, breaking the enchantment of its assumptions.

NOTES

1. See Keith Thomas, *Religion and the Decline of Magic* (London, 1971), pp. 641–63, and Jonathan Barry, Marianne Hester and Gareth Roberts (eds.), *Witchcraft in Early Modern Europe* (Cambridge, 1996).

2. See Willem de Blecourt, 'On the Continuation of Witchcraft', in Barry, Hester and Roberts (eds), *Witchcraft in Early Modern Europe*, p. 339. In fairness, it should be noted that Thomas briefly examined the continuation of witchcraft and magic in the modern period in *Decline of Magic*, pp. 581–83, pp. 663–8.

3. James Sharpe, *Instruments of Darkness: Witchcraft in Early Modern England* (Philadelphia, 1996), especially pp. 278–94. See also Anya Taylor, *Magic and English Romanticism* (Athens, 1979). For changing perceptions of witchcraft see Diane Purkiss, *The Witch in History – Early Modern and Twentieth Century Interpretations* (London, 1996).

4. Marijke Gijswijt-Hofstra, Brian P.Levack and Roy Porter, *The Athlone History of Witchcraft and Magic in Europe: Volume 5 The Eighteenth and Nineteenth Centuries* (London, 1999), p. 145.

5. Owen Davies, *Witchcraft, Magic and Culture 1736–1951* (Manchester, 1999). Malcolm Gaskill pursued this decline to its legal conclusion with *Hellish Nell: The Last of Britain's Witches* (London, 2001) exploring the case of the last person to be tried under the witchcraft laws before their repeal in 1951. Ronald Hutton's *Triumph of the Moon* (Oxford, 1999) brings the study of witchcraft into the present, albeit in a thesis that argues for a discontinuous history that revolves around the (re)invention of witchcraft tradition.

6. For examples see John Brand, *Observations on Popular Antiquities of Great Britain* (London, 1813), vols 1 and 2, and Charles Mackay, *Extraordinary Popular Delusions and the Madness of Crowds* (London, 1841).

7. Terry Castle, *The Female Thermometer – 18th Century Culture and the Invention of the Uncanny* (New York, 1995) p.125, p. 184.

8. Maureen Perkins, *The Reform of Time – Magic and Modernity* (London, 2001), pp. 6.

9. Perkins, *Reform of Time*, pp. 130.

10. See E.P. Thompson, *Customs in Common* (New York, 1993), and John Rule 'Against Innovation? Custom and Resistance in the Workplace, 1700–1850', in Tim Harris (ed.), *Popular Culture in England c.1500–1850* (Basingstoke, 1995), pp. 168–88.

11. Willem de Blecourt and Owen Davies (eds), *Witchcraft Continued – Popular Magic in Modern Europe* (Manchester, 2004), p. 2 and p. 5.

12. Pamela Thurschwell, *Literature, Technology and Magical Thinking, 1880–1920* (Cambridge, 2001), p. 2, p. 6.

13. See J.G. Frazer, *The Golden Bough* (London, 1922), and Marcel Mauss, *A General Theory of Magic* (London, 1972).

14. See Jean and John Comaroff, *Modernity and its Malcontents: Ritual and Power in Postcolonial Africa* (Chicago, 1993).

15. Peter Geschiere, *The Modernity of Witchcraft* (Charlottesville, 1997), p. 16.

16. Wim van Binsbergen, 'Witchcraft in Modern Africa', in George Clement Bond and Diane M. Ciekawy (eds), *Witchcraft Dialogues* (Athens, 2001), pp. 229.

17. See Davies, *Witchcraft, Magic and Culture*, pp. 238–43.

18. For stage magicians see Simon During, *Modern Enchantments – The Cultural Power of Secular Magic* (London, 2002). For phantasmagoria displays see Castle, *Female Thermometer*, ch. 9.

19. Stuart Hall, David Held, Don Hubert, and Kenneth Thompson (eds), *Modernity: An Introduction to Modern Societies* (Oxford, 1996), p. 17. Literature also demonstrates the transforming etymology of key words such as 'witch' and 'enchanted' during the eighteenth century. By the 1840s Manchester street ballads could proudly refer to alluring young women as 'Lancashire witches' without the negative connotations of their namesakes who were put on trial at Pendle in 1612.

20. With the exception of Owen Davies, 'Urbanisation and the Decline of Witchcraft: An Examination of London', *Journal of Social History*, 30 (1997): 597–617, one feature of modernity that has been markedly absent as a focus of magical research is the expanding urban environment. My current research is largely directed towards initiating inroads into this area.

21. The Society for the Academic Study of Magic can be contacted at http://www.sasm.co.uk/. Some of these assumptions have been re-evaluated in David Vincent, *Literacy and Popular Culture: England 1750–1914* (Cambridge, 1989) and Ralph Merrifield, *The Archaeology of Ritual and Magic* (London, 1987).

22. In this they seem to echo Nash's recent work with regard to the viability of secularization as a satisfactory grand narrative. See David Nash, 'Reconnecting Religion with Social and Cultural History: Secularization's Failure as a Master Narrative', *Cultural and Social History*, 1 (2004): 302–25.

BOOK REVIEWS

Medicine and Colonial Identity. Edited by Molly Sutphen and Bridie Andrews. London and New York: Routledge. 2003. pp. xi + 147. £55. ISBN 0 415 28880 0.

Scholars have devoted much attention to the processes involved in the formation of group or collective identities, focusing on how people sort their environment into like and unlike, self and other. This book, originating in a conference, is ably introduced by the editors who suggest that consideration of topics in the history of medicine – professionalization, choice of therapy, medical education and practice – provide a way to bring together multiple aspects of identity, usually treated separately, such as gender, class, race, ethnicity, nationality. Focusing on medical pluralism in different colonial settings, the editors argue that the search for health is not merely based on a rational choice model of assessments of medical effectiveness, social and monetary cost; instead, medical choices and discourses are key ways in which colonized and colonists define themselves and others. The papers in this collection avoid broad narratives of colonial history, and emphasize local stories of specific individuals as they confront changing circumstances, stressing the contingency and complexity of the construction of colonial identities and unexpected local manifestations of global changes.

The six papers display a wide geographic spread primarily, but not exclusively, across the British Empire – South Africa, India, New Zealand, Australia and the Netherlands – and across a range of aspects of individual and collective identity. David Gordon examines the practice and career in South Africa of an individual British doctor, John Patrick Fitzgerald. Fitzgerald was in charge of the King William's Town hospital from 1854 until 1891. At the hospital, set up to undermine rebellious native Xhosa healers, Fitzgerald taught the healers foreign healing practices, which they assimilated into their own therapeutic cultures without destroying indigenous practices or yielding to colonial hegemony. When colonial policy changed, Fitzgerald continued to see value in teaching Western medicine to African students and he continued to be willing to learn from his African colleagues even later in the century when Western medicine became more technologically sophisticated and separate from indigenous healing methods.

Maneesha Lal uses the influential Hindi women's journal *Stri Darpan* founded in 1909 to provide a new perspective on the process by which women and men constructed nationalist identity in India under British rule. Authors were concerned with health maintenance and hygiene, and drew on both traditional Ayurvedic ideas of health management and Western medical knowledge. At the same time, authors, many of whom were men, agreed that changes to Indian women's role were essential for the modernizing Indian state, including education in nutrition, hygiene and physical education, subjects central to rearing healthy young citizens. The articles, however, referred neither to women physicians nor to colonial initiatives (such as the Countess of Dufferin Fund) to bring Western medicine to Indian women.

Phillippa Mein Smith's wide-ranging chapter brings together empire, nation, gender and race to show how milk became central to the clean, healthy, green image of

Cultural and Social History, Volume 4, Issue 1, pp. 123–132 © The Social History Society 2007

New Zealand's national identity. Sculptures of cows grazed on the lawn of the New Zealand High Commission in Australia, reminding onlookers of a wet, green country in contrast to Australia's dry, red landscape. From the First World War until Britain entered the European Union in 1973, Britain was the main market for New Zealand's dairy products, and milk came to be seen as necessary for children to become strong, healthy citizens of the empire; after 1973 men became the target for milk marketing, for whom it was said to increase their strength and productivity.

Medical concerns were central to the establishment of a white colonial identity in northern Australia in the first half of the twentieth century, separate from that in the 'civilized' south and from the aboriginal population. Suzanne Parry shows vividly how white settlers brought infectious diseases with disproportionately devastating effects among aboriginals. The white population came to see aboriginals as a source of disease and hence a threat, leading the settlers to impose measures that forced exclusion, detention and relocation of aboriginals. Subsequently, aboriginals not surprisingly used the medically justified oppression in shaping their own identity.

Roy Mcleod provides a thoughtful chapter about medical biography generally and colonial medical biography in particular in the context of biographical nationalism. Using the entries on medical practitioners in the *Australian Dictionary of Biography*, he argues that they have helped to establish Australian stereotypes that are likely to be challenged in the future.

Finally, in a fascinating chapter, Hilary Marland compares state provision of midwifery services to the predominantly Catholic southern provinces of the Netherlands, with provision to the Dutch East Indies. She shows that the introduction of state provision in the late nineteenth and early twentieth centuries was a way for the state to establish its identity as modern and civilized. Northerners, mainly Protestant, also saw it as a way to civilize the poorer, Catholic southerners and the indigenous peoples of the Dutch East Indies who engaged in 'dangerous' and 'superstitious' traditional practices surrounding childbirth. Education was designed to train midwives for work in poor, rural districts, but Marland demonstrates that their education encouraged a particular version of national identity that made practice in these areas particularly difficult.

The range and consistently high quality of the introduction and chapters justify their publication, and the editors should be congratulated for putting together a book of interest to a wide range of social and cultural, as well as medical historians. It is a shame the publisher's price is bound to limit the book's distribution.

University of Glasgow   Marguerite W. Dupree

Sacred Cow, Mad Cow: A History of Food Fears. By Madeleine Ferrières, translated by Jody Gladding. New York: Columbia University Press. 2006. pp. xiii + 399. £19.50. ISBN 0 231 13192 5.

The high profile of food quality and food safety in contemporary public and scientific debates has stimulated scholarly interest in their historical aspects. Ferrières's study, originally published in France in 2002, offers an ambitious, diverse and broadly comparative perspective covering the thirteenth century to 1900, in the main using European evidence relating to meats of all description, bread and cereals. Its range provides valuable insights into the nature of food fears and their fluctuating incidence and focus so that the study places contemporary concerns into a fuller and more nuanced historical context. This is achieved primarily using evidence drawn from state and local regulations, medical texts and opinions, cookbooks, household manuals and contemporary accounts of adulterations. The approach is historical rather than theoretical and the mix of local vignettes and a broad canvass provides an engaging read. Throughout care is taken to distinguish between the requirements and rhetoric of formal regulations and their actual impact as well as to note local differences and the divergences between the diets, attitudes and options of elites and the mass of the population. In addition the book deals with different aspects of food supply including reactions to new commodities, the implications of changing medical opinions, attitudes to different animals and individual campaigns to promote food hygiene.

Ferrières offers a variety of interpretations and insights. Long-term continuities are indicated such as the debates over consumers' capabilities for evaluating food quality and safety and what information ought to be provided to consumers and their representatives. Overall Ferrières detects a general preference for relying on limited intervention and market mechanisms, although some regional differences are noted. Sources of information and reassurance for consumers included the movement of live animals, which allowed inspection close to the point of consumption, and the later emphasis on labelling, brand names and inspection by analytical chemists. Nineteenth-century regulations on adulteration are then explained as a reflection of new ideas on nutrition and regulatory concerns that certain consumers, especially children, required protection because they lacked the capacity to make fully informed judgements. In this respect a fuller discussion of milk products and infant diets would have been valuable. The impact of market incentives is explored in interesting ways. Food shortages or low incomes, it is argued, often led consumers to accept higher risks in relation to food quality in a rational trade-off between the hazards of starvation and those of food poisoning or such dangers as ergot in rye flour. More routinely, lower grade or unsafe products were cheaper, concealed in pies, pasties or other mixtures and circulated in distribution systems aimed at less affluent consumers or sometimes provided for acquired or institutional diets. Tensions surfaced regularly between commercial rivals and health reformers as well as among the competing interests within each of those groupings. Another continuity was the rhetorical tendency to proclaim past golden ages of food quality, although Ferrières suggests that European food supplies and diets did deteriorate from the 1550s to the 1700s. There was also a recurring tendency to assert that urban consumers were increasingly distanced from the sources of food supplies and, thus, from direct experience of product quality. In this respect, the expansion of international trade in foodstuffs and industrialized production in the nineteenth century are presented as a further stage rather than a completely new departure. Even domestic production did not guarantee safety if premium produce was sent to market in order to maximize incomes or where consumers engaged in forms of adulteration in order to stretch their food supplies further or to provide their food with a desired colouring. Similarly the use of salt or specific cooking practices was believed to counteract any hazards from diseased or deteriorating foodstuffs. In this respect the study usefully extends the scholarly literature on nineteenth-century adulteration into the kitchen and beyond its usual focus on the practices of food producers and distributors and the rhetoric of campaigners for reform. Such careful attention links elements of the vast literatures on food history to those on food safety more effectively than usual. More attention might have been given to the development of cooperatives, socialist groups and other reformers to balance the emphasis on medical opinion. Gaps in the coverage of more recent studies on Britain are more than compensated for by the access provided to extensive European evidence. Overall this is a valuable addition to the literature providing its own food for thought about the factors shaping attitudes, practices and policies in Europe.

University of Glasgow   MIKE FRENCH

The Greatest Fight of Our Generation: Louis vs Schmeling. By Lewis A. Erenberg. New York: Oxford University Press. 2006. pp. x + 274. £16.99. ISBN 0 195 17774 6.

In modern times professional sport has become intimately linked to politics and ethnicity. In his excellent and unpretentious monograph, Lewis Erenberg interrogates boxing- and race-related tensions between the US and Germany in the interwar era. His study enhances a reputation as an acute and versatile observer of the shaping of popular mentalities in mid-twentieth century urban America. The book also reveals an ability to fuse biography, political analysis and cultural interpretation to trace the shaping of collective attitudes towards homeland and race. Erenberg demonstrates the ways in which professional sport – the fight game was the most intensively commercialized (and criminalized) mass spectator pursuit of all – and its stars and symbols have been discursively appropriated and recycled by political regimes, whether democratic or totalitarian.

The approach is deceptively simple. Erenberg draws on a massive volume of contemporary reportage and instant biography concerning Joe Louis, the 'Brown Bomber', and Max Schmeling, the 'Black Uhlan', to recreate the social, economic and cultural contexts and meanings of two memorable fights in 1936 and 1938. Excellent use is also made of the *Ring* magazine, 'boxing's bible', edited by the influential Nat Fleischer and its German would-be equivalent, *Box-Sport*, first an independent and then Nazi-controlled publication. The core of the book focuses on the second encounter, for which a contemporary commentator coined the phrase 'the greatest fight of our generation'. Erenberg uses his extensive knowledge of boxing to provide vivid, no-holds-barred description of what actually went on in the ring. This material makes for uncomfortable reading for a generation that has witnessed the rise and physical and mental collapse of so many mainly non-white champions, and which is now also fully aware of what incessant volleys of perfectly timed killer punches can do to the human brain and to the neurological system.

The first fight, a championship eliminator, was won by Schmeling and led to his being adopted and nationally and internationally publicized – only later to be humiliated and caste aside – as a lauded symbol of perfect Aryan manhood. Victory over Louis was used to confirm Nazi propaganda. At the same time, American journalists resorted to hoary racist prejudice and claimed that Schmeling had proven himself too canny a tactician for a black fighter heavily reliant on physical strength and speed and lacking an 'innate' moral and intellectual ability to outthink an opponent and absorb, then come back from, savage physical punishment. By the time of the second encounter in 1938 American public opinion – both white and black – had become greatly better informed about Hitlerian racism. The implications of the Jesse Owen affair at the Berlin Olympics had been absorbed and more was now known of the Nazis' blatantly anti-Semitic obsessions and policies. (In the world of boxing, Jews had been champions in the lower weight divisions and had also become highly successful managers and trainers.) When Louis tore the ageing Schmeling apart in 1938, the victory was trumpeted as a triumph both for democracy and an emergently incorporated 'black America'.

In the short-term, the Nazi regime used the shattering defeat – after an alleged but not fully proven kidney punch Schmeling was hospitalized for more than a week – to depict Louis and his camp as cheats who had been briefed and manipulated by anti-German Jewish interests in America. Sooner rather than later, however, Goebbels and Hitler agreed that the Black Uhlan must be relegated from incessant headline adulation to no more than brief mentions on the sports pages. Exiling himself to the Polish border, Schmeling watched his circle of sporting, entertainment, business and bohemian friends – many of them Jewish – fall victim to ever more draconian racist persecution. After the war, he outfaced accusations of collaboration, became a successful mink farmer and then – irony of ironies – an executive for the German wing of the Coca-Cola Company. Generous to a fault and hounded by the Inland Revenue Service and many ex-wives and lovers, Joe Louis descended into penury and paranoia before taking up a steady though still menial job as a celebrity greeter in Las Vegas. (Erenberg interprets these final years in a more upbeat style than earlier writers.)

The author is surely correct to claim that Louis's magnificent example made it possible for the first time for white Americans to 'celebrate the black male body' (230). He is also right to emphasize that it was the Brown Bomber's unprecedented financial pulling power, rather than any sudden or universal transformation in white attitudes towards black athletes, that brought boxing in from the cold during the dead days of the Depression. Nevertheless, Louis undoubtedly paved the way for great champions like Henry Armstrong, Sugar Ray Robinson and Muhammad Ali. At the same time, we need to remember that his early career – like those of the iconic Louis Armstrong, Duke Ellington and Billie Holiday – coincided with astonishingly high levels of unprosecuted lynching in the south. Not the least of the merits of Erenberg's book is that it draws subtle comparisons between the realities of race, power and violence both in Germany and America during the 1920s and 1930s.

CHSTM, University of Manchester   BILL LUCKIN

Luxury and Pleasure in Eighteenth-Century Britain. By Maxine Berg. Oxford: Oxford University Press. 2005. pp. xvii + 373. £25. ISBN 0 19 927208 5.

Since McKendrick, Brewer and Plumb first published their seminal *The Birth of a Consumer Society: The Commercialisation of Eighteenth-Century England* in 1982, historians of a certain caste, and particularly those with an economic and social history background, have had a love affair with luxurious 'things'. The 'Consumer Revolution' became the natural heir to the 'Industrial Revolution'. Business history with a new emphasis on marketing was one of the beneficiaries, but most of the early explorations of eighteenth-century consumer society were focused on counting possessions and fixing their monetary values. As with the analysis of the Industrial Revolution, the 'revolutionary' character of change in material consumption was shown to be overstated. At the end of the eighteenth century the ordinary working population in most parts of Britain still lived in states of profound material impoverishment. But, as many historians soon came to see, changes in information about goods had an impact on ways of thinking and on behaviour that preceded changes in actual experience. In short, the 'revolution' had as much to do with ideas and culture as with realities. Exploring the intellectual and cultural dimensions of consumer behaviour has been a flourishing enterprise of the past fifteen years, bringing new types of historian to the field, inspired by the so-called luxury debates that were a product of the Enlightenment, along with the interest in gender and the growing emphasis on objects and images. A more intimate engagement with the material world of the past – through the analysis of personal motivations, the psychology of groups and anthropology of group behaviour relative to goods, or, indeed, the very specific 'social life of things' – has been established as a broad field of research that is still ongoing. And very recently there has been another shift in direction, back to the earlier preoccupation with the detailed mechanisms of production and design.

Each of these threads of historical enquiry is reflected in this book, by one of Britain's foremost practitioners of economic and social history. Indeed, as Berg describes at the outset of *Luxury and Pleasure*, the ideas explored here saw their first genesis in her important monograph of 1985, *The Age of Manufactures*, and her subsequent involvement during the 1990s in the 'Luxury Project' at Warwick University, which brought together scholars from a range of disciplines, hosted a series of important workshops and conferences and gave rise to the publication of two very rich collections of essays, both coedited by Berg. In the past few years, Berg has published major articles in *Past and Present* and in the *Economic History Review* that explore, respectively, her interest in international, particularly Oriental production for the British consumer market and the detailed processes of design and manufacture of new wares at home. Inevitably, therefore, this book is more a work of synthesis than an original statement – but it is a synthesis by the author of her own very considerable published output on the subject – a drawing together of the many strands of research that Berg has explored over the last twenty years. It is a very useful volume for those familiar with the field and an excellent introduction for those who are new.

The book is divided into three sections. Part 1 'Luxury, Quality and Delight' begins with the now well-known luxury debates that centred on issues of morality and threat to social hierarchy. It tries to reconcile these cultural preoccupations with the agendas of economic history. A chapter on 'Goods from the East' – particularly textiles and china – shows the connection between oriental production and the European market, which involved so many of the modern manufacturing and marketing techniques that we still assume were British inventions. The relationship between exotic consumer goods and the spawning of newly invented British products and production techniques – a national 'project', with issues of nation and economy at its heart – is also considered. Part 2, 'How It Was Made' explores the 'endlessly variable, individualized and customized, fashionable and affordable' (113) commodities of the age, ranging from glass and china to a vast array of metal wares. With rich details on 'what', 'how', 'by whom' and 'how much', this is classic Berg territory. Part 3, 'A Nation of Shoppers' explores the middle-class consumers who purchased so many 'things' and the processes of shopping. The final chapter on British products and the North American consumer was perhaps inevitable but shifts the balance from the main preoccupation of this book and is not entirely successful.

My criticisms are few. The title is perhaps a little misleading, particularly as there is no real exploration of the issue of 'pleasure' relative to the world of goods. Indeed, one could argue that the 'luxury' of the age was as much connected with anxiety and exhaustion as people yearned for and laboured for those things they could not afford – but perhaps I am viewing this through the gloom-tinted spectacles of our present consumerist age. As is often the case in such texts, the illustrations are disappointing. Small black and white reproductions do not convey a great deal when the arguments are built on the colours, textures and visual feasts that were the essence of much contemporary consumption. Though with such a reasonable cover price, it is perhaps unrealistic to expect otherwise.

University of Edinburgh STANA NENADIC

History and the Media. Edited by David Cannadine. London: Palgrave Macmillan. 2004. pp. vii + 175. £21.99. ISBN 1 403 92037 0.

The choice of writers in this volume – exactly half of whom are knighted or ennobled – perfectly illustrates the point familiar to conference organizers everywhere: that the more senior the contributors, the less easy it is to impose coherence on the contributions. The resulting volume is a curate's egg, but nevertheless ought to be required reading for any social historian who wants to know as much as possible about the way that popular treatments of history are disseminated.

Television history dominates this book, in the shape of tales – by producer Taylor Downing, Jeremy Isaacs, and Melvin Bragg – of how it has been done, and defences – by Simon Schama, Tristram Hunt and Ian Kershaw – of its merit. David Puttnam ventures outside the medium of television to ask 'Has Hollywood stolen our history?' and answer that it has simplified it, as part of a process of general simplification of reality that is its stock in trade. Jean Seton's essay on the history of broadcasting and John Tusa's on the use of the historian's techniques during a career in public service do not really fit with the rest of this volume, whatever their other merits: history of the media is different from history in the media in almost every way. Max Hastings engages entertainingly with the writing of history for the newspapers but the medium of radio is almost entirely absent; a serious omission. Melvin Bragg, however, shoehorns a mention of the virtues of *In Our Time* into his piece on the making of *The Adventure of English*. And he is right to do so: this programme, which, despite its reluctance to 'dumb down' inherently difficult subjects, attracts audiences of more than a million, does more than just demonstrate the value of public service broadcasting. It also shows that radio, untrammelled by the need to find pictures, can range over the past with a great deal of freedom. Television, however, is a visual medium. Roger Smither of the Imperial War Museum answers the question 'Why is so much television history about war?' by pointing out that content is driven by the availability of archive footage, and 'wars generate larger volumes of material than other events, and . . . a higher proportion of that material is unencumbered by private copyright.'

The defences of television history in *History and the Media* do not always strike the mark. Schama's defence against his critics would be more worthwhile if he were to identify them and detail their criticisms. Tristram Hunt claims that television history automatically democratizes and empowers. But it does not: it disseminates, but that which is disseminated is more likely to be tendentious and slanted than many texts. Hunt betrays what he really thinks about academe in his (unconscious?) differentiation between the Open University and the rest of higher education. He holds that TV history will have done its job insofar as it lures people into bookshops and lecture theatres. Under the guise of 'democratization', Hunt actually appears to want to keep the inner sanctum of the historical profession unbroken, though the commoners will be favoured with occasional tours inside the mural walls. He also claims that his television series on the English Civil War produced an increase in the number of applicants to the relevant Open University course. It did not.

We need no longer spend our time merely defending the presentation of history in the mass media as a worthwhile project. Instead, as Cannadine writes, we need 'a more systematic reflection and analysis' of this body of work. Yet *History and the Media* does not provide a wholly satisfactory model for such analysis, which ought to involve academics, producers, and commissioners, and to review and comment on the 'serious' history that is put out online, in newspapers, magazines, radio and television. Perhaps the museum reviews carried regularly by the American journal *Technology and Culture* could serve as one inspiration. One key audience for such critical engagement is those of us who are committed to sharing our scholarship with as wide an audience as possible, but in need of the clearest possible idea of the perils and pitfalls that might ensue when we are proffered a cheque, or worse, a microphone.

The Open University   CHRIS A. WILLIAMS

Violence and Crime in Nineteenth-century England: The Shadow of our Refinement. By John Carter Wood. London: Routledge. 2004, pp. xii + 204 £80. ISBN 0 415 32905 1.

This volume joins recent work by Clive Emsley (*Hard Men*) and Martin Wiener (*Men of Blood*) who also seek to explain the historical relationship between the English and violence. Derived largely from contemporary commentary and from the records generated by the legal system, it examines plebeian and elite attitudes to violence; the reality of disorder and the evolution of these factors during the nineteenth century. Carter Wood seeks to explain the overall shift in attitudes that occurred over the long nineteenth century, whereby a society that had seen violence as an essential prop of the social order and source of social power changed into a society that condemned most of its manifestations and sought to limit their effect. His consideration of the issue is perceptive and rewarding. It is illuminated throughout by his conviction that 'power and authority are products of negotiation as well as imposition', and that violence has a 'syntax' which can be studied.

As the upper and middle classes withdrew from 'what previously had been a shared culture of violence', the notion of violence became increasingly problematic, and attitudes to it became bound up to the process of differentiation known as 'civilizing'. Thus, concern about violence increased rapidly at a time when actual violence was in all probability static or decreasing slightly. Civilization in its various forms was not necessarily non-violent: it espoused a different and (crucially) conflicting definition of the limits of acceptable violence from those deriving from the 'traditional' view. By the end of the century, even the call for a return to the infliction of pain as a punishment 'had to be clothed in the language of refinement'. In many cases, the image of brutality was approached and continually re-defined as the binary opposite to civilization, hence the subtitle of the book. Violence was also seen increasingly as a problem with social causes that could thus be tackled, rather than an inevitable aspect of life. As violent actions became taboo, the portrayal of violence grew more vivid and was more likely to be fixed as a property of the 'unrestrained' lower orders. Yet the pursuit of violence had its limits, even in the opinion of so liberal an intellectual as J.S. Mill, who worried that excessive celebration of the 'man of feeling' might result in 'cultural emasculation'.

Carter Wood begins with Norbert Elias's model of the 'civilizing process' but extends the model bequeathed by Elias and his followers to consider, inter alia, the effects of class, and the fact that customary violence was not merely a passive counterpart to the advances of a 'civilized' sensibility. Rather, it too was a complex phenomena with an agency, contested nature and a continuing evolution all of its own. Customary violence was characterized by physical retribution, expressions of community autonomy and the maintenance of domestic and public norms. It was reflected and shaped by oral culture, and contained elements of performance, legitimacy, exclusion and resistance. Like civilization, 'custom was a flexible construction which maintained its relevance as it faced a changing set of social circumstances'. Carter Wood considers in detail the structured nature of the often spontaneous streetfight, which, before the imposition of Queensberry rules in the 1880s, followed many of the norms of the organized prizefight. Streetfighting was ritualized: made public and open by the creation of a ring. Like prizefighting it involved seconds, and a 'fair fight' was one that avoided foul blows. With the domestication of boxing, the link was severed, and the streetfight appears in consequence to have become less restrained.

In the case of domestic violence, however, methods were far less constrained although there was certainly a community disapproval of murderous violence. Domestic violence co-evolved with the redefinition of public space: the growing importance of the threshold of the worker's house led to more orderly public spaces but may have increased the level of violence by removing it from the view of the neighbourhood. Here, Carter Wood's problem is that he is arguing that domestic violence was less 'grammatical' than that between equals: but the nature of his evidence, overwhelmingly derived from homicide cases, makes this a difficult case to prove even as it remains a fruitful hypothesis to advance. The other major frustration in the book is the relative lack of space given to examining the extent to which working-class people themselves independently adopted 'civilized' viewpoints and fitting this development into the wider explanatory framework. By the conclusion, the traditional model of the 'civilizing process' has been comprehensively rewritten. Notably, Carter Wood questions the place of 'impulse' in Elias's work: defining customary violence as 'impulsive' rather than a response to structural considerations was itself a central part of 'civilizing' discourse, which appears in Elias's work as an objective fact. This work, though, fits snugly into the Eliasian tradition of empirically based historical sociology, which seeks to explain the reality as well as the image. Overall, it is an essential complement to Weiner's work on the civilizers; it deserves a wide readership and has an accessibility and relevance that makes its prohibitively high cover price all the more tragic.

Open University

Chris A. Williams

CULTURAL & SOCIAL HISTORY

NOTES TO CONTRIBUTORS

SUBMISSION GUIDELINES

Submissions to *Cultural and Social History* should be sent in electronic format. To submit a manuscript electronically, please send it either in WORD or in RICH TEXT FORMAT to **culturalsocialhistory@bergpublishers.com**. All submissions should include a 100 word abstract and four to five keywords. Copies of any statistical tables, maps, or illustrations that cannot be sent electronically should be sent to *Cultural and Social History*, c/o Centre for Contemporary British History, Institute of Historical Research, Senate House, Malet Street, London WC1E 7HU. Provide your name(s), address(es) and contact information on a separate title page. Articles should be no more than 9,000 words (inclusive of notes). The total word count should be added at the end of the manuscript.

Reviews and review articles should be submitted direct to the Book Review Editor.

LAYOUT

All material should be formatted for A4 or quarto paper, in double-spaced typing. Ample margins should be left. Each page of the typescript should be numbered. Notes should be kept to a minimum, and supplied as endnotes. They should be numbered consecutively and double-spaced, beginning on a new page at the end of the article. Please do not use any endnote/footnote formatting which may be available with your software. Please avoid cross-references as far as possible.

In Reviews, all material should be incorporated into the text: there should be no endnotes. In Reviews, the author's name should appear at the end of the review, together with the name of his/her institution.

SPELLING AND PUNCTUATION

Please use UK English spelling and punctuation. In general, *The Concise Oxford Dictionary* is our arbiter of spelling, especially for hyphenated words, words in italics, etc. Use 'z' spelling for all words ending in '-ize', '-ization' (organize, organization). However, alternative spellings in quoted material, book and article titles should not be changed. We also recommend *The Oxford Dictionary for Writers and Editors* and *Hart's Rules* (both published by Oxford University Press) as useful reference works.

Please see the website http://www.bergpublishers.com/uk/cshistory/cshistory_submissions.htm for full details regarding which conventions to use.

FIGURES AND ILLUSTRATIONS

If your article is heavily illustrated, please liaise with the Assistant Editor in advance of submission to discuss how many images can be accommodated in the final text.

Artwork MUST be submitted with the final draft of the article. Please note that while Berg Publishers will make every effort to ensure that your artwork is carefully handled and returned to you as soon as possible, artwork must, of necessity, be sent out of house and we can accept no responsibility for loss or damage. Therefore, we suggest that you if your artwork is irreplaceable DO NOT send us the originals. Instead images should be submitted on disk or via email as either TIFFS or JPEGS (scanned at 300 dpi for photographs/half tones and 600 dpi for maps, line drawings or artwork containing text). Images embedded in Word documents can NOT be used. Similarly, graphics downloaded from Web pages are not acceptable for print reproduction. These graphics are low-resolution images (usually 72 dpi) that are suitable for screen display but far below acceptable standards for print reproduction.

If you have any questions about the artwork you are sending, please contact the Assistant Editor or the Berg Production Department direct. The numbering on the artwork must be clearly marked, as must its position on the manuscript. Keep artwork separate from the text, with the figure number penciled in on the back of each figure. A separate list of captions and copyright information etc. should also be included. It is the author's responsibility to clear any necessary permissions. Although the print version of the journal will ordinarily only reproduce images in black and white, authors are encouraged to submit artwork in colour, since images will be available in colour in the online version of the journal. There is, however, a small budget for reproducing colour illustrations in print. Authors should liaise with the editors about any plans to include illustrations in colour in the print version of the journal.

NOTES AND REFERENCES

Use the short-title system of referencing for endnotes. Provide a full reference in the form of a note in the first instance, and thereafter a shorter version of the title should be used. Do not use 'op. cit'.

1. Mary Hamer, *Writing by Numbers: Trollope's Serial Fiction* (Cambridge, 1987), p. 25.

…

3. Hamer, *Writing by Numbers*, p. 27.

COPYRIGHTS/OFFPRINTS

In submitting an article to *Cultural and Social History* an author recognises that, on its acceptance for publication, its exclusive copyright shall be assigned to the Social History Society and operated on the Society's behalf by the publisher. In consideration of this provision, the publisher will supply the author with 25 offprints of his/her article (offprints of reviews are not supplied). The publisher will not put any limitation on the freedom of the author to use material contained in the article in other published works of which he/she is author or editor. It is the author's responsibility to obtain permission to quote material from copyright sources.

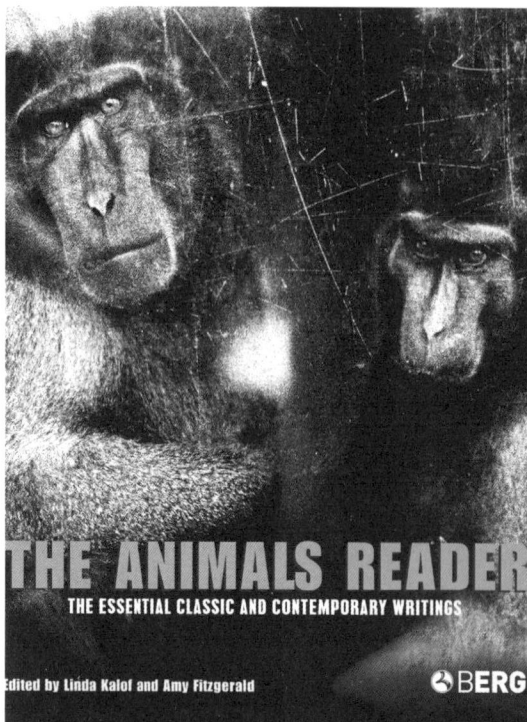